East Goshen Mennonite
Eating Disorders Group

D0108808

Maintenance
for compulsive overeaters

by Bill B.

CompCare® Publishers

MINNEAPOLIS, MINNESOTA

© 1986 by Bill B.
All rights reserved.
Published in the United States
by CompCare Publishers.

Reproduction in whole or part, in any form, including storage in memory
device system, is forbidden without written permission . . . except that
portions may be used in broadcast or printed commentary or review
when attributed fully to author and publication by names.

Excerpts quoted from *Alcoholics Anonymous,* ©1939.
Reprinted by permission of Alcoholics Anonymous World Services, Inc.

Library of Congress Cataloging-in-Publication Data
B., Bill, 1931–
    Maintenance for compulsive overeaters: The Twelve Step way
    to ongoing recovery .

    1. Obesity—Psychological aspects.   2. Reducing—
    Psychological aspects.   3. Obesity—Patients—United States—
    Biography.   I. Title.
RC552.025B22 1986   616.3'986   86-9681
ISBN 0-89638-091-2

Inquiries, orders, and catalog requests should be addressed to
CompCare Publishers
2415 Annapolis Lane
Minneapolis, Minnesota 55441
Call toll free 800/328-3330
(Minnesota residents 559-4800)

        3   4   5   6   7   8   9

88   89   90   91   92   93   94

*God waits for man to regain
his childhood in wisdom*

— Rabinadrath Tagore

THE TWELVE STEPS

1. We admitted we were powerless over (problem)—that our lives had become unmanageable.

2. Came to believe that a Power greater than ourselves could restore us to sanity.

3. Made a decision to turn our will and our lives over to the care of God *as we understood Him.*

4. Made a searching and fearless moral inventory of ourselves.

5. Admitted to God, to ourselves, and to another human being the exact nature of our wrongs.

6. Were entirely ready to have God remove all these defects of character.

7. Humbly asked Him to remove our shortcomings.

8. Made a list of all persons we had harmed, and became willing to make amends to them all.

9. Made direct amends to such people wherever possible, except when to do so would injure them or others.

10. Continued to take personal inventory, and when we were wrong, promptly admitted it.

11. Sought through prayer and meditation to improve our conscious contact with God *as we understood Him*, praying only for knowledge of His will for us and the power to carry that out.

12. Having had a spiritual awakening as a result of these steps, we tried to carry this message to addicts and to practice these principles in all our affairs.

THE TWELVE STEPS OF ALCOHOLICS ANONYMOUS

1–We admitted we were powerless over alcohol—that our lives had become unmanageable. 2–Came to believe that a Power greater than ourselves could restore us to sanity. 3–Made a decision to turn our will and our lives over to the care of God *as we understood Him.* 4–Made a searching and fearless moral inventory of ourselves. 5–Admitted to God, to ourselves, and to another human being the exact nature of our wrongs. 6–Were entirely ready to have God remove all these defects of character. 7–Humbly asked Him to remove our shortcomings. 8–Made a list of all persons we had harmed, and became willing to make amends to them all. 9–Made direct amends to such people wherever possible, except when to do so would injure them or others. 10–Continued to take personal inventory and when we were wrong, promptly admitted it. 11–Sought through prayer and meditation to improve our conscious contact with God *as we understood Him*, praying only for knowledge of His will for us and the power to carry that out. 12–Having had a spiritual awakening as the result of these steps, we tried to carry this message to alcoholics and to practice these principles in all our affairs.

(Reprinted for adaption with permission of AA World Services, Inc.)

Acknowledgments

This book would not have been possible without the generous sharing of others. During the last fifteen years, *thousands* of people have shared with me their most precious gifts: innermost thoughts, feelings, fears, failures, successes, and—most important in a work like this—their secrets. I'd like to express my undying gratitude to all of these people for their trust, their willingness to share their stories with me, and their willingness to allow me to share my story with them.

I will never be able to fully express the love and appreciation I feel for the dear friends of mine who have shared their lives on the pages of this book. I feel so fortunate to have found a number of people willing to open up and talk freely about their pain and their achievements for one purpose only: to help others. These wonderful people have paid their dues; I wish them peace and serenity.

Special thanks to my dear friend, MaryEllen, who not only shared her story, but also shared her time and energy in typing and retyping page after page of the manuscript. Special thanks, also, to MaryEllen's "boss," Don, who allowed much of this work to continue during business hours, while she put aside his work to meet my deadlines. Not many employers would have been so tolerant and understanding.

Most authors do the best they can just to *survive* the ordeal of having their work edited and prepared for publication. It is rare to find a publisher such as Comp-Care Publications and an editor such as Ronelle Ewing;

they understand the message I am trying to convey in this book. Their patience, understanding, and care are rare in the publishing business. Without their faith in me, this published work would not have been accomplished.

To Doris, my sponsor, my friend, and my supporter, I give special thanks for always being there for me with words of wisdom. She has been a source of energy and inspiration to me and to countless others as well.

Most of us who struggle through life trying to change ourselves through the Twelve Step Program somehow expect our families to appreciate the great strides we've made. We seldom realize the deprivation our families have gone through while we "changed." It is no different in my case. I have saved the best for last:

For the last fifteen years, I have given up many days and nights with my family in order to learn how to live the Program. My family didn't bargain for all the time I would spend away from them.

My children have grown up somehow, and for the better. I cannot adequately put into words the love I feel for them and the pride I have in their humanness, their accomplishments, and the real contribution they have made to my spiritual awakening. *I see my children as living examples of maturity and love.* I am proud of each one of them.

To my wife, Enid, who has stuck with me through good and bad, success and failure, change and more change, and who has stayed home night after night and weekend after weekend while I led a retreat or a marathon somewhere in this world, I can only say "Thank You." Thank you for sticking with me; thank you for crying with me; thank you for your patience and understanding (especially when you were *out* of patience and understanding); thank you for inviting into our home Twelve Step friends who had no family and "adopted" ours; thank you for the hours and hours you spent editing this book. Most of all, thank you for being you. I love you.

Love and Peace,
Bill

Editor's Notes

Maintenance for Compulsive Overeaters features individual applications of the Twelve Steps of Alcoholics Anonymous (AA). This book is not intended to replace the Big Book (titled *Alcoholics Anonymous* and published by Alcoholics Anonymous World Services, Inc.) as a resource for Twelve Step Programs. What the author said in his first book, *Compulsive Overeater*, still holds true for him today: "There is no substitute for the Big Book. For me, nothing could ever replace that book as a guide for recovery. Reading it was the most important thing that ever happened to me."

Each of the twenty people profiled in this book, including the author, has developed his or her own application of the Twelve Steps by working the Program, reading the Big Book, and using the Twelve Step principles in his or her own life. Whereas Bill B.'s first book, *Compulsive Overeater*, applies the concept of the Twelve Steps to the process of identifying and coping with compulsive overeating, this book applies the concept of the Twelve Steps to the challenge of *long-term recovery* from compulsive eating behavior.

Bill B. and the other nineteen people who tell their stories in *Maintenance for Compulsive Overeaters* share how the Program has worked for *them*—by helping them to find happiness and serenity, by helping them to lose weight, and by helping them to maintain that weight loss over time.

For readers already familiar with the Twelve Step Program, this book represents an opportunity to renew and deepen their understanding of the Program.

Readers not acquainted with the Twelve Steps may want to read the Big Book and other Twelve Step literature and/or participate in a Twelve Step fellowship.

Maintenance for Compulsive Overeaters, like *Compulsive Overeater* before it, was written and published independently of Overeaters Anonymous and, therefore, has neither the endorsement nor the opposition of *Overeaters Anonymous.*

Excerpts from *Alcoholics Anonymous* (the Big Book) are reprinted with permission of Alcoholics Anonymous World Services, Incorporated. Page references to the Big Book are placed in parentheses directly following the quoted excerpt and are from the Third Edition, twenty-first printing, 1985.

Author's Notes

The following introduction to terminology, resources, and concepts used in this book may be helpful for readers not familiar with the elements of the Twelve Step Program, its dynamics, and fellowship:

Two dictionary definitions are particularly useful:

compulsion - "A strong irresistible impulse to act."

obsession - "Compulsive preoccupation with a fixed idea or unwanted feeling."

Alcoholics Anonymous (the Big Book) and *Twelve Steps and Twelve Traditions* are two important resources referred to in this book. Written by recovered alcoholics in 1939, the Big Book is a classic Twelve Step work that even today is recognized as the basic text for Alcoholics Anonymous (AA), as well as for other groups working with one of several adaptations of the original AA Twelve Step Program. The recovered alcoholics who tell their stories in this book show precisely *how* they recovered. *Twelve Steps and Twelve Traditions* is another Alcoholics Anonymous classic that not only explains the Twelve Step Program, but also how members recover, how AA functions, and the conditions that govern the operation of the Twelve Step group.

Overeaters Anonymous (OA) is a self-help group adapted from the original concept of Alcoholics Anonymous. OA is a fellowship of men and women of all ages who come together and share how they work a program of recovery to solve the problems of overeating and unhappiness in their lives. OA was founded in 1960. Starting with one small group, OA has grown in twenty-six years to include thousands of groups in more than twenty countries throughout the world.

Some of my own interpretations:

When I discuss compulsive behavior in this book, I am referring to behavior that is repeated time and time again, to the point that a person feels that he or she is unable to prevent the behavior and is actually *controlled* by it. (I believe that all compulsive behavior is preceded by obsessive thoughts, whether they are conscious or subconscious.) A *compulsive overeater* is a person who eats compulsively or obsesses about eating. *The Twelve Steps* represent an approach to obtaining relief from compulsive behavior by removing the obsessive thinking that precedes that behavior. This approach was introduced by Alcoholics Anonymous and is now utilized by Overeaters Anonymous and other Twelve Step groups as well. Indeed, the Twelve Steps have become the basis for several other Programs dealing with the problems of compulsive behavior—Al-Anon, Alateen, Overeaters Anonymous, Narcotics Anonymous, Emotions Anonymous, Emotional Health Anonymous, Gamblers Anonymous, Parents Anonymous, and Families Anonymous. The Twelve Steps are still as inspired, as effective, as uncompromising, and as practical now as they were when they were first presented more than fifty years ago. The Twelve Step Program is one of single purpose that deals with an illness which is threefold—physical, emotional, and spiritual. The Program is, however, first, last, and *always* a spiritual program.

Working the Program means following the Twelve

Steps in everything one does and having a willingness to really work the Twelve Steps, one day at a time, in order to recover from obsessive thinking and compulsive behavior and maintain that recovery. *Anonymity* is one of the Twelve Traditions of AA which governs the operation of the Twelve Step group. It is generally understood in anonymous Programs that members of a Twelve Step group are not to publicly divulge, at the level of the media, their membership in that group, even though it might sometimes be necessary to divulge their membership on a one-to-one basis in order to attract new members. In addition to anonymity with regard to membership, what is said at a meeting or in other confidences relating to the Program is never revealed, even to another member, nor is the fact of one's membership discussed with non-members.

Whether or not we choose to refer to our *Higher Power* as God, this power is the source of our ability to do that which we have been unable to do before. *Inventory*, as referred to in the Fourth Step, is a comprehensive self-analysis. *Character defects* are patterns of thinking, flaws, and adaptive and self-defeating behaviors that have outlived their usefulness in our lives. A *sponsor* is a recovering member of an anonymous Twelve Step group who shares with another member of the group how he or she recovered and maintained that recovery. Instead of telling others how to work the Program, sponsors share by the example of their lives how the Program works for them. *Twelve Step work or service* refers to helping other individuals in the Program or helping the Program as a whole. In the long run, though, the best service one can give to others is the power of example—recovering and maintaining recovery by living the Twelve Steps, each day, to the best of his or her ability.

For the alcoholic, of course, abstinence means refraining from the consumption of any alcohol whatsoever. But we compulsive overeaters cannot similarly refrain from eating. For me, abstinence means freedom from food compulsion—that is, freedom from the desire to eat compulsively. But in order to abstain from compulsive eating, a person must be able to stop doing what he or she acknowledges powerlessness over in the First Step. Our Program states that in order to abstain—in other words, to stop the compulsive behavior—a person must get in touch with a power that will enable him or her to do what he or she had been unable to do alone.

When I talk about *recovery* in this book, I am referring to a state in which a person has attained and continues to maintain freedom from obsessive thinking and compulsive behavior by having worked through the first Nine Steps and by living his or her daily life on the basis of the Tenth, Eleventh, and Twelfth Steps. Another important concept referred to often in Twelve Step Programs and literature for compulsive overeaters yet subject to many interpretations (and misinterpretations) is *maintenance*...and that is what this book is all about...

Preface

We began our journey to recovery with a fervent hope that we would soon feel better, eliminate compulsive overeating behavior from our lives, and gain some measure of self-esteem.

How far have we come?

Most of us came to Overeaters Anonymous (OA) in generally the same condition: *overweight and overwhelmed*. Whether we were 10 pounds overweight or 200 pounds overweight, we seemed to share a similar pain. Many of us came to OA with similar histories: countless unsuccessful and successful attempts at losing weight, followed by feelings of despair when we failed to achieve or maintain our goal weight. Many of us came to OA having lived lives of embarrassment, humiliation, and loneliness. For most of us, OA represented the last resort, *our last hope*. We attended our first OA meetings and heard strange words there. In fact, for most of us, OA was not at all like we anticipated it would be. We heard a new language spoken there based on unfamiliar phrases: "God did it; I didn't"; "Let go and let God"; "food plans"; and "calling in food". We heard words like "Program", "abstinence", and "sponsors." The "members" of this "group" seemed to be in some kind of euphoric state: they applauded when we would have booed; they greeted people when we would have ignored them; they hugged people when we would have pulled away. When I attended my first OA meeting more than fifteen years ago, no one there seemed to be losing weight very fast, so even *minor achievements* were applauded. (At least the achievements seemed minor to me *at the time.*) For example, not gaining weight was considered a major accomplishment. *But I knew I wanted much more than that.* I wanted my weight off, and I wanted it off immediately, if not sooner. Truthfully, though, I was unwilling to do the things most everyone else at the meetings was doing. I was not willing to applaud anyone, hug anyone, or even greet anyone.

When I came to OA, my life was a classic example of swimming against the stream, and I was completely worn out from the constant struggle. On the other hand, I certainly didn't want to give up my "gregarious personality." I was the consummate clown in those days and assumed that no one would like me if I were to lose the identity I had so carefully built and reinforced. I literally had to buy affection. *We compulsive overeaters don't have friends; we hold hostages.* At that time, my philosophy was something like this: hang on for dear life to anyone or anything—just tell me the emotional price to be paid. But, ironically, I usually ended up doing things *my way.* The price I ultimately paid for all this conflict and inconsistency? Obesity and profound loneliness.

The real moment of truth for me came after the OA "language" that initially seemed so strange began to have meaning for me, and after I had contributed a few aphorisms of my own to the Program. (I really believe that a similar moment of truth comes to all of us.) Whether we lose all the weight we want to or not, the *real* thrust of this Program is not how to lose weight, but *how to keep it off*. In other words, how do we *maintain* what we've worked so hard to achieve in the first place? The answer is a simple one that is probably familiar to most everyone: *eat less and exercise more*. Why is it, then, that even when people learn to do these things and see them working, they *still* don't incorporate them into their lives on a permanent basis?

I've promised myself hundreds of times that if I lost a specific amount of weight, I would never gain that weight back again. But regardless of my good intentions and steely self-will, each time I lost weight, I gained it back again. When I came to OA, I was promised that this was the last stop, that I would never regain the weight once I lost it. But as I spent more time in the Program, I saw the highly disciplined "abstainers" fall by the wayside. The excess weight these people were fighting so hard to lose came off, then returned—along with a sense of personal humiliation for having broken abstinence.

Could this possibly be the Program of recovery AA and the Big Book gave to us? Why the failures? Look around. How many people do you know who have lost weight and continue to maintain that loss? I'm not talking about ninety-day wonders; I'm talking about people who have been active in the Program for two, or five, or ten years. *When we talk about long-range success and maintenance in the Program, where are those highly disciplined, almost perfect abstainers?* The overall purpose of this book is to address that very point. If we can somehow learn to achieve sanity and recovery and *maintain* it as well, then perhaps the day will come when we can present a program to newcomers that fulfills the promises: weight loss and self-esteem forever.

The real evidence of maintained recovery is not weight loss or even abstinence, but *re-birth*, a new way of life attained through an ongoing awareness of the real power of the Twelve Steps.

I don't intend to spend much time in this book discussing the traditional tools of OA: meetings, telephone calls, service, and abstinence. For at least some people, these tools are an effective excuse for staying busy, yet not really being *within* the Program. Instead of tools, I've tried to offer readers new motivation, insight, and hope. I have written this book to give you as a reader an opportunity to raise questions, then proceed on and answer those questions for yourself. I hope and pray that as you read this book, you will come to feel a renewed and joyful sense of being in charge of your own life. At the very least, I hope that you will come to know—perhaps more clearly than ever before—what it is that you want out of life. There is nothing more liberating than to leave guilt, fear, pain, and the bondage of the past behind us—and reach out for a path to happiness and fulfillment.

Contents

Personal Stories of Maintained Recovery

Chapter 1

Introduction to Living Without Compulsive Overeating

If you are here to learn how to stop eating compulsively or to lose weight, we have nothing for you. If you are here to learn how to live without compulsive overeating, you are in the right place.

After fifteen years of sharing at OA meetings, conventions, retreats, and through my writing, I still wonder how to start, what to say, and what people expect of me. Everyone who shares probably wonders about these things from time to time. I used to share with only one goal in mind and that was to tell other people what *I* thought the Program was all about. At that point in my life, it was very important for me to feel that I was helping other people understand and appreciate the Program. That priority was perhaps appropriate for where I was at the time. I believed then—and still do—that the quality of life improves *dramatically* for people when they really understand this Program and epitomize it in their lives. The major difference in my sharing *now* is this: I realize that nothing I say or do will ever change someone else. I have learned that even when a person is open to new ideas and ways of doing things, nothing much changes unless a person

1

chooses to change. I now understand that in sharing with people, our goal is just to *be there for them*, not to get them to stop eating compulsively and not to convince them to *start* eating a certain way.

On more than one occasion, I've been listening to someone speak at an OA meeting and said to myself, Oh, here we go again. I've heard this person speak *dozens* of times. I'm sick and tired of hearing his/her story. Then, all of a sudden, I hear that same speaker say something for the first time that he or she has probably been saying for years. *Insight.* Each of us grows at different times and in different ways. After fifteen years in OA, I have learned at least this much: I don't play for the audience. I'm not there for them; I'm there for *me*. At this point in my Program and in my life, I know that whatever I do, *I do it for me*. Selfish? I don't see it that way. To me, "selfish" means doing something at the *expense* of another person. On the contrary, my Program is *self-awareness*. I share for myself, but now I do it with a different attitude. I no longer try to change or "convert" people or give them some special "word" or "message." Sharing with others is now an *integral* part of my life.

The Twelve Step Program as conceptualized in the Big Book of Alcoholics Anonymous underlies everything I say in this book. That Twelve Step concept is the same whether it is used in OA, AA, Gamblers Anonymous, or any other Twelve Step group. The first time I read the Big Book, I realized that the Twelve Steps could free me from unnecessary anxiety and pain. Each day since then has reinforced my belief that the Big Book and the Twelve Steps have all the answers I need. Over the years, I've sought help from many different sources. Even though I have found other things useful and encouraging at times, *I always come back to the Big Book.* I deeply believe that, in the long run, the solution to whatever is wrong with us will be found only through working the Twelve Steps and living the Twelve Steps. When I introduce people to the concept of the Twelve Steps, I tell them about the time my young daughter decided to make a cake. She had a recipe for guidance, but instead of following it step by step, she mixed all the required ingredients in a bowl together at the same time. Then, when the cake didn't turn out as she expected, she was puzzled and disappointed. She told me that she had used every single ingredient the recipe required. I explained to her that in order to get the result she wanted, she'd have to add and mix things in the order specified in the recipe. When you think about it, the same principle applies to the Twelve Steps: we cannot skip around or lump all the Steps together and still get the result we want. Some people follow only the directions they're comfortable with and they change or eliminate the "ingredients" they don't like. They get results all right, but not the results they desire. We can make amends, write inventories ad infinitum, and provide service in a variety of ways, but unless these things are done to reinforce the change of thinking as epitomized in the Twelve Steps, they will not mean all that this Program *can* mean to us. The Twelve Steps are designed to tear down the walls that exist between us and the kind of life and feelings that are available to us.

My son came home very enthused one day after

hearing a speech given by a famous man. He told me that he was very inspired by this man and what he had to say. I was pleased with my son's response to the speech but I asked him to think about what it had *really* done for him and for his life. "I understand," I said, "that you feel good when you hear this man and you're impressed with him as a person, but two weeks or four weeks or a year from now, will you still be drawing inspiration from his message that will help you in your daily life?" The real value of any information we receive is how we can use it in times of need. Most of us enjoy hearing inspirational messages because they make us feel positive and hopeful. But these messages don't always carry over to the next day, the next month, or the next year—times in the future when we really *need* inspiration or are tempted to eat compulsively. Let's say you attend a weekend retreat and leave feeling encouraged and inspired. I maintain that the feeling you leave the retreat with does not represent its *real* value. The value of *anything* we read or hear or observe is how we can, in practical terms, internalize it and utilize it in our lives. The real test of the new information we receive is this: when things are terrible and life falls apart, can we reach *inside ourselves* for that new information or insight and get the strength to go on? My sharing is of little value unless I can do it simply and practically, and in such a way that others can grasp it whenever they need it in their lives. My words have value if what I say somehow leads other people to a way of life that enables them to stay in touch with themselves and with God's power, and in that way keep things in perspective through good *and* bad times.

Actually, some of the most difficult and destructive times in my life have been the times when things appeared to be *wonderful.* Until I came to OA fifteen years ago, my life had not been terrific, so on the rare occasions in those days when things *did* go well and I felt good, *I just didn't want to let go of the feeling.* Now I can see that my compulsive overeating may have been, among other things, an acting out of my desire to sustain good feelings. For example, somewhere along the way, I learned that eating one pretzel gave me a good feeling. The pretzel tasted good, but it didn't take long to chew and swallow it, *then it was gone, along with the good feeling.* I soon discovered, though, that if I ate a gigantic bag of pretzels, I could *prolong* that good feeling. Then I'd think, I've eaten that bag of pretzels, now what? *"Now what"* was usually another bag of pretzels and the chance to perpetuate the good feeling until my supply of pretzels was completely gone. Then I'd just find something else to eat, and something else...and something else. When my food supply was gone or I was physically unable to eat another thing, I could look in the mirror and feel disgusted with myself.

Whether our problem is compulsive overeating, alcoholism, or other drug abuse, *low self-esteem* is likely to be an important underlying factor. Somehow, we have come to believe that we will achieve self-esteem if we can just manage to get thin and get approval from others. But I think we run into problems when we lose sight of the real *meaning* of self-esteem. Approval from others cannot give us *self-esteem.* It is counter-productive to depend on approval from other people, for that just sets us up for having to meet *their* standards. And if a person has low self-esteem to begin with, then basing the development of self-esteem on "perfect abstinence"—an impossible goal—only sets the stage for failure. I once heard a young woman at an OA meeting tearfully share that she had broken her abstinence by eating *one strawberry*. Other people at the meeting seemed to agree with her assessment. At the same meeting, I heard a man say that without abstinence, *he was nothing.* I thought it was very unfortunate that other people at the meeting shared the perception that the Program is all about perfect abstinence. Not one person at that meeting even *attempted* to put abstinence in perspective. I'm aware of the fact that many people believe abstinence is the key to recovery and that without abstinence there is no Program. *But abstinence is only one facet of recovery and the ability to maintain recovery.*

An oldtimer in AA once said, "If you are in AA to learn how to stop drinking, you are in the wrong place. If you are here to learn how to live without drinking, you are in the right place." I like to paraphrase that statement for compulsive overeaters: *If you are here to learn how to stop eating compulsively or to lose weight, we have nothing for you. If you are here to learn how to live without compulsive overeating, you are in the right place.*

I think that some OA groups spend a little too much time and energy adapting the OA Program for the newcomer, possibly at the expense of those who are already *in* the Program. I believe that we do a disservice to ourselves and to others each time we mask what we are so as not to scare the newcomer away. For instance, one OA group I know of doesn't say the Lord's Prayer at the end of their meeting in deference to any newcomers who may not believe in God. Now, if the newcomer's resolve is that fragile, he or she probably won't continue on in the Program anyway. In the meantime, why deprive other people in OA who may appreciate having the opportunity to pray together? When I hear it said during OA meetings that newcomers are the most important people present, I always feel a bit uncomfortable. Some newcomers respond favorably to all the attention they receive at their first meeting, then wonder what has changed when the attention shifts to someone else at the *next* meeting. Other newcomers recoil from the spotlight at that first meeting and never return.

Role models are important in the Program because they give us an opportunity to see that someone else has accomplished what we want. We don't always believe what we read in the Big Book. We don't believe, for example, that recovery and *maintaining* recovery are possible. We don't trust the Program; we tend to trust only what we *know. And we know for a fact that if we eat less, we are going to lose weight.* Consequently, we diet instead of working and living the Program. We don't know whether or not another person has a good Program because we're unable to walk in that person's shoes. What seems like an insignificant thing to us may be a *major accomplishment* to someone else. I am not an alcoholic, but my role models are the people in the Big Book of Alcoholics

7

Anonymous. I understand that it is not their drinking behavior I should relate to, but their sobriety and their maintenance of a powerful, life-affirming, day-at-a-time Program.

One thing should be clear: each and every one of us has the opportunity to achieve recovery and *maintain* ourselves in recovery. With all our weaknesses and faults, we strive to reach that goal. Even when perfection appears to be remote, beyond our limited potential, the Program gives us the opportunity to progress and improve. Probably the biggest change that has come into my life by working the Steps and the Program is that now I know it's OK to be imperfect and it's OK to accept myself as I am. God has *already* taught us how to live without compulsive overeating, but we either deny this or we are unable to see it. We compulsive people are so busy trying to grasp at things—food, people, jobs, material goods—to enhance our lives and "give" us happiness that we're unable to see that we have *within us* the very things we have been seeking.

There was a time when I couldn't stand being with *me* and nobody else seemed to want to be with me *either.* In those days, I couldn't stand the voices in my head telling me how bad I was, how terrible life was. I used to think those negative voices were God talking to me, so I had no faith in Him. To me, God was punishing and judgmental. I knew I hadn't done anything terribly wrong, so there seemed to be only two explanations for God's negative messages to me: either the very fact that I was alive was wrong, or everything I *did* was wrong. (Unfortunately, I believed both.) I continue to hear those negative voices from time to time, but now I know they're *mine*, not God's. Now I'm involved in *celebrating* life. Nothing has changed out there—the world is still the same; the people in it are still the same. *The real difference is me.* I am *alive* and not just existing for the next meal or the next excitement.

In the Program, we work to follow the natural laws of the universe. We learn to open ourselves to God, as we understand Him. We learn to disclose ourselves—our joys and tears; strengths and weaknesses; fears and doubts; the qualities of ourselves we love and the qualities we dislike. In doing this, we tear down walls, drop our masks, and join with all mankind in the ongoing journey to live life and strive to become all that we can be. Even if we can manage to do this only one step at a time, we *must* do it because, in the end, this journey is what makes life worthwhile.

Our Program promises that when we live the Twelve Steps, we join hands with all God's creations and, in doing that, we are fulfilling God's gift of life to us. The Program promises that we *can* recover and maintain recovery, and that we can begin to do it *now*.

Chapter 2

What Is Our Problem?

The Program teaches us to become part of humanity, not to separate ourselves from it.

Not long ago, I heard a man at an OA meeting share how much he loved being there and how difficult and unpleasant life was for him at home. He explained that OA meetings meant so much to him because he felt he could be himself there and could find the support and comfort he *needed* so much but wasn't getting anywhere else. As he spoke, people in the room nodded, then smiled and gave him looks of sympathy and understanding. I listened and watched for awhile, then realized that I could not hold back any longer. So I spoke up and said to him, "It's not up to me to burst your bubble, but I think you're in the wrong place. If you come to OA to seek refuge from the world *out there*, you are using us for the wrong purpose. OA is not a refuge; *OA is a philosophy.* How can we recognize maintenance if our Program is a 'thing' rather than a continuing experience, a way of life?"

I emphasized "we" as I spoke to this man because I made the very same mistake he did during my early years in OA: it was *my* OA meeting, *my* OA sponsor, *my* OA friends. I had a life over *here* in OA; over *there*

11

was the rest of my life. I was *determined* never to combine the two. Eventually, though, I learned that compartmentalizing my life in that way only prevented me from practicing what the Program teaches. OA is now so much a part of my life that I don't even know where *I* end and the Program begins. *We have to learn how to live in the world by becoming a part of the world.* Using OA as a cocoon of safety not only doesn't help us, it actually *deters* us from applying the practical aspects of the Program to our lives. *The Program teaches us to become part of humanity, not to separate ourselves from it.*

The Program also teaches us a way to work through what is a terribly difficult thing for most of us—to change habits that are so much a part of our lives that we find it *painful* to give them up. Many of us feel that as compulsive overeaters we are unique. In some ways, OA *may be* the most difficult of the Twelve Step programs to practice. It's true that we *are* different from alcoholics, drug addicts, and compulsive gamblers because we must deal with the object of our compulsive behavior—food—on a daily basis. We *must* eat in order to survive. Also, compulsive overeaters just don't get the kind of support alcoholics get as they begin to work on their problem. Take the case of an alcoholic who goes to an AA meeting and stops drinking that same day. After two weeks of sobriety, no one can *believe* the dramatic change in this person. Other people begin to comment about how terrific he or she is, and even if he or she did nothing at all during that two week period but *not drink*, family, friends, and co-workers think this person is wonderful for admitting the problem, *then doing something about it.* It seems that no matter what else alcoholics do or don't do, they are given a great deal of positive reinforcement for not drinking. On the other hand, a person could be active in OA for *two months*, abstain from compulsive overeating, and still not lose a noticeable amount of weight. That person simply isn't going to get enthusiastic support from other people. It is estimated that there are ten million problem drinkers in America today. Those ten million people, in turn, directly affect at least forty million other people. I've heard estimates that there may be as many as forty million people in America today who have eating disorders (compulsive overeaters, bulimics, anorexics.) But the effects of compulsive overeating usually don't have the direct and dramatic impact on other people that the effects of alcoholism do. Denial, blackouts, poor judgment, defensiveness, and other behaviors characteristic of alcoholism certainly affect the lives of the alcoholic's spouse, parents, children, employer, and/or employees. The symptoms of compulsive overeating affect compulsive overeaters *themselves* because they don't like the way they look or feel, but the symptoms don't generally affect the lives of other people in the same way that alcoholism does. In summary, I think it can be said that the social incentives and rewards for a person who stops drinking are more immediate and tangible than the social incentives and rewards for a person who stops eating compulsively.

On the other hand, the punishment is not as great for compulsive overeaters as it is for alcoholics. I can eat as many corned beef sandwiches as I want to, then

13

drive home, and nobody is going to arrest me because of it. My children are not going to be hesitant to bring friends home for fear they might see me eating corned beef sandwiches. The boss isn't going to say, "I can tell that you had corned beef for lunch; you're fired!" Many of us surround ourselves with people who *accept* our compulsive overeating behavior. We may have parents, children, a spouse, friends, co-workers, and other associates who have absolutely no problem with our compulsive eating behavior. And it's unlikely that other people would say anything to us about our behavior. As compulsive overeaters, our *state of mind* is similar to the state of mind of the alcoholic, the drug addict, and the compulsive gambler, but the consequences of our compulsive overeating behavior usually don't have the same kind of impact on the people in our lives that these other compulsive behaviors do.

Despite the obvious and not-so-obvious differences between compulsive behaviors, each and every one of us has similar opportunities and tools to bring about positive change in our lives.

People who join anonymous groups in order to deal with their alcoholism, drug addiction, or compulsive gambling are given clear and concise rules—*don't drink, don't use drugs, don't gamble.* But we cannot set or observe a *don't eat* rule. Unfortunately, the absence of a single clear-cut rule in OA seems to have resulted in an adaptation of the Program for compulsive overeaters. In time, food plans, diets, rules, and assignments were added. Through the years, attempts have been made to clarify and simplify OA, but the addition of rules and regulations only seems to make the Program *more difficult.* I've given up trying to convince people that these program adaptations are actually a *deterrent* to understanding and working the Twelve Steps; I've come to the conclusion that people just have to discover this for themselves. I'm not saying rules and regulations are right or wrong; I'm saying they're not OA.

I have found that when people tell me they need a "strong sponsor," they usually mean they want someone to tell them what to *do.* They want a program that could be called "Doctor, Do It For Me." It's almost as if they want someone to *command* them to do certain things so that when they fail, they can conveniently blame the person who issued the commands. But I have found that the more commands and requirements we add to the Program, *the simpler it appears and the more difficult it actually becomes.* Indeed, some of us think we *need* rules, regulations, and rituals in order to work the Program effectively. In some ways, these things make the Program easier to understand because they offer guidance for what to do from the moment we get up in the morning until the moment we fall asleep at night. But this highly structured and regulated interpretation of the Program also emphasizes guilt and failure. Each time we fail we can say, "Oh, it happened because I didn't do this ritual or observe that rule." (On the other hand, if things go well and we are *successful,* we know it is only because we did what we were instructed to do.) If things go badly when we have observed all the rules, rituals, and regulations then we say, "Well, I really don't know why God does these things. There must be some meaning to it, or else I just didn't do what I was told in the right way. I'd better do it right the next time."

Sometimes OA rules, rituals, and regulations have the effect of making people *more comfortable* with their old behavior and, therefore, more resistant to changing their thinking. *"Keep it Simple" is a legacy of our Program, yet we find that this essentially means we have to do it for ourselves.* When I first came to OA, I thought I was just *fat*. I didn't know I had this "disease." When I was told that I was a compulsive overeater—as if I were a diabetic or a cancer patient—I felt a tremendous sense of relief because then I "knew" for the first time that I wasn't just a fat person with a problem, but a *diseased person*. And somehow I knew even then that I could always fall back on that "diagnosis" to explain my insanity. If I discovered that I was eating too fast or too much, I would say, "Oh, that's just my disease." This disease concept was comforting to me as it is to many people. I hate to take a crutch away from anyone, but I don't believe that compulsive overeating is a disease like diabetes or cancer are diseases. Our compulsive overeating is a *spiritual* disease. Unfortunately, all the rules and food plans and assignments in the world simply cannot give new life and depth to our spiritual health. *Only the Twelve Steps allow us to achieve a spiritual beginning.*

For a long time, I went to OA meetings only to hear personal "horror" stories from others and to have an opportunity to tell my own. I'd share the details of my "terrible" life, then everyone would empathize and sympathize with me and wonder how in the world I had survived my ordeal. Now, as I look at my life from a different perspective, I realize it wasn't so *terrible* after all. I believe that I survived because I learned to *adapt* to my life. And it just so happens that at one time, *overeating* helped me to adapt. I thought my entire life had been terrible until I began to see for the first time that eating compulsively was not *wrong*, it was just something I did that had outlived its usefulness. Overeating had once been useful to me. In fact, there was a time when I felt that overeating was absolutely *necessary* for my survival.

Most of us have done an awfully good job of justifying our behavior. Our Program teaches us a way to go through one of the most difficult processes in life: changing ways of thinking that are so much a part of us they're almost impossible to give up. I was at a three-day retreat one time during very warm weather. I noticed that in spite of the intense heat, one woman in the group wore her sweater throughout the weekend. At one point when it was especially uncomfortable, we took a break. Then, just as we were assembling again, the woman with a sweater on asked if someone could lower the air conditioning because she was freezing. Everyone else in the room was terribly warm. I said, "I'm kind of warm and you're wearing a sweater. Everyone else here is warm." She said, "Well, I guess it's an old habit of mine. When I was a young child, my mother always used to say, 'It's cold; wear a sweater,' so I just got into the habit of doing that." This woman had actually *created* a feeling in order to justify wearing her sweater. Not to wear the sweater would have made her feel strangely uncomfortable for "disobeying" her mother. The woman then told me that

17

she was fifty-eight years old and that her mother had started telling her to wear a sweater when she was about eight. I said to the woman, "For fifty years, you have been listening to your mother's message. When you were eight years old, obeying your mother was appropriate and rational. Your mother was protecting you and perhaps it *was* cold. But now it is fifty years later and very warm."

Later that same day, this woman mentioned to me that she had removed her sweater, but was still feeling cold. I told her that it was OK to feel cold without doing anything about it. I also told her that if she could begin concentrating on the *facts*—whether or not it was cold and, therefore, whether or not it was appropriate to wear her sweater—she wouldn't have to deal with imagined thoughts that her mother wouldn't like her if she didn't obey. (As children, we sometimes have the perception that our mothers won't like us unless we obey them.) It struck me that this woman probably was still hanging on to that kind of childhood perception. In my opinion, this brief dialogue made the whole weekend worthwhile because this woman was doing exactly what so many of us do all the time. We still hear messages—direct, indirect, or even completely fantasized—that we first heard ten, twenty, thirty, forty, even fifty years ago. We are acting out long after "Mommy" or some other voice has stopped protecting and advising us. I believe that those old, now-irrelevant messages create the kind of conflict in our lives that generates and perpetuates compulsive behavior.

Recovery means getting our sanity back. At first, I couldn't even grasp the concept that I ever *had* sanity.

Frankly, I don't remember *ever* having a day of sanity prior to my recovery from compulsive overeating. *Eating* certainly didn't give me sanity. I didn't even regain my sanity when I started attending OA meetings. In fact, during my first three years in the Program, I was more obsessive than I had been when I thought I was alone in my compulsive behavior. I had kept my compulsive overeating a secret from other people, and I had also kept it a secret from *myself.* When I came to OA, it was like getting a license to go ahead and *be* obsessive, and glory in it. I was delighted that I had found a whole "club" of the same kind of people.

Now I understand a lot of things about the Program so much better. I understand that when we talk about regaining our sanity or being *restored* to our natural state, we mean being restored to what it is we were created for. The Big Book says we are "reborn," getting a fresh start. In the Program, we say we are recovering. I don't *want* to be powerless and I don't want my life to be unmanageable. I want a power that will give me what I'm supposed to have in this life. I want a power that will allow me the opportunity to be mature. I want a power that will allow me to develop, to grow, and to enjoy children, friends, flowers, and life itself. By reading the personal stories in the Big Book, I was able to see that this power was something that *could be achieved.* The first time I read the stories, I could see that these people had a sense of well-being that I wanted, but didn't have. It was not just that these people didn't *drink* that attracted me to them, *it was their new attitude.* Through a miraculous change, these people developed a capability to handle adversity.

They learned to survive and *grow* from adversity and had a sense of wellness in their lives *besides*.

Unlike the alcoholic, the compulsive gambler, or drug abuser, we do not have clearly defined parameters of behavior. So what? I still eat too much sometimes and I still eat too fast sometimes. Certainly there will be occasions in my life when I won't be able to deal effectively with food. Nobody is ever going to have perfect abstinence at all times—I don't think we should even lay that kind of burden on ourselves. For too long, we have identified "bingeing" as a decisive mark of shame that we wear almost with pride. We figure that bingeing behavior shows the world just how "sick" and "bad" we really are. Throughout our lives, we are going to encounter desserts, bread, potatoes, butter, and other tempting things to eat. We can eat all we want and nobody is going to arrest us or even force us to stop. We must learn to live with going to restaurants and parties and having our former binge foods readily available to us. We must learn to find the power to say, "No, I'm just not going to eat it." Our Program is of little value to us if we cannot deal with food, and deal with it under *ordinary, real-life circumstances*.

Actually, regular mealtimes rarely present a problem for compulsive overeaters. Instead, our problem usually arises when we are *alone with food*. Suppose a person who is a compulsive overeater was served all of his or her favorite foods while completely alone in a private room. The problem is not whether that person eats the food or doesn't eat the food; the problem is that compulsive overeaters think they are so sick that they cannot deal with food by themselves and actually feel the need for *protection* from food and certain situations.

We cannot live our lives using OA as an excuse for failure *or* success. We should not run to our meetings (or our sponsors) as if they represent safety and comfort in a terrible world. *The world isn't so terrible.* Sometimes, in fact, *the only problem we have with the world is our reaction to it.* Life isn't so bad, and it isn't so good sometimes. But if we cannot deal with having cake or bread or potatoes or gravy in front of us, then we have learned nothing. Think about it: if we're unable to deal with dessert being placed in front of us, how in the world are we going to deal with children who don't do what we'd like to have them do, or with a call in the middle of the night telling us that someone we care about is ill, or with our own illness? If we cannot deal with the food at parties and restaurants, how in the world are we going to deal with adversity? How are we going to deal with success when we don't feel worthy of it? How are we going to deal with common annoyances like flat tires when we are in a hurry, or people who don't show up on time when we're counting on them? *Living is having a problem, solving it, and going on to the next problem.*

People often ask me now how I manage to do so much. That question represents a real change for me because in the past, my whole life was spent *thinking* rather than *doing*. I did the things I did either to *create* a feeling for myself or to *get rid* of a feeling. My behavior was never based on *choice*, it was based completely on my reactions to people and circumstances.

21

Consequently, I got almost nothing done. I was like a hamster on a wheel. When I received a phone call in those days, I would automatically think to myself, "Why are they calling me? What do they want? Can I give it to them?" In fact, whenever I got a phone call, I also got a sinking feeling that *it couldn't possibly be good news.* Some of us become so adept with this kind of automatic reaction based on fear and negativity that we completely lose sight of the fact that other ways of thinking *do exist.*

We cannot learn how to deal with life unless we learn how to deal with *living.* And the way we learn to do this is by having someone instruct us, *preferably through the example of his or her life.* Learning by example is sometimes a little threatening to us because we have been tilted in the wrong direction for so long. *We perceive things through smoky glasses.* Years ago, for example, I got word while I was at work one day that a policeman was in the building and waiting to see me. I immediately panicked, broke out in a sweat, and thought to myself "Oh God, what did I do wrong? What terrible thing has happened?" Before I even knew the *facts,* I automatically went through the process of experiencing fear to the point that I actually began considering what I could do to protect myself from a completely fantasized fate.

Somehow, we have mistakenly learned that when we get feelings of fear that *necessarily* means something is wrong. Then, if nothing *is* wrong, we think, "What a relief; I feel so good because nothing is wrong." All these thoughts are going on in our heads and we have used our time and energy dealing with something that has no basis in reality. I think that our minds actually become *cluttered* with that kind of thought process. As a consequence, we perceive everything through a distorted view, and we spend so much energy preparing for fantasized events that when something *real* happens, we are totally unprepared and without the energy we need to deal with it effectively. Would you want to have a cab driver, a security guard, a lawyer, a doctor, an accountant, a computer expert, a banker, or a teacher for your children whose mind is cluttered in the way our minds were cluttered when we came to the Program? At that time, most of us used our minds primarily to beat ourselves or to create an impression for others. Would you want to have someone teach your child who is busy working out his or her own feelings at the expense of children? Would you want your accountant to discuss your personal tax problems with another client in order to satisfy his or her own ego?

I'll share a very simple example of the change in my thinking that has given me a gift of time. Suppose I buy a new suit, then realize I don't have a shirt in my wardrobe to match it. Based on that determination, I decide to buy a new shirt and I simply go to the store of my choice and purchase it. The decision and transaction take me all of fifteen or twenty minutes. In the past, I would decide to buy a shirt for no real reason other than that I wanted it or wanted to feel good, or powerful, or spontaneous. I'd spend time and energy trying to decide what store to go to, whether or not to have my initials embroidered on the shirt, and whether or not to buy the style I *thought* I wanted in a silk fabric. Instead of considering what items in my wardrobe I could wear with the shirt, I would spend my time and energy thinking about how people might perceive me with this shirt on and how I would feel if they didn't perceive me the way I *wanted* them to. When we think this way, *nothing* is dealt with in perspective and we eventually wear ourselves out. If I spend fifteen minutes buying a shirt instead of fifteen minutes buying a shirt and an additional two hours *thinking* about buying a shirt, I save two hours that I used to waste. Now, because of my new way of thinking, I have more time in my life.

It used to be that I never left for home after a day of work until at least seven o'clock in the evening. And those extended workdays didn't mean that I was a *workaholic*. I stayed as late as I did because I never completed my work during regular hours. I told myself that I needed a reward for *every* hour I worked during the day. I just *had* to go out and do *something* to reward myself for my diligence. I wasted so many precious hours that way, then always wondered why my business day was endless, tiring, and unproductive. My lunch break typically lasted for two hours. Now that I am dealing with things in perspective, I work a full day with just a few short breaks. I now leave work at a reasonable hour and I find that I have time to get involved with activities I was hardly even aware of before—like gardening. In fact, gardening has become an important part of my life. Every morning now, I dash out into my garden to see what's happening there, and I actually rush home from work each day to see how my flowers are doing. If someone had told me several years ago that I would actually get *excited* about flowers, or that I would willingly spend my time digging in a garden, I would have said they were *crazy*. Today I feel so good about myself and my garden. My mind is focused more often on *pleasurable* things. And my activities are natural, not forced like when I used to chastise myself for being inactive and say, "*Bill, you've just got to get into these things.*" There is a natural flow to my activities now; they just happen. Without much thought or effort, I continue to get interested and involved in new things.

The result we all want—to be happy, joyous, and free—has always been *available* to us. But we have in some way interfered with that result. *We are entitled to be happy, joyous, and free. We are entitled to have the power of choice.* God has set everything before us and, in effect, has said to us that He wants us to choose life, happiness, and freedom for ourselves. We compulsive overeaters were programmed by our past experiences and we chose a living death. In time, we lost the power to choose another way. This Program gives us enough power and freedom of choice to choose a path in life that will bring us that happiness, joy, and freedom. Our relationship with God is all about the feelings we get that are natural to us. *Feeling good is natural to us.* If we can really see our relationship with God in this way, then letting go makes sense because letting go doesn't mean letting go of anger or resentment or friends or food, it means letting go of *having* to do something in order to feel good. We need to learn to let go of using food for our only gratification, *because gratification is a natural part of our life.* We

25

need to learn to let go of manipulating people and our environment in order to feel that we have value, because we already *are* of value. Sometimes we are so busy trying to capture life that it passes us by...

The Twelve Steps *

Adapted for compulsive overeaters

Step One
We admitted we were powerless over our food compulsion—that our lives had become unmanageable.

Step Two
Came to believe that a Power greater than ourselves could restore us to sanity.

Step Three
Made a decision to turn our will and our lives over to the care of God, as we understood Him.

Step Four
Made a searching and fearless moral inventory of ourselves.

Step Five
Admitted to God, to ourselves, and to another human being the exact nature of our wrongs.

Step Six
Were entirely ready to have God remove all these defects of character.

Step Seven
Humbly asked Him to remove our shortcomings.

Step Eight
Made a list of all persons we had harmed, and became willing to make amends to them all.

Step Nine
Made direct amends to such people wherever possible, except when to do so would injure them or others.

Step Ten
Continued to take personal inventory and when we were wrong, promptly admitted it.

Step Eleven
Sought through prayer and meditation to improve our conscious contact with God, as we understood Him, praying only for knowledge of His will for us and the power to carry that out.

Step Twelve
Having had a spiritual awakening as the result of these steps, we tried to carry this message to other compulsive eaters, and to practice these principles in all our affairs.

* The Twelve Steps reprinted for adaptation by permission of AA World Services, Inc. © 1939.

The interpretations which follow are those of the author, not those of AA, and are neither endorsed nor opposed by AA.

Chapter 3

The Program

The Twelve Steps are not for people who need them, they are for people who want them.

I believe that the OA Program can help people find a positive and practical way to create a better life for themselves. I also believe that the Program can help people accomplish much more than just worrying about the next meal or just "getting by" when life isn't so great. I realize now that I didn't come to OA to lose weight. Like most people, I came to OA to feel the way I thought losing weight would make me feel. For some reason, we think that if we lose weight, we will *automatically* feel good. It's true that some people lose weight and feel good. It's also true that some people lose weight and feel *terrible*.

I have come to believe that losing weight, in and of itself, is not the most important thing in *anyone's* life. If, after all my years in the Program, I believed that losing weight was the key to feeling good, I would certainly use every opportunity I had to say so. The fact is, I know thin people who feel bad all the time and I know fat people who are *happy*. Despite the glorification of thinness in this country, there is nothing inherently *bad* about being fat. Being fat is not bad, and being thin is not necessarily good. The simple fact is that we compulsive overeaters have utilized eating for something beyond nourishment and gratification. We have used eating as one of our few sources of happiness *and* as a source of our pain. *To learn how to feel well—or learn how to feel bad and go on anyway—is perhaps the most important lesson we can learn. What does that have to do with losing weight? Everything!*

I've always found it helpful to think of the OA Program in four parts: *the attitude, the foundation, the working steps, and the living steps.*

As I see it, *the attitude* is the first part of the Program. Unfortunately, I have found that relatively little time is spent in OA discussing the attitude a person must have before he or she can effectively begin working the Program. The Big Book says, "If you have decided you want what we have and are willing to go to any length to get it—then you are ready to take certain steps" (p. 58). I maintain that if a person does not yet have this attitude, he or she is not ready to begin working the Twelve Steps. What I'm referring to here is the attitude people have in deciding they really *want* what the Program has to offer and are willing to go to any length to get it. *The Twelve Steps are not for people who need them, they are for people who want them.* Too often, it's *assumed* that newcomers at an OA meeting want what we have. But newcomers rarely get to see just what it is we have because there is so much emphasis at meetings on before-and-after stories and photos, "horror stories," and foodalogues. At most meetings, there seems to be very little sharing of long-term recovery and how people actually *achieve* recovery through the Program.

The second part of the Program is what I call *the foundation*, Steps One through Three. I've discovered that when some people conceptualize and work on the first three steps, they tend to focus on only *one part* of the First Step. For these people, the work begins and ends right there. I've seen so many newcomers carefully acknowledge their powerlessness in the First Step, then either slough off the Second Step and Third Step *entirely* or work on them only very casually. These steps presuppose that we acknowledge a Higher Power and that we understand what "turning it over" and "letting go" *mean* in terms of our own lives. But many people haven't had the opportunity to develop a clear understanding of these concepts before coming to the Program. Those of us already involved in OA should probably make more of an effort to talk about these things when we present the Program to newcomers. Of course, no one has all the answers, but then I think it's more important and helpful to pose questions anyway—questions like this: *How do we really get in touch with and grasp God's power? Where is God and what is God?* People need to achieve an understanding of these concepts that they're comfortable with *before* they go on in the Program.

The third part of the Program is what I call *the working steps*, Steps Four through Nine. This is the part of the Program that we use in our lives each day; it carries us forever. This is the part of the Program in which we cease to be a "members" of OA, and OA becomes an important element of our everyday lives.

The fourth part of the Program is what I call the *living steps*, Steps Ten through Twelve. These Steps represent much more than meetings, phone calls, writing, and sponsorship. To me, the Program is really all about how we relate to other people, how we talk to others when we share, how we handle the times of challenge, disappointment, and failure, and how we handle the times of joy and triumph. *It is important to understand that our success in the Program is measured not only by how much weight we lose physically, but also by how much weight is taken off our shoulders.*

Recently, a friend of mine was working on a thesis titled "Long-term Abstainers in OA." (After some discussion, we agreed that only those people with more than five years of abstinence should be included.) Of course, the first challenge my friend encountered in her work was finding enough long-term abstainers. After some searching, she *did* locate a sufficient number of people to interview. She also conducted extensive research on the subject and reviewed many written contributions from professionals in the field. Through her interviews with long-term abstainers and her study of research by professionals, she ascertained that less than 10 percent of the people who lose weight maintain that weight loss for more than two or three years. Furthermore, she found that less than 5 percent of the people who lose weight maintain that weight loss for more than four years. She concluded that an individual's chances for losing weight and keeping it off for more than five years are practically *nil*. Of course, there's another way to look at this conclusion:

people can succeed. A glimmer of hope is represented by the 5 percent who *do* maintain their weight loss. In OA, we have *proven* that if the Program is followed, it will always succeed.

Based on her interviews with people who *did* succeed in maintining weight loss, my friend listed sixteen possible reasons for their long-term success. Then she asked the people she interviewed to rank those reasons in order of importance (to their success.) In other words, given the fact that the chances for maintained weight loss are practically nil, to what do they attribute their long-term success? Of the sixteen possible reasons for success listed, *sharing with another person* ranked number one for both men and women in her research as well as in all other research she studied.

Sharing with another person—one person working with another—is the basis of the Program. We can make phone calls, speak at meetings, diet ad infinitum, do all the assignments in the world, write everything perfectly, and yet those things alone *are not enough.* I know people who can cite page and line from the Big Book just as they might quote chapter and verse from the Bible, yet this mastery hasn't done them one bit of good except that they *appear to be smart.* Sharing ourselves—not just talking with another person—is the most important part of the Program. Not surprisingly, one of the *least* important reasons for success cited in this study (number 15 for men; number 16 for women), was *calling in food* (reporting by phone to another OA member—a "food sponsor"—exactly what you plan to eat that day.) I know some people who have reported their food plans to another OA member *every* day for periods of time up to *five or six years*. These people will probably stay thin if they continue to call in their food plans for the rest of their lives. But why do that when there are so many other ways to use time that are more affirming and enjoyable than talking about food items and intake?

I once participated in a panel discussion with other long-term abstainers as part of an anniversary celebration for one of the original OA meetings. Now, a lot of people at that meeting had been in the Program for a long time and had been successful in losing weight and keeping it off. As I talked with these long-term abstainers, I discovered that we all had one major thing in common: even after ten, twelve, fifteen, or *eighteen years* in OA we still shared on a daily basis with someone in the Program and expressed the Program in our lives, on a continuous basis, to the best of our ability. Looking back on it, there's hardly been a day in fifteen years that I've not had at least *some* contact with an OA person because I needed that person or that person needed me.

I would guess that there are very few long-term OAers who have not, out of necessity, helped to organize a new meeting. I've helped to start about fifteen different OA meetings. Some of these meetings still convene on a regular basis. I work in an area where there are about 100,000 office workers within a four-block radius. Several years ago, it occurred to me that it might be a good idea to organize an OA meeting in this area. Today, people continue to attend this meeting and share during lunchtime. Other OAers have started breakfast meetings or early morning meetings.

34

I started a Monday evening meeting seven years ago and still attend that one myself. Certainly, starting meetings can be an exciting part of our Program. But this organizational activity is only one expression of our desire to put into effect what we have learned in the Program. Regardless of the form it takes, sharing with others makes us feel good.

Our interpretation of reality is, to a great extent, determined by how we *feel*. We human beings *are* our feelings. Unfortunately, many compulsive people allow the circumstances and events around them to dictate how they feel. When compulsive people feel *bad*, they often try to change the situations and circumstances in their lives in an attempt to alter their feelings—a single person gets married; a married person gets a divorce; another person relocates; another quits his or her job. *Compulsive people will do almost anything to change the bad feelings and somehow make them good.* Furthermore, we compulsive overeaters sometimes are like computerized programs in that we react in a predictable way when our "buttons" are pressed. In effect, these "buttons" say, "Pain, Please Press Here." But remember, we are accountable for the emotional buttons that stimulate our own automatic reactions. We cannot blame the people who happen to press these buttons, just as we cannot blame the newspaper, world events, or our own life circumstances. Our job is to get rid of the buttons entirely. Through the Program, we learn to create good feelings *naturally* instead of always being the effect of everything that is going on around us.

The OA Program can also help us get in touch with

both good and bad feelings. Many of us have some-how developed a belief that it's wrong to feel bad, but obviously *there are times in life when it is perfectly natural and appropriate to feel bad.* The fact is that *everybody feels* depressed at times, and the more we do to deny our depression, *the more depressed we become.* We must learn how to *accept* feelings that exist—good and bad—and we must learn to change our thoughts so that we can *live through* those feelings. We must learn to accept the fact that it's perfectly nor-mal to have an unhappy day now and then. We needn't feel guilty or that we have to take decisive action to make the bad feelings go away. Instead, all we need to do is *acknowledge* our feelings of depres-sion, then try to live through the day as best we can.

One morning a few months ago, I woke up feeling terrible. For some unknown reason(s), I felt horribly depressed and discouraged. More than anything, I wanted to stay in bed that morning, physically and emotionally pull the covers over my head and say, "the hell with everything." I had been ill a few weeks before that, so I could have justified a day of with-drawal from life by saying, "Hey, I feel bad, and I'm going to pretend that this day never even happened." But I realized that I had another clear-cut choice that morning: I could get out of bed, go about my business for the day, and just see how things would turn out. I *did* choose to get out of bed that day and face the world. It wasn't a wonderful day by any means, but it wasn't nearly as bad a day as I *thought* it would be, either. Instead of feeling sorry for myself and lamenting the fact that I was down and not feeling my best, I chose to *participate* in life that day.

To many people, joy is merely the absence of pain. I used to think that I was the only person who considered a day good simply because it was free of pain. Then I found out that most people in OA think that way—good days are just days that *aren't bad*. Still, a genuinely good day was a unique occurrence for me because the goals I set for myself were practically unattainable. But genuinely good days do exist for me now. Quite often, I experience *whole days* that are just about perfect. I have more good days now because I no longer allow myself to get caught up with insane delusions.

Learning to stop being the effect of everything going on around us is one of the most difficult jobs in life. I'm convinced that the difficulty of this job and the desire to feel good motivate millions of people to spend great amounts of time and money each year consulting with therapists, psychologists, and psychiatrists. But the person who succeeds in changing his or her approach to life and who is able to find joy where there was no joy before has essentially lost two hundred pounds. *Weight will come off when it no longer serves a purpose in our lives—that is the only diet I know of that ever really works.* Very simply, our Program is a Twelve Step approach to changing how we think so that we'll feel good naturally. And when we feel good to begin with, we are not dependent on food, alcohol, drugs, relationships, or specific events to create or perpetuate good feelings.

THE SERENITY PRAYER

God grant me the
Serenity
to accept the things
I cannot change
Courage
to change the things
I can
And
Wisdom
to know the difference.

— *Anonymous*

Chapter 4

Distorted Reasoning

For a number of reasons, we have learned to withdraw from life. And when we withdraw, we don't get an opportunity to grow up.

Obesity continues to be a major health problem in the United States and a serious personal concern for millions of people. One look at the diet and fitness industries in this country tells us that Americans are actively fighting fat and flab, and they're spending millions of dollars in the process. Unfortunately, *they're having to fight this battle over and over again.* Research clearly shows that most weight-loss programs have dismally low success rates *in the long run.* (Remember the statistics in Chapter Three: only 10 percent of the people who lose weight maintain that loss for as long as one year; after two years, the percentage drops to 5 percent, then lower with each subsequent year.) Experts in the field of diet and weight control say that the voluntary breaking of dieting—bingeing as we call it—occurs under mood pressure due to strong emotional stress which is preceded by distorted reasoning.

Distorted reasoning is really the key to our problem. Before we binge, we rationalize why we need to do so using a thought process that is, at that point, distorted and irrational. Each time we eat compulsively, our behavior is preceded by distorted reasoning, and that *results* in emotional stress and mood pressure. Rather than dealing with just the *results* then, why not go right to the source and do away with the distorted reasoning? Our Program is based on the process of eliminating distorted reasoning.

Most compulsive overeaters understand the basic principles of fitness and weight loss. But given an opportunity for "secrecy" (being alone with access to their binge foods,) I believe that most of them *would* binge. *Knowledge just isn't enough.* In fact, knowledge about overeating and obesity used to make me feel even *worse.* I certainly knew the facts about overeating and obesity long before I came to OA. But the bottom line was a self-defeating message I kept replaying in my mind: "I can't do it. I know what is right. I know how to do it. I know all the facts, *but I just can't do it.*" I guess I've *always* known that it's really pretty foolish to eat when I'm not hungry or to eat junk food at all, *but there were times in my life when I just couldn't stop.* That is a key phrase: "*...but I can't stop.*" We know it. We realize how irrational our thinking is at the moment we reach for food, but we can't stop. Our Program tells us that at this point we have lost the power to change our irrational thinking. When we begin to think rationally, we can see our behavior more clearly and decide when it's appropriate and when it's not. We see the *results* of our irrational behavior, realize it isn't working for us, and decide that we need to change. *We have the ability to change.* Our problem is not the way we eat but the irrational, distorted, immature thinking that takes place before we eat. *Irrational behavior is preceded by irrational thinking.* It follows, then, that we are working *backwards* if we deal with irrational behavior first. *Changing our behavior does not change our thinking.* Because our problem is essentially the way we think, then it just stands to reason that *the solution to that problem is a change in our thinking.*

Immaturity accurately describes distorted reasoning and most other irrational behavior as well. Indeed, immaturity is a fundamental problem for compulsive overeaters. *For a number of reasons, we have learned to withdraw from life. And when we withdraw, we don't get an opportunity to grow up.* As the years pass, the reasons *why* we withdrew in the first place disappear, yet out of habit and conditioning we continue to withdraw.

Before I really began to work the Program, I actualized myself based on conditions only, not based on conscious decisions. For example, if someone looked at me a certain way or wanted something from me, I felt compelled to react. Regardless of what I did or didn't do, it was invariably a *reaction* on my part rather than a conscious decision. If my team won, I felt a certain way; if my team *didn't* win, I was depressed all day. If I got some money, I reacted one way; in order to *get* money, I reacted another way. If I had friends, I reacted one way; in order to *get* friends, I would do *anything.* I was a *victim* of my environment, and I didn't even realize that I could *choose* not to live my life that way.

I'm aware of the fact that some people say positive

41

things about me and other people make negative comments about me. I *understand* that now, but in the past I didn't. One time, I asked my OA sponsor why people said unkind and critical things about me, sometimes for no apparent reason. And she said: *"Bill, if you put yourself out there, that is the price you pay. You can be quiet and you can sit back. You really don't have to say a word. Then nobody will criticize you at all. But if you put yourself out there, you pay a certain price. Some people will love you, and some people will hate you. If you withdraw, nobody will criticize you, but nobody will love you, either."* Through the years, I have made the decision that I can't afford the *price* of withdrawing.

When we get our first look at the world as young children, it seems very mysterious to us and our parents are all-knowing and powerful. When we are one or two or three years old, most of us know nothing but the environment of our own home. Even then, however, *who we are has already been determined* to a great extent. Everything that happens in our lives after that tends to compound and accentuate what we already *are*. Whatever we are, we were then. Now, chances are we didn't eat compulsively at that time in our lives. It wasn't until later in life that we learned compulsive behaviors to express what went on in the past. Our compulsive behavior is just an *expression* of the lessons we learned, so changing the behavior cannot change what we learned. Our compulsive behavior will not change until we eliminate the distorted reasoning that continues to make it necessary.

Most newcomers ask what abstinence really *is*. This

is certainly a logical question that deserves a good answer. But many of the answers people get are distracting, for they *seem* to be rational, but they're really just distortions in a new form. For instance, we hear that OA is a spiritual program and we think, "Oh, great; this Program is different." But then we're handed printed material that focuses on weight loss through controlled, systematic eating. This is only another *form* of distorted reasoning and, what is worse, it's given to us at a time when we desperately need *rational thinking*. You'd think *somebody* would get up at a meeting and say, "My understanding is that this is not a diet and food program, but a *spiritual* program."

I remember going to an OA convention during my early (still insane) days in the Program and actually trying to convince OA to adopt a particular food plan as the *definitive plan* for abstinence. Many of us believed that we could not *have* abstinence unless we *defined it*, so we tried to promote one particular way of eating as a kind of "working definition" for abstinence. *We thought it would be so simple.* We gave a copy of our food plan to newcomers with the encouraging (but unintentionally erroneous) message that if they followed this plan, they would *succeed* in OA. The plan we devised failed to achieve its purpose at that convention. Unfortunately, however, our plan actually *did* achieve its purpose in the long run, because many people are now told either at their first OA meeting or soon thereafter that there *is* a certain way to eat in the Program.

I realize that food plans seem like a clearer, easier way to work the Program, but they're rarely successful in the long run. I wish food plans *did* work. I wish things *were* that simple and I could say: "Here it is. This is the way to eat. Eat this way. Do this Step this way and that Step that way and you will succeed." If by some miracle these commands gave us power to think in a mature and rational way, I'd be the first one to say, "Go ahead and follow them to the letter." But people tend to become resentful when they feel they must do exactly as they're told. And when people are not in touch with their feelings, their resentment is likely to surface in the form of compulsive behavior. The Big Book says, "Resentment is the 'number one' offender." (p. 64). We compulsive people often come to resent *ourselves* when we sit back, look at our lives, and see that we could have freed ourselves from a negative thought-behavior cycle and that we didn't have to go through all that misery.

I disagree with the concept that God sends us problems because He knows we are strong enough to handle them. When we do try to deal with problems by ourselves—through self-will—we find that we're weak. We get tired and overwhelmed and we begin to wonder how we will *ever* make it. But then, just when we reach the limits of our own strength and courage, *something unexpected happens.* We find new resources coming from somewhere *within us* and also from the knowledge that *we are not alone.* God is on our side, and He always has been. Because of that knowledge, we somehow manage to go on. *The God I believe in doesn't send us problems, He gives us the power to solve the problems we encounter in the process of living.* But solving problems doesn't *undo* them

44

or make our world perfect; solving problems just allows us *to go on.* Where do we get strength to go on when we've used up our own strength? Where do we turn for patience when we've run out of patience, when we've been patient for years and the end is nowhere in sight? I believe that God gives us strength, patience, and hope; I believe that He renews our spiritual resources when they run dry. How else could a person manage to find new strength, patience, and hope in the face of catastrophic illness? How else could a hopelessly frightened person find a new source of courage that allows him or her to pick up the pieces and go out to face the world alone? How else could the parents of a sick child wake up every morning and turn again to the routine responsibilities of daily life? *I am constantly reassured that God is real because of the fact that so many people who have prayed for strength, hope, and courage have found resources they did not have before.*

Why is it that two people can have the same terrible things happen to them, yet one of those people becomes an alcoholic or a compulsive overeater and the other one works through the adversity, goes on with his or her life, and continues to grow and mature. The difference between these two people is that one of them wallows in adversity while the other one experiences the power to *overcome* that adversity. Where do people get the strength they need to overcome these terrible things? I have learned that we certainly don't have to bribe or bargain with God in order to get the strength, hope, and patience we need. Instead, we only need to turn to Him, admit that we can't do it all on our own, and understand that our ability to bear up under adversity is an extension of God's power within us. The kind of power I'm talking about here is not the ability to control food intake, but the courage to think rationally about things and then go on. I'm talking about having the power *not* to eat compulsively in order to deal with resentment, because harboring resentment is not an effective way to live.

I deeply believe that unexpected, just-in-time surges of power, courage, and serenity represent God's power within us. Are you capable of loving and forgiving people, even when they let you down? Can you forgive people and love people, even if they're not perfect? Are you able to love God, even when you feel that He has created an imperfect world, even when you feel He has let you down and disappointed you by permitting unhappiness and injustice in your life and in the world around you? Can you learn to love and forgive God, despite the limitations He has imposed upon Himself? He will not intercede, certainly not by doing things *for* us. He has given us all the power we need to intercede *on our own behalf*, and to help other people when they lack the courage and strength to change. If you can do these things—forgive and learn to love imperfect people—can you see that the *ability* to forgive, and the *ability* to love constitute the power God has given us? This power enables us to live in a less-than-perfect world. Can you acknowledge that you *have* power by virtue of the fact that you are here and reading this book? Can you acknowledge the power that comes from the people who have been here before us, not only those who succeeded but also

those who failed and then came back? Can you acknowledge the power that comes from the people who
have been around for years and keep coming back,
and are *there* for us, doing the best they can?

How do we reach out and find that source of power
within us? Where do we find the strength to go on?
What is the key to it all? When the alcoholics who
started AA first got together more than fifty years ago,
they realized that they needed to make some fundamental changes in themselves. In order to break the
habit of distorted reasoning and develop an awareness
of God's power within them, they decided that they
needed to adopt a *new mental attitude* that would enable them to see the power of God and get in touch
with it. Steps Four through Nine represent the process
they designed to allow themselves and others to adopt
this new mental attitude. These Steps were not designed to drag up the past or otherwise use it to
rationalize or explain present behavior. People who
think, Poor me, my past experiences explain why I am
the way I am, are accomplishing nothing. In fact, these
people are actually blinding themselves to the resources God *has* given them.

I believe that all human beings have within themselves the power of God, courage in the face of adversity, the quality to love even when it is not returned,
and the ability to reach out to other people. In the long
run, isn't that what was said more than fifty years ago
when one alcoholic worked with another and together
they developed the AA Program? Isn't that what our
Program is all about? Think about it: over fifty years
ago, two alcoholics got together. But AA didn't begin

when Bill Wilson stopped drinking; AA began when Bill Wilson *helped another alcoholic* (Dr. Bob) to stop drinking. AA began when two people worked together to help each other and themselves. *Our new life begins not when we stop overeating, but when we start practicing being there for another person.* Our new life begins when we extend ourselves, but only when we do so without indignation or resentment.

Our Program enables people to find a power to live by so that they can continue to mature and change and grow. The Twelve Steps are not designed to be an ordeal that, once completed, leads us to a beautiful horizon. That beautiful horizon is *within us* and, furthermore, *it always has been.* The Twelve Steps are designed to tear away the walls built of lies and fantasies so that the power of God within us can emerge. Once people have this understanding, the Twelve Steps actually take on new meaning for them and they become much more interested in completing them. Writing an inventory is no longer done with a sense of beating oneself over the head. Instead, writing an inventory becomes an opportunity to tear down the walls that have been built. Through the years, we have built these walls to protect ourselves from what we thought was a horrible world that existed "out there." Somehow we learned that the world was filled with pain and anxiety. We learned to protect ourselves from a world that was real to us as children, then we continued to protect ourselves because we continued to view the world in the same way we did as children. Ironically, the same walls we built to protect us from a world that we don't need protection from anymore have also separated us from the power of God within us. I see the Twelve Steps as an opportunity to break down these walls and become filled with what has always been there. *How* do we do it? The Big Book tells us: we find out what this wall is; we write an inventory; and we look at what we have *become.* The Big Book helps us to look at these things from a positive point of view, not in the spirit of "who did us in" or "now that I see why I am the way I am, it is all very understandable." Instead, the Big Book helps us to *understand* what we have become and *it helps us to see what is real and what is not real in our lives.*

In my opinion, fear of the truth is the primary reason most people don't work the Twelve Steps. And I'd be the first one to admit that the truth *is* frightening because, in effect, it tells us *"This is it."* Suddenly we realize that no power is going to come out of the sky, zap us, and say, "Now you're in OA and I'm going to change the world for you. This is it!" No. *We are all we have.* Nobody is going to protect us from the consequences of our own distorted reasoning and irrational behavior just because we go to the "right" church, pray the "right" prayers, or take part in the "right" rituals. I cannot believe that God resides only in certain places. I cannot believe that the power of God resides in some people and not in others. I have come to believe that His gift to us is the power to go on, and change, and grow, in spite of what we believe and in spite of what we have been taught. What does the Serenity Prayer *really* say? Note that it doesn't ask for abstinence. It doesn't ask God to do things *for* us; it asks Him to *grant* us the serenity, courage, and wisdom we need in this life.

In this Program, we deal with our problems by bringing out the lies and distortions that have ruled our lives and by looking at these lies and distortions—really seeing them—for what they are. This process helps us to mature. And when we mature, we begin to understand that the world *isn't* what we learned it was when we were children. The world is cruel, but the world is also beautiful. This Program helps us focus on the beauty in the world.

"Rarely have we seen a person fail who has thoroughly followed our path. Those who do not recover are people who cannot or will not completely give themselves to this simple program, usually men and women who are constitutionally incapable of being honest with themselves. There are such unfortunates. They are not at fault; they seem to have been born that way. They are naturally incapable of grasping and developing a manner of living which demands rigorous honesty. Their chances are less than average. There are those, too, who suffer from grave emotional and mental disorders, but many of them do recover if they have the capacity to be honest" (p. 58).

From Chapter Five
Alcoholics Anonymous (the Big Book)

Chapter 5

Some Thoughts on How It Works

. . . we have thought for so long that if the problem is being fat, then the recovery is being thin.

Chapter Five of the Big Book ("How It Works," pp. 58-71,) beautifully captures the essence of the Program. Too often, though, people take this extraordinary chapter for granted and they add and omit words to suit their own interpretations. When I first read "How It Works," for example, I substituted words I thought *should* be there and ignored words I didn't want to deal with. Now I know that when we read the Big Book *we need to read the black letters, not the white spaces between them.*

I always find it interesting to listen to people read the first paragraph of Chapter Five, because each person reads it in a slightly different way. For example, I hear many people accentuate the word *rarely* when they read the first line: "Rarely Have we seen a person fail who has not thoroughly followed our path." I think this emphasis somehow transmits a subtle message that says, "Whew, I don't have to do it." Consequently, this is what many of us actually hear when we read the first sentence: rarely do we see a person *succeed* unless he or she *follows this path.* When reading the second sentence in this paragraph, many people accentuate the word *completely:* "Those who do not recover are people who cannot or will not *completely* give themselves to this simple program..." This emphasis has the effect of obscuring the word *recover.* As I see it, recover is the key word in this sentence. People *do* recover and, of course, that is what our Program is really all about.

People in OA often comment about frequent use of the words *honesty* and *truthfulness* in the Program. I think that the emphasis intended is on the *capacity* for honesty and truthfulness. The Big Book refers to "having the capacity to be honest." Indeed, people who have been involved in the Program for a long time almost always emphasize their *capacity* to be honest with themselves. If "rigorous honesty" were a prerequisite for working this Program, I would never make it and neither would anyone else. There *are* times when we cannot or choose not to be rigorously honest. In fact, I think it's permissible for me to lie at times: I would lie if my country depended upon it; I would lie to protect my family. What the Big Book is really talking about is whether or not we have the *capacity* to be honest. *The Big Book describes a manner of living which demands rigorous honesty, not rigorous honesty that would result in a manner of living.* Many of us set ourselves up for failure in the Program by establishing goals that are not only impractical, but *impossible.* Even if a specific goal we set for ourselves in the Program *is* achievable, it might be very impractical to incorporate it into our lives for an extended period of time. This is why the Program emphasizes *capacity, capability, and ability*, rather than specific actions and goals.

Many of us share a common experience in that we were first introduced to Overeaters Anonymous by the media or in conversation with another person. I was introduced to the concept of OA by someone who described it as being, "Similar to Alcoholics Anonymous" (AA). At that point in my life, the only information I had about AA consisted of stereotypes collected from movies and television through the years. I assumed that when I became a "member" of OA, I would "join" an organization and go to meetings where other people would provide me with all the inspiration, motivation, and incentive I would need. I also assumed that OA would have a handy "help-line" I could call whenever I felt like bingeing, then someone on the other end would promptly talk me out of it.

In reality, very few people call someone else in OA to report that they feel like bingeing; most people call *after* bingeing. In my own case, I was much more likely to call someone at times when I was anxious, or lonely, or just wanted to reach out and make contact with someone. But instead of admitting the *real* reason(s) I was calling in, I would just tell the person I talked to that I felt like eating. I did this because I had been taught as a newcomer that the desire to eat compulsively was an appropriate reason for calling in. I never *did* disclose myself and the real reason I was calling by saying, "I want to talk with somebody; I'm lonely." And I didn't reach out in this way at times when I *really* wanted to eat compulsively. Many of us fail to reach out when we want to eat compulsively because we know that someone might talk us out of it. *What we really want at those times is to be talked out of feeling bad about eating.*

Many people want to lose weight, but very few people want to give up compulsive overeating. This basic inconsistency helps to explain the immense popularity of diet plans, pills, and programs. The development and marketing of these "tools" for losing and maintaining weight are based on the fact that *most people really don't want to stop eating the way they choose to eat for any extended period of time.* Basically, these "tools" are promoted with a heartening message: "Here—take this pill/program/plan. You may continue to eat the way you have always eaten and we will somehow manipulate or reduce the caloric content of what you eat so that you will lose weight." Beyond the fact that this premise fails to take into account the need for a change in thinking, there is another fundamental problem with it—a person can be on a diet plan, pill, or program, and still eat or drink compulsively! (I know this from my own experiences with dozens of "miracle cures.") Several years ago, a new diet drink was introduced and promoted in such a way that I actually believed it was the "magic answer" for my weight problem. To me, this diet beverage tasted just like a chocolate malt, and I managed to convince myself that I'd finally found something I could consume with impunity. I loved that "magic potion" so much I gained twenty pounds enjoying it!

People are likely to lose weight at the beginning of

a diet, food plan, or other weight-loss program primarily because they have a new commitment, with fresh goals and motivation to match. But merely changing eating habits usually doesn't work for long. In fact, I believe that people fail in OA because they direct all their energies into trying to change *habits*. People get phenomenal support and reinforcement when they go to meetings and report, for example, that they've been working the Program for four weeks and have lost eight pounds. But enthusiastic support from others eventually wanes. Other people naturally grow tired of hearing personal weight-loss stories and, in time, even the people who have lost weight tire of talking about it. Then, after the initial novelty and motivation wear off and the "easy" weight is gone, the "hard" weight is usually much more difficult to lose. We may look better, and if we have worked the Program for a time, *we feel* better. But we don't see things changing fast enough. So, we get discouraged. *We compulsive overeaters are not known for our patience.* Eventually we fail. We fail because nobody told us the truth in the beginning about how it works. *It works by working it.*

How can we begin to recover or know when we *have* recovered when we don't even know what our problem is in the first place? It took me a long time to really understand my problem and recognize my recovery. It's true that many of us could have been helped had we been told what our problem was at the outset. Instead, we spent time and energy trying to identify our problem as well as our recovery: "I lost twenty pounds—were the twenty extra pounds my problem and is weight loss the recovery?" "I divorced my husband—was my marriage the problem and is divorce the recovery?" "I got a new job—is my old job the problem and is my new job the recovery?" "I began a new career—was my old career the problem and is my new career the recovery?" The problem and recovery are not as clear as they might be because *we have thought for so long that if the problem is being fat, then the recovery is being thin.* But our problem is essentially a spiritual one.

When I tell people that I tried unsuccessfully to lose weight *many times* before I came to OA, I usually get nods and knowing acceptance. Most of us have had the experience of losing weight. When a person tells me about losing a significant amount of weight, I usually ask how long he or she is going to keep it off *this time.* That comment really seems to hit home. Before I do anything else, I make it clear to the newcomers I share with that we are not here to help them lose weight or teach them *how* to lose weight. I tell them that the Program is designed to deal with *changing* so that when they *do* lose weight, they will keep it off forever. I never again discuss diets and weight loss. I remind them that maintenance is a spiritual issue, not a physical issue. Then I invite them to attend an OA meeting.

At OA meetings we are told to share our experience, strength, and hope, or what we were, what happened, and what we are now. The Big Book says, "Our stories disclose in a general way what we used to be like, what happened, and what we are like now" (p. 58). I believe that the key here is the word "*disclose.*" Our task is not to *tell* people what we were like, what happened, and what we are now. Instead, we're supposed to *disclose* ourselves like the people in the Big Book do. By disclosing ourselves, other people will then be able to *perceive* what we were like and what happened. Many of the stories in the Big Book disclose how people lived their lives as if in the middle of a hurricane and how they, in turn, affected the lives of others. We read these stories not so that we can say: "Look how that person changed; he doesn't do that anymore." Instead, we read these stories so that we can say: "Look how a person can change. If that is achievable for him or her, then it is achievable for me."

So, how does it work? How do we maintain our emotional well-being? The Big Book tells us quite simply that we all share similar Twelve Step experiences and that all of us have hit our personal lows. The Big Book also *shows* us how *real* people went from despair to wellness, and it shows us that hopelessness need not be a chronic condition. It works the way they tell us it works. And it works by doing what the people in the Big Book *did*, not by being what they were. There was a time when I thought I had to be an alcoholic in order to relate to the people and the stories in the Big Book. But now I know that these people were sharing their recovery, not their alcoholism, with me. Now I am trying to share my recovery with others; the Program works for me by doing that. In sharing recovery, I *maintain* recovery. But as the Big Book says, we cannot share what we don't *have*. Even in recovery, we must continue to grow in awareness, wellness, and maturity.

Chapter 6

Choosing How To Eat

There's a world of difference between choosing foods rationally and craving foods while being forced to eat a certain way for the rest of our lives.

For many of us, OA represents a last resort. Before I had even *heard* of OA, I just considered myself fat and I felt bad. Then when I first came to OA and failed, I felt even *worse*. If our Program is designed and carried out in such a way that we fail, then why in the world would we want to continue on with it? If we fail in OA, what else *is* there? Why not work the Program in a way that will encourage success? Remember, compulsive overeating was somehow *necessary* to us at one time in our lives. This behavior will change only when we see that it is *no longer necessary*. Eating compulsively and getting gratification, then feeling bad becomes a less attractive option when we see that we can think and act in ways that *don't* result in bad feelings. Our Program gives us a Twelve Step approach to feeling good *without* having to feel bad later. Behavior changes naturally when *thinking* changes.

In some ways, my life became *more difficult* when I began to recover, because the parameters I set for appropriate thinking and behavior became narrower and

61

more specific. Behavior that had been allowable or even unnoticeable to me—lying, for example—is now very obvious and unacceptable to me. There was a time in my life when I was so adept at lying and deceiving myself that I was unable to get in touch with what I was doing or saying until it was too late. In the past, I wasn't even *aware* of the fact that I had learned to shut out feelings. Now I have feelings I never even knew existed!

When I wrote my first inventory, I didn't have the feelings of resentment that so many people talk about. I was so deeply into denial and deception that I didn't resent *anybody*. I either liked a person or I didn't, and my feelings depended on only one thing: whether or not that person liked *me*. I simply didn't have the tools to make an independent judgment.

Some people talk about uncovering jealousy when they write their inventories. I was so out of touch with myself and my feelings that jealousy was unknown to me. If someone rejected me for someone else or took something from me, I just told myself that I didn't want that person or object anyway. Years ago, I had a relationship with a woman I cared about very much. But after we'd been together for a period of time, she met another man she liked. As always, I assumed that the new man in her life was superior to me in every way. This woman subsequently left me and went to him. And when she left, I didn't feel the least bit jealous about having been replaced by someone else. Instead, I was noble and magnanimous about the kind of personal loss that would normally be a very painful one. After she left me for the other man, I actually said this to the woman I cared so much about: "I'm glad you found somebody. I'm no good for you." I was so completely out of touch with myself that I never even experienced the feelings of jealousy and sadness that would have been natural in that kind of situation.

Feelings of guilt were also unknown to me. I usually knew when I was doing something wrong, but I never had the *feeling* of doing wrong. Instead, I focused on intellectual observations: "This is wrong." "It's against the law." "It's against nature." "It's against common decency." But it was the fear of getting *caught*, not what I *did*, that kept me awake at night. In fact, during my insane days, fear was really all I knew. I was a sick person, a person who blocked out perfectly normal feelings. I was programmed early in life to block out normal feelings, and I continued to block out feelings long after it was practical for me to do so.

Through punishments and rewards, we have learned to *react* to people and situations. Some of us learned to react in order to survive painful, abusive situations. But other people learned to react too, people who did *not* experience pain and abuse as children. For a long time, I just couldn't understand how people with loving parents and pleasant childhoods could possibly become "reactors" in need of OA support. Then I met a lovely woman in the Program whose story helped me understand how this pattern of reacting begins and takes hold. This particular woman came from a close and caring family. Her father was a clergyman and she grew up in an atmosphere of love. Abuse and intimidation were not at all a part of her childhood. Until I really looked at her background, I was terribly surprised that this woman had problems with compulsive overeating. Then I realized that oftentimes the programming that leads to compulsive overeating actually evolves from love and protection.

This woman's parents had come to the United States from a country which, at that time, valued stoicism, restraint, and passivity as important tools for personal survival. Being "survivors," her parents came to value the survival tools they had mastered and they reinforced their daughter's behavior accordingly. In the family home, this woman learned that she would get approval and love from her parents when her behavior was most like theirs. Her parents reinforced her quiet, passive nature with love. But when she went off to school, she encountered new situations, new feelings, and new ways of responding to the world. She subsequently learned to express herself in ways that were unacceptable to her parents—assertiveness, enthusiasm, anger, sadness, and unbridled joy. A situation developed in which she could freely express certain feelings with her friends at school, yet she was not free to express those same feelings at home. For example, when she *was* assertive or even just physically active at home, her father would try to change her behavior with simple but firm directives: "Now sit still;" "Don't move;" "Don't mess your dress;" "We're having dinner;" "It's time to be quiet and contemplate."

Perhaps the lifestyle this woman's parents advocated for her was completely appropriate in the family home, but her life was developing outside the home, too. As she grew older, she spent more and more of her time in a world that included school and peers and community activities, in a culture that tends to reward self-expression, cheerfulness, and assertiveness. In time, this woman learned to withhold feelings at home. As a mature adult, she began to understand that the conflict in her life came, at least in part, from the love of her parents. In fact, many of us experience conflict between the survival skills we learn and need at home and the survival skills we learn and need in the world *outside* the home. Compulsive eating behavior is one of the ways we deal with this kind of conflict. When we're programmed to withhold feelings but the reason for doing so has long since passed, we tend to find other reasons to *continue* withholding feelings. After a time, the feelings are actually gone, but we continue to do what we have *always* done in order to avoid them. Then, food itself, the contemplation of eating, the process of eating, and the anxiety *after* eating completely control us.

Everything that touches our lives contributes to who we are. We are products of moment-to-moment experiences and some of us are *victims* of our history. People who have somehow learned that being out of control is intolerable seek to always be *in* control and to always have their finger "on the button," even if that means *creating* their own pain just to control it. As compulsive people, we cling to ghosts, fairy tales, secrets, stories, and misinterpretations from our distant past. Unfortunately, some of us even believe that we can read people's minds. Instead of responding to reality, we just press an emotional "button" and get our automatic reaction. ("They don't like me because...;" "I'm liked because..."). At times, we may be right, but we'll never know for sure and it really isn't important whether we're right or wrong. What *is* important is the fact that we continue to press our own button, or we seek out someone else to press our button for us. If there are 500 people in a room, we will intuitively seek out just the right "button-presser" for us. We will use any means available to us to ensnare that person. What evolves, then, is a destructive interdependency that sometimes even masquerades as "love." And this connection makes for a seemingly compatible situation: "You play my game and I'll play yours. You press my button and I'll press yours." In the beginning, the realities of this kind of relationship are masked with powerful feelings. A warmth flows over us and we may even "feel" that we're in love. We compulsive overeaters always want to be in charge of feeling good, yet it seems we always feel so *bad*. That irony brings many of us to OA in the first place. We come to OA because we want to feel good, but *we will always fail if losing weight is our ultimate goal.*

The problem we face in overcoming compulsive behavior is how to shed the thoughts and behaviors that no longer work for us and replace them with healthy and realistic new thoughts and behaviors. *Why* we do things becomes the most important consideration as we begin to make this fundamental change in ourselves. Behavior may be the same, but the *reasons* for that behavior change. A person who is working to change his or her motivation may say, "I still do eat sweets but I do it for different reasons now." This kind of thinking helps us simultaneously lighten up and control our feelings and actions.

There are people who say, "I don't know how to eat properly." I can't accept that. I believe that we instinctively know how to eat properly and that we quickly learn which foods are fattening to us and which foods are not fattening to us. Newcomers often ask me what they should eat and my response to them is simple: "Don't eat anything fattening; don't eat between meals; don't take second portions." I think that's about all we need to say on the subject of eating and food. We are not here to learn how to eat or what to eat. *We are here to be at one with the power of God.* I know that most people think they come to OA in order to lose weight; *I certainly did.* Actually, though, I was totally *unwilling* because I did not have the ability *or* the willingness to do what thin people do. No matter how much I wanted to be thin, I could not put down a piece of food I wanted because I knew if I did, I'd feel empty. Our problem is not that we don't have the power to put down the chocolate cake; *our problem is that we don't have the power to live with the feelings we're going to have if we don't eat the chocolate cake.* We're unable to deal with those feelings because we don't understand them. As compulsive people, the most important thing to us is being in control of our own pain. We can't stand deprivation of any kind and we can't stand not getting our way, even if "our way" is rife with pain. How many of us can go against the pain? How many of us can resist rewards? How many of us are willing to *live with* that terrible emptiness we feel when we don't eat what and when we want to eat?

Even as we struggle to abstain, we are still fighting

67

food and dealing with it. I'm not willing to argue whether this portion of food weighs three ounces, or that portion of food measures a cup, or whether or not I should even *eat* this or that food item. I just don't want to know about those things. Nobody can tell me that we are *different* because we have to deal with food in the way we do. It's just a little more difficult for us, that's all. So what? Oftentimes, people don't want to give up the game of dieting and food plans because then they will have lost the power. I understand that. What I *don't* understand is why, when we have a Program that so clearly shows people a way they can regain that power, they *still* don't choose it. Instead they say, "Yes, but... somewhere down the line, I may get around to it."

People can be in OA *forever* and keep saying "Yes, but I want to lose weight." My response is this: "So, you want to lose weight. You've *always* wanted to lose weight. How come you haven't? If wanting to lose weight is that important to you, how come you haven't lost it yet?" *We can want forever.* But *wanting* won't mean a thing until we have the willingness and power to change our thinking. The important thing is not whether we do or do not eat a certain way, but that we don't have to lie to ourselves anymore. We can learn to say to ourselves (or to others) honestly: "You know what? It isn't worth not eating candy in order to be thin." I used to fantasize that I could eat candy and *also* be thin, or that I could continue to eat candy because I knew I would *never* be thin. But now I know that I *can* be thin; I choose to be thin. I may decide to eat candy, but I will not lie to myself about it anymore.

If I *do* eat candy, I will acknowledge that it is more important for me to do that than to be thin. It just so happens that in my case, it's more important for me *to be thin* than to eat candy. For this reason, I choose not to eat candy, or chocolate cake, or doughnuts, or ice cream, or any of the other foods I used to binge on. It has now been over fifteen years since I've eaten those things compulsively. This long-standing ability to control my compulsive eating behavior is not a function of my sense of right or wrong or an irrational fear of fat, but *the result of my power to choose.*

I have lived as a fat person and as a thin person, and I know from experience that I just don't enjoy being fat. There is nothing *wrong* with being fat; there is nothing *right* with being thin. What *is* right is my ability to make my own decisions, free from emptiness and free from fear. I want to be free to choose to live *my* life, not the life *others* expect me to live. The primary thing that happens as we begin to mature and think more rationally and sanely is that we get to feel well. Being mature and sane is an option and it doesn't require us to give up employment, spouse, family, or friends. *Being mature requires that we give up a certain way of thinking.*

Even though we aren't required to give up people in our lives in order to change, we may find that when we begin to *think* differently, our relationships change: we may look at people in a new way and they may look at us in a new way. It's possible that people who were once very important in our lives will become much less important to us when we begin to think in a different way. As the change in a person becomes

69

apparent, dramatic things can happen: some relationships may change and others may even come to an end because the people involved are no longer necessary in each others' lives. But when people change *together*, a better relationship may result that is characterized by a new capacity for mutual tolerance and understanding. How can we accept someone else just the way he or she is if we can't even accept *ourselves*? We have used people and situations in our lives as excuses to justify our bad feelings: it's the fault of our spouse, our children, or our parents; it's because of the weather, the city, our house, our job, our unemployment. Whatever the excuse, the point is that the situations in our lives usually are not the fault of *anybody* or *anything*. Situations in our lives are the result of *life itself*...and, really, what's the point of wasting time and energy thinking about *that*?

Nowhere is it written that we must be mature and sane. We can be as crazy as we want to be. I happen to choose sanity and now I also can choose to stop eating compulsively. I choose not to eat compulsively and I choose to avoid some foods *entirely* because they metabolize a certain way in my body and make me fat. *There's a world of difference between thinking and choosing rationally, and craving foods while being forced to eat a certain way for the rest of our lives.* I don't weigh, measure, or count calories. If, by mistake, I'm given three times the amount of food I'd usually have, I just leave the portion I don't choose to eat. (In the past, I would have eaten the entire serving just because it was there in front of me.) I control myself now, not because it is right or wrong, but because I know thatfeeling good will be the result. I can choose that. With God's power, I am in charge of my life.

That is it: that is my "food plan." I know it's not the precise and dramatic answer some people would like to have, but it's the best one *I* can give. In time, I hope that it will also turn out to be the best answer people can receive.

Chapter 7

Attitude

...some of us come to realize that our real goal is not losing weight or keeping it off, but changing our thinking so that losing weight and keeping it off become as natural to us as gaining weight and keeping it on used to be.

Failure is practically *inevitable* for newcomers when they begin working the Program without fully understanding the problem they're dealing with or the nature of the changes they will need to make in their lives. In fact, many people already *in* the Program don't fully understand these things and therefore don't have the attitude that is necessary to really work the Program. This gap in understanding can lead even oldtimers in the Program to lose confidence in themselves and their Program. Naturally, people begin to have some doubts when they share themselves with newcomers and then those newcomers are unsuccessful in their attempts to lose weight, or they regain the weight they *do* lose. Most of us come to OA with the expectation that it is somehow different from other things we've tried. But how different is OA, really, if we come to feel that we have failed in our quest for serenity, peace, and joy? No matter how long we've been in and around the

Program, I think we all need a reintroduction to it from time to time.

Most of us come to OA with a desire to lose weight. And what we get rather quickly from the Program is a method that helps us realize this desire. At first this method appears to work quite well, because when we follow it we lose weight. *But then some of us come to realize that our real goal is not losing weight or keeping it off, but changing our thinking so that losing weight and keeping it off become as natural to us as gaining weight and keeping it on used to be.* It's important that we develop this attitude and then *maintain* it as we begin to see results. Thinness is no more an indication of a healthy mind than tallness or blue eyes or curly hair are indications of a healthy mind. If a person is thin only because he or she has been abstinent and that abstinence is what he or she gets accolades for, then what happens when abstinence is broken? (Almost *everyone* breaks abstinence sooner or later.) You know what happens then? This "abstainer" feels that he or she is a failure. And, really, what good is a Program that sets an unachievable goal—long-term abstinence—for people who *already* have low self-esteem?

What do those of us who are in OA *really have*? What do we present to people when they come to the Program? On a personal level, what do I give to others—the information that I've been in OA for over fifteen years and haven't had a piece of cake or candy during that time? The fact that I've lost a significant amount of weight and *kept* it off? The words I share with others? *None of these things.* In this case, the most obvious things are *not* the most important. The really important things are my thoughts, attitudes, and demeanor—as they are expressed *through the example of my life*. In other words, it's not what I say or how I say it that's important, but what I *am*.

I think that the most unproductive attitudes newcomers can have are the following: "Who am *I* to question anyone?" "I know it all; you can't tell me anything," or "What does all this discussion about God have to do with my losing weight?" In my opinion, an attitude of trust in the power of God and a basic belief that recovery can be achieved are *absolute prerequisites* for recovery. But these essential things are not achieved by just attending meetings or having a ninety-day wonder as a sponsor. The old AA approach of one person working with another is what is paramount here. How can we understand and practice *any* important new attitude if no one bothers to take the time to *share* it with us. What usually happens is this: someone hands us a "newcomer's" kit, or a sponsor tells us *exactly* what to do. Instead, each newcomer should be approached by a person who has recovered—not someone who just lost weight, but someone who has gone through *all* Twelve Steps and practices them, every day, to the best of his or her ability. In this way, the newcomer and the oldtimer have a clear message, *not in what is said but in what is practiced*. The recovered person exemplifies—*in action*—love, caring, calm serenity, and trust in the power of God.

How can newcomers possibly decide they want what we have if those of us who share with them aren't even in touch with what we have ourselves? We've become so accustomed to belittling and chastising ourselves that we even find it difficult to *talk* about our success and our recovery. Instead, we stand up at meetings and talk about how much *weight* we've lost. But our success in the Program is determined by the fundamental changes in our lives that *result* in a loss of weight. When the Big Book refers to a willingness "to go to any lengths," I think that means *living* the Twelve Steps and giving up the kinds of thinking and behavior that are in conflict with the Twelve Steps. The willingness spoken of here must come from knowing what it is we have to give up in order to work the Twelve Steps effectively. And living the Twelve Steps doesn't mean that we *can* work them or *might* work them; living the Twelve Steps means working all of them, and working all of them as effectively and deliberately and completely as possible. It's really amazing, though, how people will try almost anything—dieting and complicated rituals, for example—just to avoid twelve simple steps.

I've heard it said that the *real* contest in a professional basketball game often takes place during the last four minutes of play. At that time, it is likely that the competing teams are only a few points apart and, of course, under the right conditions, even eight or ten points can be taken care of in a matter of seconds. I think many of us work the Program in a similar way: we just play around with it for years until we get to a very precarious point in our lives and we feel that we're heading for catastrophe. Then we say, "Well, after all these years, maybe I'd better *concentrate on this Program*—write an inventory, make amends, and *really work* the Twelve Steps." When we *really work* the

Twelve Steps, we focus on changing our thinking rather than our behavior.

When we change the way we think about ourselves and our lives, we come to understand that we can continue to feel what we feel, yet we no longer need to invest time and energy trying to find out *why* we feel the way we do. There is nothing wrong with feeling uncomfortable, anxious, afraid, or angry. There is nothing wrong with feeling hungry immediately after eating. What *is* unnatural is to think and act as if food and eating will "fix" our feelings. One of the most difficult things to understand at first is that our behavior may be perfectly acceptable socially, while our motivation for doing what we do is *insane*.

I once heard a psychologist who had lost a lot of weight talk about eating disorders. He told us that his mother was a native of France and an enthusiastic gourmet cook. She moved to America when she was a young woman, married, became a housewife and mother, and continued her experiments with gourmet cooking by preparing exotic French meals for her family. At times when her son was reluctant to eat the food she had prepared, she'd say to him, "Don't you love your mother?" So, very early in his life, this man developed a habit of eating everything his mother prepared in order to "keep" her love. Eventually he became a fat person. But his training in psychology helped him understand *exactly* why he became fat, and he was able to lose the extra weight and keep it off. Years later, his mother again prepared a rich gourmet dinner and served it to him while he was visiting in her home. He ate only until he was satisfied, then stopped. His mother tried to lay the old "guilt trip" on him saying, "Aren't you going to eat all of it? I made it just for you." And he answered, "No; I love you mother and I appreciate the lovely meal you took the time to prepare for me. But I've eaten enough now and I'm satisfied. I don't choose to eat anything else."

Now if this man had been told that he *absolutely had to stop* eating the exotic French meals his mother prepared, he never would have had the opportunity to deal with his erroneous belief—that his mother wouldn't love him if he didn't eat everything she served him. While this kind of thinking is irrational, *it appears to be rational.* One could argue that this man was pleasing his mother. That may have been true when he was a young boy, but it's irrational for him to think that his mother would withdraw her love for him at *any time* in his life because of his failure to eat all the food she prepared for him. It is likely that early in his life this man somehow came to believe that his mother would like him only if he ate the food she prepared. Then and now, his mother may not *like* the fact that he doesn't fully appreciate her cooking, but assuming she is a rational person, her love for him will not be affected by his decisions about what to eat and how much to eat.

This is where many of us are before we begin to really work the Program: the only thing we can see clearly is the problem we have created to obscure the *real* problem. And the problem we compulsive over-eaters usually create for ourselves involves the conflict generated by the never-ending cycle of losing and gaining weight, complicated by unsuccessful attempts to change eating behavior. But the Program clearly tells us that our thinking, reasoning, emotions, ideas, and attitudes must be changed before behavior *can* or *will* change. My hope is always that the appropriate attitude will be described to people in such a way that they will be willing to see it, accept it, internalize it, and clear everything else out of their way to focus their energies on working the Twelve Steps. It's not an easy task, I know. But instead of complaining or boasting at meetings about how much weight we've lost, we should spend our time talking about the importance of changing our thinking.

Sharing with others is vital to the Program, but as we work the Program we must make decisions *for ourselves*. We cannot allow other people to make decisions for us or force us to make decisions through intimidation or rejection. If we do what we're told under these conditions, we are not making a decision, but merely reacting in order to avoid the judgment of another person. Our decisions must be our own and they must come from a conscious awareness of what is taking place in our own lives. People in the Program just don't have opportunities to make clear-cut decisions for *themselves* when they're told things like, "Here is what to do; that's all there is to it." It's very important for me to understand and accept the fact that the people I sponsor will (and should) develop tools of independent judgment. I *want* the people I sponsor to feel free to disagree with me. Similarly, my sponsor does and says some things I don't agree with. *My sponsor and I work the same Program*, but sometimes we see things differently. I know that I don't have to emulate her in order to work the Program and fully appreciate it. She shares her point of view with me and there is really no need for me to argue with her about it. I listen to what she has to say and consider it an expression of her perception and opinion. Then I proceed to think about it and balance it with my own perception and opinion. My relationship with my sponsor is not affected by whether or not I agree with her. Regardless of what I say, think, or do, she is always there for me—tolerant, caring, and non-judgmental.

I have more self-awareness now. (I use the word "self-awareness" or "self-esteem" instead of "self-worth," because self-worth implies evaluation and judgment.) What is natural to me now is the feeling of wellness—regardless of whether I'm feeling happy or unhappy. Now I choose to stay with my feelings and work through them rather than running from them, denying them, or desperately trying to fix them. Most of us have spent so much of our time trying to avoid feelings and doing things to avoid, deny, or otherwise "fix" the experiences we had as children that we don't even allow ourselves an opportunity to find out that our lives have changed. (Of course, many of the experiences we had as children will not occur again in our lives.)

When we adjust our behavior or try to control it in order to feel (or not feel) a certain way, we are interfering with our natural selves. Unless something undesirable is happening to us, being well and feeling happy is natural. But sometimes we feel unhappy for no particular reason. We don't know the source of our unhappiness. We only know that we feel "bad" and "unhappy," perhaps even depressed. If we do something in an attempt to make ourselves feel good again, we are interfering with the naturalness of our lives. *We interfere with our natural selves each time we try to adjust our behavior rather than our thinking in order to create or alleviate feelings.*

I certainly don't enjoy it when I wake up feeling bad, but so what if I do? I no longer allow the rest of my day to reflect this feeling or what I theorize might be the underlying cause. Most times, I don't even *know* the cause of my bad feelings. I just go on. And I don't have to spend the rest of my waking hours *striving* to feel good because I understand that my feelings—good or bad—are *natural* feelings. Most of us compulsive overeaters have become accustomed to extremes— feeling either very good or very bad—instead of living with an ongoing feeling of wellness. When somebody asks me how I feel now, I can honestly say, "*I feel well,*" regardless of whether I'm feeling good or bad at the moment. I think this Program is extraordinary because it opens up a window for us. As we continue to work the Program, we see new possibilities through that window—new vistas of wellness. We want what we see through that window, and so we go on.

Chapter 8

Spiritual Experience

Dieting is just another form of compulsive behavior...

Spirituality has absolutely *nothing* to do with losing weight unless we understand and accept the concept that what we weigh and how we eat to decrease, increase, or maintain that weight is *directly* related to our thoughts and emotions. What we do is the result of our motives for doing something and our motives are based on what we think and how we feel before, during, and after we do something. In other words, our actions, "behavior," and "habits" are determined by what we think and feel. It stands to reason, then, that if we want to change our behavior, we must first change our thinking.

Our *unwillingness* to see ourselves as we really are has been a major part of our problem. Contrary to what we might believe, we have been protecting ourselves not from the real world, but from the fantasy world we have come to believe is "out there." Distorted reasoning and irrational thinking have dominated our lives. We had a battle going that we consistently lost: we *wanted* to eat, but we knew that we shouldn't. Part of us said, "Don't eat," and another part of us said, "Go ahead and eat." It seemed that we always succumbed to the latter because we didn't have the power to resist the temptation. We are striving to achieve that power. Dieting is just another form of compulsive behavior and our goal is not to substitute one form of compulsive behavior for another; our goal is learning to live *without* compulsive behavior. *We need to be able to change our way of thinking and engage the power to fill ourselves up with living instead of with food.* And it all begins with taking that First Step.

In the Biblical story about Moses leading the Israelites from bondage to freedom, Moses comes to the Red Sea and waves his staff as God commanded. But the sea didn't part until one man trusted, *took the first step*, and entered the water. In the same way, the sea of despair will not part for us until we take a trusting First Step. Virtually *no* change takes place in a person until he or she takes that First Step. But so many people are discouraged when they *do* take that Step and nothing dramatic occurs. The Big Book tells us that dramatic occurrences are unlikely. In other words, we're probably not going to have the mystical experience of waking up one morning, looking in the mirror, and discovering that we've become thin. In fact, when we really *experience* the change in our thinking, we don't even *notice* that we're losing weight.

Like many other people, I always thought that a spiritual experience was, by definition, a *religious* experience. But the Big Book says that most people in the Program think that "...an awareness of a Power greater than ourselves is the essence of spiritual experience" (p. 570). The Big Book goes on to say that "Our more religious members call it 'God consciousness'."

What happens when we have this awareness of a Higher Power or conscious contact with God? I always assumed I'd feel a warm glow enveloping me, that I would feel God surrounding me, and that I would see His miracles with my own eyes. But those things didn't happen. I didn't hear voices or see images; I didn't really have a religious feeling at all. In fact, it's only when I reflect on the changes that have occurred in me that I feel the existence of God. I have come to believe that the *awareness* of change is the real spiritual experience. What does this awareness do for me? It gives me a sense of well-being.

When I first began working the Program, I felt the need to draw attention to the changes in my life and talk about them. I'd say things like, *"Hey, look what I'm doing; look what I'm accomplishing in OA! I'm not eating my binge foods! I'm being patient and understanding! I'm driving within the speed limit!"* I was absolutely *amazed* that I could make these changes, but I was still very self-conscious about them. Now I actually *experience* change. I'm no longer amazed or self-conscious about the changes and it's only as I look back that I can say, "Yesterday I did this, but at an earlier time I would have done that." I can say this only when I reflect on something that has happened.

One morning a few years ago, I arrived at my first appointment out of the office for the day and immediately received a phone call from my secretary. She said, "Did you forget that you scheduled yourself for another meeting *at this same time* on the other side of town?" (I had completely forgotten the other appointment, and it was a very important one.) She went on to say that the man I was supposed to be meeting with at that moment had just called my office wanting to know where I was. He told my secretary that there were several people waiting for me and the meeting was being delayed until I arrived. I asked her to give them a call, tell them I was delayed elsewhere and that I'd be there in a half-hour. I finished with my first appointment as quickly as I could. Then, as I drove to the other meeting, I began thinking to myself, Boy, these people are really going to be upset with me for being so late. What kind of excuse can I give them so they won't be angry with me and *might even feel sorry for me?* I considered all the elaborate lies I could tell to justify my lateness and avoid embarrassment. Of course when I got to the meeting, everyone was assembled. I was then almost two hours late. As I took my place in the room, a man who had traveled several hundred miles to attend the meeting said, "We've been waiting here for a long time. You could have called us last night to tell us you'd be late so that we'd know!" Out of sheer force of habit, I immediately thought to myself, How can I get out of this? But I paused, that reaction passed, and I said this: "I'm terribly sorry; I forgot and double-booked myself this morning. *I have absolutely no excuse.* Please accept my apologies."

Several days later, I thought about that incident and realized that I had, indeed, told the *truth*. At the time I hadn't said to myself, "Now, Bill, you're in OA and you've got to quit lying," or "You're going to get fat if you don't tell the truth." The truth just came out of me—naturally. As I reflected on that experience, I felt good about it. Of course, most rational people wouldn't think that *not lying* was such a big deal. But at that time, I had a long history of lying to avoid the realities in my life. It was a habit that had become an important part of my life. Actually, I could have told some very convincing lies that day that may have garnered some personal support and sympathy: I could have said that I'd been sick the night before, or that I had to rush someone to the hospital in the middle of the night and had no time to call, or that I was busy doing research for the meeting. But I told the truth that day because telling the truth was becoming the *natural* thing for me to do. That is what sane people do. Looking back to that day, I could reflect on the change that had occurred in me. When I thought about it, I *experienced* a change in my thinking. I felt good about not lying to the people at the meeting. I felt even *better* about the fact that when I told the truth that day, I did it *spontaneously*—not because of the fear of punishment or the promise of a reward. Because of what I had become through working the Program, my thinking and behavior changed automatically at that moment. As I thought back to that day, my awareness of the change was definitely a spiritual experience for me.

The Twelfth Step refers to a spiritual awakening, and that is the essence of what the Program offers us—*an awakening, a beginning*. When we begin to work the Program, we are essentially starting on a journey. But like all beginners, we stumble and fall and we make mistakes. Breaking abstinence is just one of many mistakes we are likely to make as we find our way. But remember, making a mistake doesn't mean that we have to start over. A woman I sponsor came to me very distraught one day because she had binged after going for nine days without eating compulsively. At that point, she absolutely could not see that she had, for the first time, accomplished nine days of non-compulsive eating. All she could see was her brief and temporary failure, not nine days of *success*. Instead of thinking that we're a Program of losers because we don't have perfect abstinence, we should think of ourselves as a Program of *winners instead*! When we work the Program, don't we begin to think and act more rationally? Haven't we started to think about what we *do* have, rather than what we *don't* have? Haven't we come to believe that recovery is *progress?*

When people begin to really work the Program and change their thinking, they discover that they have a new relationship with their environment and a new way of dealing with themselves and their world. And when people grow in this way, their self-esteem grows too. They no longer need to eat for gratification or to dull the pain they feel afterwards, because gratification now comes from living *and there is no longer remorse*. This does not mean that a person will never overeat again. On the contrary, overeating may sometimes be as natural as eating, but now it can be accepted as just that—a natural act that a person has the power to choose and the power to choose to *stop*.

Depending on continuous weight loss for self-esteem is a *setup for failure*. Since perfect abstinence is not achievable in the long run, why should it be used as a criterion that determines a person's sense of worth in his or her relationship with anyone, particularly with

self? Even the most rational, sane, and mature individual overeats from time to time. Perfection is simply
not achievable when it comes to eating behavior. It's
ludicrous to think that one can or even *should* go
through life never, ever again eating something fattening, yet many people label themselves failures when
they break their abstinence or "go off" their diets.
Many compulsive overeaters live their lives believing
that their low self-esteem is *completely justified* and
they become addicted to failure in order to perpetuate
these feelings. *"I can't help myself"*—I think that's
probably the most destructive concept of all. I wasn't
even familiar with that excuse until I came to OA and
they told me I was a diseased person. When they told
me I would never be "cured," I took that to mean that
I would never *recover.* Recovered people are not
people who are forever cured and they're not people
who have some sacred guarantee for perfect, problem-
free lives. *Recovered people are people who have
learned how to live life, and are working, every day,
trying their very best to do just that. Progress, not perfection*—I believe that is the spiritual experience we all
yearn for.

Chapter 9

When We Binge

The point is to have a program so that we will no longer want to binge...

It seems as if everyone has questions about bingeing: Why do we binge? What process do we go through? Where do we go from there? I believe that if the Program is presented appropriately to a person and that person practices it every day to the best of his or her ability, he or she will no longer have problems with compulsive behavior. I'm not talking about a complete and permanent disappearance of old ways of thinking and behaving. What I *am* talking about is this: when the Program truly becomes a way of life for a person, compulsive behavior will no longer dominate that person's life. *The point is to have a program so that we will no longer want to binge, because bingeing is no longer necessary to our sense of well-being. In fact, bingeing just isn't us anymore.* What is natural to us is maturity and growth, and rediscovering God's power within us.

At one time or another, almost everyone in OA "relapses" in some way. I've heard that this backsliding happens to people in *AA*, too. Sometimes we binge simply because we enjoy the feelings of fullness we have afterwards. Other times we binge simply because a particular food tastes good and the bad memories associated with compulsive eating are not vivid enough to deter us from repeating the behavior. But most of the time we binge because at some point in our lives we learned to "obsess" over food and eating and we simply have an uncontrollable urge to engage in an old and familiar habit. How and why we learned this behavior is not important; the important thing is to learn how to stop. We aren't here to play psychologist; we're here to accept what is real, learn to change, and create new thinking to replace the old. What follows from this is new behavior. We will stop bingeing when we stop having this irresistible urge, or when we gain the power we need to control the behavior that *results* from such an urge. If our compulsive behavior results from our obsession with food and our obsession with food is a learned way of dealing with a world which we believe to be unliveable, then the answer is really quite simple: we must learn that the world *is* liveable and that we can be in charge of our thinking. When thinking really changes, behavior changes automatically. This, in effect, is the promise of the Program. How is it done? Through an awareness of the power of God within us and learning how to use that power.

We learn the power and how to use it through the Twelve Steps. *There is no other simple answer.* Some people want to be told exactly what to do and what not to do in order to make sure they won't binge. Strict instructions like this may work initially, but experience shows us they cannot help us *maintain recovery*. We really begin working the Program when someone, with his or her *living* example, gives us the opportunity to do it for ourselves. No one is going to do it *for us.* In fact, I think we do a terrible disservice to newcomers when we treat them like children by labeling them right or wrong, good or bad, based on the way they work the Program. I really don't want someone in the Program to say to me, "Now Bill, what you have to do is write this at home tonight." I don't want instructions from other people; *I want examples from their lives.* Someone who has recovered from compulsive overeating is not a *better person* than someone who is still a compulsive overeater. We all know (or should know) that there is real potential for each of us, at any time, to turn 180 degrees and go right back to where we *were.* Just going to OA meetings doesn't constitute being in the Program. We're not really *in* the Program unless we share with others, read the Big Book, and live the Twelve Steps every day, to the best of our ability.

I often tell people that when they feel like bingeing, probably the best thing they can do is to go to an OA meeting. Unfortunately, however, the nature of some meetings actually *supports* our bingeing. At times when I feel bad or I'm uncomfortable, or anxious, or feel like bingeing, the *last* thing I want to hear is someone at OA telling me how wonderful it is that *they're not eating.* I'm not particularly inspired when someone gets up at a meeting and says, "God did it for me. I'm terrific today, and *everything* is just wonderful." When I hear pronouncements like that, I automatically feel as though I've done something *wrong. I feel bad.* On the other hand, when people get up at meetings and say they feel like bingeing, that doesn't inspire me either.

What is there to help us then? What *does* inspire me at OA meetings is people sharing their *recovery*, not simple platitudes like "God did it." *I want to know how God did it.* If I feel terrible on a day I'm at an OA meeting, I want to know how I can get to feel *good*. At least I want to learn how *not* to eat to numb my feelings. I *have* learned that I don't have to eat to *avoid* feeling bad.

People in OA are not doing us a favor by saying nothing to us each time we confess our latest binge. It would be much more helpful if someone would take the time to sit down with us and say, "Do you want to talk? I'm here to listen." Instead, people keep their distance and say things like, "Poor guy, there he is bingeing again. He really doesn't have much of a Program." We need to work *with* each other. We need to resist the temptation to say, "I don't want to go to that meeting tonight; everyone there is so unfriendly." *Whose responsibility is that*? The Twelve Traditions make it clear. Most often, we talk about our responsibility to the group as a whole, yet we also have a responsibility *to each other* as individuals. But we can't possibly act on our responsibility to others when we're worried about who's going to do us in or how someone might be taking advantage of us. We simply cannot contribute in a meaningful way when we're always involved in controlling our own pain. We can only contribute when we say, "I don't want pain anymore; I want to get rid of it. I have more important things to do with my life."

I'd like to clarify something about the OA fellowship as I know it: though many people use OA as a social outlet, it really isn't a club or a forum for socialization. I have friends in the OA Program whom I love as much as any friend I've ever had in my life. These OA friends have known me for many years now and they understand me, sometimes better than my *family* does. But as close as I feel to my OA friends, I know we can live without each other. Of course we would miss each other if we lost contact completely, but then we didn't come to OA for social contacts or friendship, or to get incentives and attention. *Our motive for being here is to learn to live without compulsive overeating.* Don't misunderstand; I think it's perfectly healthy to want friends and support and attention and incentives. Personally, I never would have stayed in OA had I not met people there I liked, people with whom I could share a camaraderie and common purpose. But the real reason I'm in OA is because I know what is right and I can do what is right. I now have clear insight. That doesn't mean I always *do* what's right, but I usually have a sense of what's *important*.

As a sponsor in OA, it is not my job to change people. I do, however, have a responsibility to *be there* for someone if that person needs me. I feel this way not because I think I'm God's answer to OA, but because the Program supports *me*. There is only one way I know of to help someone stop bingeing, and that is to convince that person to work the Twelve Steps. Without the Twelve Steps, people will not have the *power* to stop bingeing.

I'd like to make a little suggestion: immediately before eating—at mealtimes or other times—jot down the thoughts going through your mind at the moment and *exactly* what it is you're feeling. Get in touch with what is going on in your mind prior to eating—anxiety, obsessions, needs, and fantasies. Regardless of what you write down, as a compulsive overeater you will find that *not eating* leaves you with an almost overwhelming feeling of emptiness. This feeling of emptiness is *intolerable* to most of us. We compulsive overeaters believe that we must do something, *anything* to relieve that emptiness. Eating *seems* to be the only way out for us, but there *is* another way. Instead of filling ourselves up with food, we can fill ourselves up with an inner feeling, a serenity, a joy that we've possibly never even known before. We can easily learn about this inner peace. As a matter of fact, this inner peace is as natural to us as breathing. It comes to us as we practice this Program, day in and day out.

We admit; we believe; we decide. The first three Steps are mental activities, not step-by-step instructions for developing the necessary attitude to work the Program. In effect, they are Steps of *attitude under guidance*—a valuable opportunity to see how the proper attitude works in the lives of others, so that we can emulate them. There *are* people who do not binge. Everyone has the choice not to binge available to them, but many people are unwilling to do what these other people did in order to live without bingeing. And they're unwilling because they continue to say they're unable, rather than admitting that they're *unwilling*. Compulsive overeating will stop the day you can go to the refrigerator, consciously think about your feelings and say, "I'm hungry and I'll feel much better, more satisfied, if I eat something."

My life was *totally insane* before I came to the Program. Although I *appeared* to function well, there were actually very few times in those days when I was completely rational. Almost everything I did was motivated by insane delusions, negative thinking, and distorted reasoning. I still do crazy things at times, but now my life is much more natural, rational, and sane, more the way I believe it's supposed to be. I was an unnatural person before I came to OA. I was not living my life as my natural self and it seemed I was always filled with anxiety. And the times I was filled with anxiety were the times that I binged. For a number of reasons, there came a point in my life when I said to myself, "I don't *want* all this anxiety anymore. There *has* to be a better way. There just *has* to be a way to live that is not consistently filled with anxiety and emptiness. I *want* maturity because it is right and natural for me at this time in my life—it represents what God wants for me." I want to be able to stand in front of a refrigerator and make the conscious decision *not to eat*. I want to have the power to feel good and forget the refrigerator.

I still have days that are filled with anxiety, days when I feel strangely detached from the world around me. The old me would have tried to *do* something about those feelings, but now when I feel anxious I allow myself to *experience* the feeling, go through it, and focus on the fact that tomorrow is another day. Now I understand that when I struggle to "fix" feelings, I become the *effect* of my fantasies and anxieties. (And those are the times I am most likely to binge.) Feelings and how we react to them—that's a big part of the problem. I used to spend so much of my time and energy and power trying to avoid, deny, or create feelings. For example, we compulsive overeaters don't like feelings of anxiety, so when we feel anxious, we instinctively want to get busy and *do* something to rid ourselves of the feelings. Now I understand that there's nothing we *can* do about those feelings. Indeed, there is nothing *to do. In fact the harder we try to alleviate feelings of anxiety, the longer those feelings will stay with us. Now, instead of concentrating my energies on avoiding* feelings, I set myself up for positive things so that I can perpetuate feeling good. I still prefer feeling good to feeling bad; I still prefer feeling joy to feeling anxiety. Now I also prefer being well to bingeing. Now I just acknowledge feelings, then let them go and move ahead with my life.

This Program allows us to become aware of and utilize our inner strengths. In fact, the Big Book tells us that the Program is about power—how and where to find it and how and where to utilize it once we have an awareness of it. I now understand what the Big Book is talking about when it refers to recovery as "rebirth." Now I truly have come to believe that I was born in God's image with a soul, with feelings, and with the capacity to genuinely care about others with no thought about what might be in it for me. *Now I know what is in it for me: I get to feel good.* Certain events in my life caused me to build a wall. But that wall had to be torn down so that I could be "reborn" with new awareness and with the sense of God that exists in all of us. A person who has that kind of awareness has no real need to avoid life: he or she no longer has to engage in activities that serve to deny God's power. He or she no longer needs to avoid pain.

The world is filled with people who are searching for a day of happiness in their lives. In the past, I didn't even know if it was *realistic* to hope for an entire day of happiness. Now I have day after day of happiness, yet nothing in the world around me has changed. I still live in the same world with the same people around me and the same circumstances and situations to deal with. Everything in my world is the same as it always was—everything, that is, *except me*. Now I know that my worth is based upon my acceptance of myself, not acceptance from other people. I no longer give others the power to vote on me. I need to get rid of all the fantasies, lies, and secrets that have dominated my life so that I can get in touch with the power of God within me.

Now it's difficult for me to understand why binge-eating is important in a person's life, because it's gone from my list of priorities. I don't mean to imply that binge-eating isn't still tempting to me at times. It is. But at those times, I just make the decision that I'm not going to allow myself to go back to that kind of behavior. The change in me is much more than a weight loss—it's a change in my thinking, my conceptions, my attitudes, and my motivation for doing or not doing something. I have an incredible power within me that gives me the freedom to choose. What's happened to me is this: physical habits that I used for so long to help me express my feelings and my pain just don't *do* anything for me now. For me, that is the greatest abstinence in the world and that is the greatest sobriety. Chocolate is just chocolate now. It still looks good, and

I sometimes think about how much I would enjoy a candy bar or a piece of chocolate cake. But now I have the power to resist chocolate without having to tell myself that it's bad or I'm allergic to it. I have the power to resist the temptation now because the state of mind that would justify eating chocolate just isn't operative any more.

I realize that these revelations probably don't sound very exciting, but then excitement isn't a goal in this Program. Recovery comes when we practice the Twelve Steps, each day, to the best of our ability. When we begin to think and feel differently, the binge-ing is no longer necessary, so it stops. The Program also works through the feeling we get when we extend ourselves to another human being. This indescribable feeling of wholeness fills us up and replaces our obsession; we are filled with an inner peace, an inner feeling of wellness that eliminates obsessive thinking and the compulsive behavior that follows.

The Twelve Steps *

Adapted for compulsive overeaters

Step One
We admitted we were powerless over our food compulsion—that our lives had become unmanageable.

Step Two
Came to believe that a Power greater than ourselves could restore us to sanity.

Step Three
Made a decision to turn our will and our lives over to the care of God, as we understood Him.

Step Four
Made a searching and fearless moral inventory of ourselves.

Step Five
Admitted to God, to ourselves, and to another human being the exact nature of our wrongs.

Step Six
Were entirely ready to have God remove all these defects of character.

Step Seven
Humbly asked Him to remove our shortcomings.

Step Eight
Made a list of all persons we had harmed, and became willing to make amends to them all.

Step Nine
Made direct amends to such people wherever possible, except when to do so would injure them or others.

Step Ten
Continued to take personal inventory and when we were wrong, promptly admitted it.

Step Eleven
Sought through prayer and meditation to improve our conscious contact with God, as we understood Him, praying only for knowledge of His will for us and the power to carry that out.

Step Twelve
Having had a spiritual awakening as the result of these steps, we tried to carry this message to other compulsive eaters, and to practice these principles in all our affairs.

* The Twelve Steps reprinted for adaptation by permission of AA World Services, Inc. © 1939.

The interpretations which follow are those of the author, not those of AA, and are neither endorsed nor opposed by AA.

Chapter 10

A Point of Reference

The First Step is a point of reference from which we grow, not an excuse to use for the rest of our lives.

If I am "rigorously honest" with myself, I'd have to admit that there was a time when this is what the Program meant to me: "I'm going to write an inventory so I'll know who's responsible for my problems; I'm going to read my inventory to others so that I'll get sympathy; I'm going to pray as often as possible so that God will reward me for being good by making me thin, happy, rich, famous, and handsome; and then I'm going to tell other people how to live their lives." During my early years in OA, I also thought that the First Step meant I was completely and forever powerless over food. I wasn't alone in interpreting the First Step this way. Through the years, I've noticed that when people are asked what the First Step means, they invariably say, "I'm powerless over food and my life is unmanageable." But the First Step doesn't say that at all.

The First Step says, "We admitted we *were* powerless over our food compulsion—that our lives *had become* unmanageable." *Note that the First Step is written in the past tense. The First Step is a point of*

103

reference from which we grow, not an excuse to use for the rest of our lives.

The First Step gives us an opportunity to see— perhaps for the first time—that our lives *have* become unmanageable and that we haven't yet been able to get the power we need to manage our lives or to stop our compulsive overeating. But once we acknowledge our powerlessness, we need to move on. A sane, mature person doesn't *choose* to continue living an unmanageable life that is characterized by powerlessness over food and eating behavior.

I've heard people who've been in the Program for years confess at OA meetings that they feel like eating, or didn't act perfectly that day, or for that matter, acted perfectly but *thought* imperfectly. And I've heard so many of these self-disclosures conclude with the same words, "But, after all, I'm powerless over food and my life is unmanageable." When I hear oldtimers in OA say this, it makes me wonder what they've been doing if after all these years they're *still* powerless over food and their lives are *still* unmanageable. I think we make a big mistake whenever we look at the First Step as a limitation set down for the rest of our lives, or even when we say, "I have this disease called compulsive overeating. I am powerless over food and my life is unmanageable." We're misusing the Program and merely perpetuating our feelings of helplessness and hopelessness when we use the First Step to *prove* over and over again that we're powerless over food and our lives are unmanageable.

Unfortunately, many of us take the First Step, then emblazon it on our foreheads forever. When I came to

OA, I was fat. I *knew* I had a problem. Then I was promptly labeled a diseased person in OA. But instead of trying to conquer this disease, I used it as an excuse for my behavior.

It's worth reiterating that the First Step is a point of reference from which we move on, not a position we take for the rest of our lives. Unfortunately, many of us have taken this position most of our lives. The First Step translates this position into words so that we finally get to see ourselves as we really are. At some point, though, we need to be able to look at ourselves and say, "These are not just words; I *am* powerless over my compulsive eating, my life *has* become unmanageable, *and I don't want to be like this anymore. I want to change.*" The Big Book says that we "...have lost the power of choice..." (p. 24).

When we lose the ability to *choose* in order to give ourselves feelings of wellness, we begin to grasp for any feelings at all. As a result, we experience a variety of temporary, superficial feelings instead of the wellness that is natural to us. Having completely lost the power of choice when it comes to food and eating, we compulsive overeaters spend so much time trying to "buy" approval and reinforcement from other people that we have no time left to really *live*. We're able to convince ourselves of our maturity and sanity when we see proof of our achievements. As one compulsive overeater told me after his first OA meeting, "Bill, I'm not a skid-row drunk and I don't weigh 400 pounds; I have a job and a family and a nice home."

Some of us have directed whatever power we do have left into specific areas of achievement. Some of us have become workaholics, and that may give us the appearance of being "successful" and in control of our lives. As I was talking with a man about the lack of power to choose that is characteristic of compulsive overeaters, he said to me, "Bill, you say I don't have the power to choose, but I run a business that employs 8,000 people." It's true that some of us function very effectively in specific areas of our lives. But then many of us who take so much comfort in our achievements might do well to remind ourselves that at least some of our workday functions could be adequately performed by a computer. The quality that separates us from computers is not our ability to function appropriately, but our ability to function appropriately *even when we don't feel like it*. But when we're powerless and our lives are unmanageable, we lose that special ability. We have lost touch with *the power of God within us*, and we have also lost the *power to choose*.

If the purpose of the Program is to enable people to find the power of God within them, then why do people in the Program continue to concentrate on their *powerlessness*? If they haven't found the power in this Program, then what have they been doing? Our problem is a lack of power. The Program is designed to show people how to regain lost power so that they can choose not to eat or drink compulsively or engage in other kinds of insane behavior. If the Program *continues* to tell me that I am powerless over food and my life is unmanageable and always *will be*, then why would I want to stay around and continue working it? I don't *want* to be powerless over food; I don't *want* to live a life that is unmanageable.

106

Most of us *are* powerless when we come to the Program. Admitting this powerlessness is a crucial part of the First Step. We must admit and accept the position we find ourselves in on our first day in the Program before we can move on in the Program. Many of us acknowledge our powerlessness over our compulsive eating, then stop dead in our tracks and fail to take a look at the unmanageability of our lives. It took me a long time to understand how unmanageable my life had become because I *thought* I was managing pretty well. After all, I had gotten by; I had survived. (In fact, I had manipulated, cajoled, lied, denied, bargained, twisted the facts, and figured things out *my way*.) But in time, I got the opportunity to see that my powerlessness and the basic unmanageability of my life were actually preventing me from achieving fulfillment and happiness. Despite all my machinations, manipulations, and "managing" to achieve what life had for me, I wasn't even able to disclose myself *to myself*. And my powerlessness involved much more than just deciding what to eat and what not to eat. I was also powerless when it came to making mature, rational decisions. In other words, I was *just functioning*, and that is not manageability. A person who manages his or her life has the ability to choose right from wrong and good from bad.

Change and choice really form the foundation and hope of the Program. When we think about the Program in terms of change and choice, then any considerations we might have about four ounces of a certain kind of food seem insignificant. The concept of God's power within us takes on new meaning when we think of it in terms of the power to choose and change. When I came to OA and people spoke to me about the First Step, no one even *mentioned* those elements of power. They just said, "You are powerless and your life is unmanageable," as if that were the only consideration. *But there is so much more.* The First Step can give us hope because it tells us there are options. When the First Step became clear to me, I finally realized that there were more options available to me in this life than just being a thin, compliant "computer." When I acknowledged this and also acknowledged that I was an out-of-control, fat computer, I was expressing the power of God in me that I was still in touch with. *When we acknowledge these things, we have taken our first step toward sanity.*

When I emphasize the need to move beyond feelings of powerlessness, someone inevitably responds to me by saying, "But Bill, I've been in the Program for *years* and I still struggle with old thoughts and behaviors from time to time." Of course we do. There isn't one of us who won't now and then continue to engage in old thoughts and behavior. In fact, I don't believe I've ever met *anyone* who's had perfect abstinence for a significant period of time. I'm not saying abstinence is impossible; I'm saying that I don't think abstinence is achievable for compulsive overeaters in the way that it is for alcoholics and drug addicts. So what? The fact is, sometimes we *will* eat too much, but that doesn't necessarily mean that we're going to abandon OA completely. What do you want—never to feel a craving again? I can say from my own experience that we *will* continue to have cravings. But when we recover, we will have the ability to control the behavior that follows our cravings.

When I first heard the word "recover" used in conjunction with the Program, I just assumed it didn't apply to me. I couldn't recall *ever* having been sane, so what could I possibly get back or "recover?" Even my earliest childhood memories involve insane behavior on my part. By working the Program, I learned that I actually began to lose touch with God's power when I was very young. But somehow I kept in touch with enough of His power to perceive what I had lost. Now I know for certain that I was born in the image of God and that God's power is *natural to me.* People who are unable to perceive that they've lost the power of God within them are what the Big Book refers to as "constitutionally incapable of being honest with themselves" (p.58). I know that at one time or another, almost everyone says, "Well, maybe that's me. Maybe *I'm* constitutionally incapable." But people who choose to come to OA still have at least some degree of sanity. Simply stated, if an individual has enough awareness to know that he or she *wants* to change, then that person has the power to change, develop, mature, and *recover* the natural aspect of God's power within. *Awareness itself is an exercise of God's power within us.*

I felt as if a tremendous burden had been lifted from me when I finally understood that the First Step is all about freedom, not limitations. I had been working the Program with an assumption that I would continue to be powerless and continue to have an unmanageable life for the rest of my days. The Program says that we are never cured. I took that literally, but later found that I was mistaken. I think that the concept of compulsive behavior being incurable means that compulsive behavior will continue to be a *possibility* for us; there is always the potential for reverting to our old thinking and behavior. The very fact that there are people who've been in the Program for eighteen, twenty, or twenty-two years is very important. We need to know and understand that people can succeed and fail, succeed and fail, yet still come back to the Program. These people, in fact, represent the hope that exists for each one of us at every stage of our recovery.

We human beings are more than the sum total or capacity of ourselves. Within us is the *nature* of us, "God's power." The Program gives us the capacity to get in touch with God's power again. The Program also teaches us to manage our lives, to be powerful, and to have the ability to choose based on rational thinking. When people get power from the Program, they can honestly say the following about something they do: "I know *exactly* what I'm doing and why I'm doing it. I choose to do it." Now I have the power to *choose* not to eat certain foods and not to engage in certain behavior. I can choose because now I have tools to perceive myself as I really am. Now I allow myself to make mistakes.

Everyone makes mistakes, but there's a basic difference between insane people who make mistakes and rational people who make mistakes: rational people own up to their mistakes, admit them, then go on with their lives, while insane people react to their mistakes by saying, "I'm bad and I don't like the feelings."

If someone in OA who's trying to lose weight told me that she or he had eaten food containing sugar, I'd probably respond by saying this: "OK, you made a mistake. So what? The issue is not the fact that you ate food containing sugar, but *why* you ate food containing sugar. Did you know that the food contained sugar *before* you ate it? Was your behavior compulsive in that you couldn't stop yourself from eating the food, even though you knew it contained sugar and you shouldn't eat it? There's no need to be *afraid* of food, but that doesn't mean that we can or even *should* eat anything and everything. On the contrary, *we can choose* what, when, and how much to eat based on our nutritional needs and our preferences. *Choosing* is rational, mature behavior."

There are times every day and even entire days when I still feel powerless and that my life is unmanageable. But I know that I am not completely and forever powerless. I am not powerless over food and eating anymore. In fact, I can be very *powerful* when it comes to food and eating, as well as other issues in my life. Now my life functions well because I conceptualize it, organize it, and manage it through the power of God within me. Now I do things based on rational choice, not based on old fears and fantasized systems of rewards and punishments. Of course I still make poor choices sometimes, but they're *my* choices and I own up to them. For example, I still overeat occasionally. But at some point I remind myself that I'm eating too much, and then I choose to stop. I am no longer a reactor who can be manipulated and controlled by old thoughts and other people. Instead, I'm learning to respond with maturity and sanity to experiences that are happening *in the here and now.* I want to be alive and I want to *participate* in life, but I can't do these things if I just react to the environment around me.

A man once shared with me at an OA meeting that he felt absolutely *terrible* because he'd been in a state of panic for an entire day. I told him of my own experiences that day: the phone company had neglected to transfer calls from my old business number; the phone system in my new office had gone out entirely; my car radiator developed a leak and I couldn't get to a service station; and my daughter's car broke down on the freeway and was towed to a service station miles away from home. Dozens of things were going wrong for me that day and I was in an absolute panic. Was I serene and calm? Not on your life. I didn't know *what* to do. As I told this man, I finally just said, "I give up," then went on with the day and with my life.

It's completely normal to have feelings of panic and frustration and utter helplessness at times. In the past, I had actually been afraid of these kinds of feelings because I thought they meant that I was bad. I didn't like the feelings I had and as a compulsive person, I felt compelled to do *something* to get rid of them. I wish I *did* have a workable formula for getting rid of bad feelings, but of course I don't. All I can share is that there's nothing we can *do* about these feelings. If we avoid them or attempt to rid ourselves of them or hold them at bay, we only give the feelings more power. Wanting to eat is natural. Wanting to *over-eat* at times is natural, too. But being powerless is unnatural and immature. And with the power of God, being powerless is also *unnecessary*.

The Twelve Steps *

Adapted for compulsive overeaters

Step One
We admitted we were powerless over our food compulsion—that our lives had become unmanageable.

Step Two
Came to believe that a Power greater than ourselves could restore us to sanity.

Step Three
Made a decision to turn our will and our lives over to the care of God, as we understood Him.

Step Four
Made a searching and fearless moral inventory of ourselves.

Step Five
Admitted to God, to ourselves, and to another human being the exact nature of our wrongs.

Step Six
Were entirely ready to have God remove all these defects of character.

Step Seven
Humbly asked Him to remove our shortcomings.

Step Eight
Made a list of all persons we had harmed, and became willing to make amends to them all.

Step Nine
Made direct amends to such people wherever possible, except when to do so would injure them or others.

Step Ten
Continued to take personal inventory and when we were wrong, promptly admitted it.

Step Eleven
Sought through prayer and meditation to improve our conscious contact with God, as we understood Him, praying only for knowledge of His will for us and the power to carry that out.

Step Twelve
Having had a spiritual awakening as the result of these steps, we tried to carry this message to other compulsive eaters, and to practice these principles in all our affairs.

* The Twelve Steps reprinted for adaptation by permission of AA World Services, Inc. © 1939.

The interpretations which follow are those of the author, not those of AA, and are neither endorsed nor opposed by AA.

Chapter 11

Came To Believe

My willingness came from my pain; my recovery came from God.

I think we're always somewhat reluctant to change old ways of thinking and behaving, regardless of how long we've been in the Program. People who say, "I'm not completely willing," or "I binged; I guess I really wasn't willing," *are telling the truth.* Believe me, I know from firsthand experience that there are times when we are just *not willing.* But as we work the Program, we make amends more readily, we write better inventories, and our willingness continues to develop.

Obsessiveness is another matter. *Obsessiveness holds on for a long time.* In fact, our obsessiveness may become even *more* pronounced when we first come to the Program. Looking back, I can see now that I was actually more obsessive during my first three years in OA than I had been *before.* In my insanity, I felt the Program was granting me some sort of institutional permission to go ahead and be obsessive, and to do so in the company of others. I remember that I was so enthusiastic about meetings in those days. I gladly shared dramatic stories about my eating behavior, my weight losses and weight gains, my slips and my relapses. In those days, I constantly tried to be better by being worse. I was then completely obsessed with losing weight—the faster the better. Most important, I did not yet recognize the transference of my obsessiveness from eating behavior to involvement with the Program.

But even back in the days when I was still so obsessive, I perceived sanity as a state of wellness in a person, an attainment of maturity. And I knew that if this sanity and maturity were attainable, they had completely *eluded* me. Despite therapy and other things I tried, I had never been able to attain sanity. It was also clear that *no one else* had been able to attain sanity *for me*, either. And it's not that I hadn't asked for help: over the years, I had consulted with numerous psychiatrists, psychologists, and counselors. But each helping professional I consulted with failed in his or her attempts to get me to change, or mature, or develop in order to have the sanity I so desperately wanted.

Beliefs are not feelings; beliefs are conclusions based on experiences we have had and situations we have observed. (If I've been to five baseball games and have enjoyed each one of them, I then conclude that I will enjoy the sixth game. Now it may turn out that I don't enjoy that sixth game, but my belief based on experience and perception leads me to conclude that I will.) When I came to the Program, I didn't see much sanity around me and I certainly hadn't experienced much sanity myself. The only thing I knew for certain was that if wellness and happiness and joy were really achievable in this life, then I had failed in my attempts to attain these things. I had not been able to attain these things on my own and I know for a fact that no one else had been able to give them *to* me. I finally reached the conclusion that wellness, happiness, and joy were perhaps not available to me *after all*, or that they must come from a source other than those I had tried. In some circumstances, I think it's possible that therapy or proper training might lead us to this sanity, for God works in many ways. The point is, however, that at this stage in my life, I knew sanity was there but I couldn't see it.

Now it's so easy for me to see the absolute futility of my single-minded and misguided self-will, but during my first years in the Program, strong self-will represented the only alternative I could see in my quest for sanity. The reason I held out a belief that there was sanity at all was that the people in the Big Book clearly showed me through their powerful words how they achieved it. Why wasn't there sanity around me? Let's face it, crazy people don't generally tend to associate with the sane people of this world.

We might say the following about our failure to achieve sanity: "I'm not mature. I can see that my habits are not appropriate, and if my habits are not appropriate and I can't stop them, then I'm not in charge. And if *I'm* not in charge, then who or what *is* in charge? Am I in charge of some things and not others?" Maybe we continue on and rationalize things a bit by saying: "I'm in charge of some things. I don't yell or scream anymore and I get to work on time every day. I function well." At the same time, we're probably well aware of the fact that we have not been successful in our attempts to control our behavior and break certain undesirable habits.

It isn't really behavior that we're talking about here, but how we *feel* about the behavior we engage in and what we subsequently do about the feelings we have. There is nothing inherently *bad* about being overweight. We *make* our excess weight a problem and consequently we feel bad. When our behavior and related feelings are out of control, we can sometimes see how they are out of sync with respect to what is really happening in the environment: perhaps we feel depressed when there is nothing to be depressed about, or we feel euphoric and idealistic when we need to be functioning rationally and logically. These incongruities between reality and our feelings and behavior surface in our lives and we might say, "That is not the way a human being is supposed to function. I've gone to therapy, but I'm still unable to resolve the conflict between my reality and my behavior and feelings."

In time, I began to see that if sanity could be achieved and if the people in the Big Book got sane, then that sanity had to come from a source other than those sources I had already *tried*. As I continued to work and develop in the Program, it became even more apparent to me that the sanity I sought would have to come from a source *other than my own efforts and willingness*. Only through a gradual—and sometimes painfully slow—process of developing this logic did I come to believe that there *had* to be a power greater than myself that could give me sanity. A power greater than me had to be available, *or all those stories in the Big Book were lies.*

Believing is more than just a theoretical or practical acknowledgment of the existence of a Higher Power.

The real assurance of this Higher Power is its reliability: Can I rely on it? Can I trust in it? Can I be certain of its existence? When I came to the Program, my experience had been that when I asked God to do something for me or give me something in order to prove His existence, I never got what I requested. It took me a long time in the Program to see that the proof of God's existence and power is evident not in what He does for me or gives me on demand. The *real* proof of His existence and power is in what already exists around me: the look and touch of a loved one, the sunsets, the morning dew, the warm spring sunshine, *the millions of recovered alcoholics and recovered compulsive eaters.* This proof was really there all along, but it eluded me because I was not actually looking for proof of God's power. Instead, I was looking for some evidence of His judgment and His failure so that I could blame Him for my misfortunes and my pain.

Wellness—I really like that word! It represents so many life-affirming, positive concepts and behaviors to me. Maybe wellness *is* achievable and maybe it isn't. But I'm willing to explore the possibilities. What I *do* know is that if overall wellness can be achieved, it must come from God, not from man. I want to *know* about this God. This is why the Third Step says, "Made a *decision* to turn my will and my life over to the care of God as I understood Him." I struggled with this concept for such a long time that the questions I asked are still familiar to me: "What does it mean, this 'Make a decision?' How in the world can I make a decision to give 'my will and my life' over to the care of a power when I don't even know for sure if that power exists?"

119

And, furthermore, I have no assurance that I will get the results I desire or feel entitled to if I *do* give my will and life over to the care of God. Really now, how can I make the decision to give my will and my life unless there is some kind of logic or support or reasoning to tangibly support that decision?"

This is what I have come to believe: we were created in God's image. Our purpose in life is to tap the source of power that He gives us. I don't know about other people, but I seem to need something more concrete than just verbal reassurance that God exists. I really believe that it makes no difference who we are. Our motives and our deeds are the most important things. Good deeds generated by selfish motivation don't work, and neither do good motives without the deeds to bring them to life. I believe that a person can profess to be an atheist yet still be close to God, because closeness to God has everything to do with motives and behavior and deeds and experiences and very little to do with words and rituals and the formal institutions organized in the name of religion. People mature in many different ways in the Program; this Program does, in fact, reinforce freedom and latitude. When we talk about power in the Program, we mean our own individual understanding of power. One person in the Program might perceive this power as cosmic energy and another person in the Program might perceive this power as acceptance or love. The point is that both people are in OA because they haven't been able to conceptualize a way of life that is different from what they already had. Most of us have thought in terms of right and wrong, not in terms of *being well*. Wellness

120

is not right or wrong; it is the state of being well.

I came to believe that God did not want me to have pain. He gave me all the tools I need with which to love life, but I lived on this earth for years completely blind to those tools. Only in my willingness to see and believe the lessons of the personal stories in the Big Book did I come to believe that God could and would restore me to sanity. All that was required of me was a willingness to work with Twelve Steps. *My willingness came from my pain; my recovery came from God.*

The Twelve Steps *

Adapted for compulsive overeaters

Step One
We admitted we were powerless over our food compulsion—that our lives had become unmanageable.

Step Two
Came to believe that a Power greater than ourselves could restore us to sanity.

Step Three
Made a decision to turn our will and our lives over to the care of God, as we understood Him.

Step Four
Made a searching and fearless moral inventory of ourselves.

Step Five
Admitted to God, to ourselves, and to another human being the exact nature of our wrongs.

Step Six
Were entirely ready to have God remove all these defects of character.

Step Seven
Humbly asked Him to remove our shortcomings.

Step Eight
Made a list of all persons we had harmed, and became willing to make amends to them all.

Step Nine
Made direct amends to such people wherever possible, except when to do so would injure them or others.

Step Ten
Continued to take personal inventory and when we were wrong, promptly admitted it.

Step Eleven
Sought through prayer and meditation to improve our conscious contact with God, as we understood Him, praying only for knowledge of His will for us and the power to carry that out.

Step Twelve
Having had a spiritual awakening as the result of these steps, we tried to carry this message to other compulsive eaters, and to practice these principles in all our affairs.

* The Twelve Steps reprinted for adaptation by permission of AA World Services, Inc. © 1939.

The interpretations which follow are those of the author, not those of AA, and are neither endorsed nor opposed by AA.

Chapter 12

As I Understand Him

Our task is to reflect and echo the light and spirit of God within us.

I don't see God as a puppeteer who dangles me on a string, tests me, then assigns punishments or rewards for me, and I don't see Him as a cosmic waiter who is there to respond to my wishes and commands. I don't think that God made me fat because I did something wrong, and I don't think that He will make my weight magically disappear forever because I work hard in the Program. I just don't see God working with a system of rewards and punishments. A common theme that runs through my comments in this book and elsewhere is that I have come to believe that God has created everything we need in order to have lives of sanity and wholeness, but He does not interfere: He doesn't move cars out of our way, or hold back the storm, or pull strings so that we can avert a sudden financial reversal. God doesn't reward or punish behavior.

Note that the emphasis of the Third Step is not the *act* of turning one's will and life over to God, but *making a decision to do so.* I truly believe that if I live a life of punishment, it is because I *choose* a life of punishment. Furthermore, I believe that God gives us the power to *reward ourselves* and to essentially change the face of the earth by changing our perception of it and our reaction to it.

God doesn't create the problems and misfortunes in our lives. Instead, He gives us the strength and His power—if we seek it—to grow, develop, and mature from those challenges. *The choice is ours.* We can choose to go on loving when things are difficult; we can choose to continue to grow even when life doesn't go our way; and we can choose to mature from years lived in insanity. We can choose to say, "If there is a way out, if there is something I can choose other than pain, suffering, and unhappiness, then I want to find it." We can talk forever, say the right things, go to the right churches, participate in the right rituals, never hurt anybody, and still not achieve sanity. Just doing these things and not hurting anyone is not *enough*. We cannot be idle; we must be *doers*. But if we perform good deeds either to receive a reward or out of the fear of punishment, we are not exercising free choice. God doesn't give us problems; He gives us the power to cope with and solve problems that are so much a part of living. If we accept this concept, internalize it in our lives, and learn to look inside ourselves as the source of that power, then we begin to achieve sanity.

I have come to believe that God exists in all of us, but that in the process of living we put barriers between ourselves and His presence. I think that a fundamental problem for many of us is this: we believe that God exists, but we are not willing to make a decision to completely turn our will and lives over to Him because, we reason, if God is all-powerful and has already determined the outcome, then what is the use? I don't think

God uses His power in such a way that He preordains that people will die in concentration camps, or that a generation of people will die of starvation, or that there will be injustice in the world. I just don't believe that we are forever being judged and tested by God. If He *did* test and judge us in that way it would mean, for example, that the poor innocent child who darts out into the street and is run over by a truck has somehow failed. Why do perfectly innocent children die? I have come to believe that God does not intervene: if a child runs out into the street and a truck is coming down that street and the driver doesn't stop, then that child is going to be hit. Think about it—if God could and would stop all trucks from killing all children everywhere, then why would he not halt starvation, injustice, and unfairness in our world? In more personal and less dramatic terms, why doesn't God make me happy? Why doesn't He just make everybody in the world rich, healthy, and good-looking? Why doesn't *everyone* have a wonderful life? Why doesn't He do all these things for us?

As I began to work the Third Step, I finally came to believe that *God does indeed give us everything we need.* It is always within us to be happy, joyous, and free. We don't even have to put a tremendous amount of energy into seeking and finding God's power because it has never been lost. I believe that God's power is within us and, furthermore, it has always been there. I never really lost God's power within me, I interfered with God's power through my own self-will and I covered it up with barriers and obstructions to the point that I didn't even *recognize* it anymore. In order to

125

reconnect with God's power, I had to go within myself and become aware of what was already *there*, rather than to search outside myself for something that was lost. In order to regain what was already there, I had to get rid of all the things that interfered with my awareness of myself. I made a decision to turn my will and my life over the the care of God's power within me.

Not long ago, I received the following letter from a friend of mine; this letter serves as a powerful reminder to me of the way many of us desperately struggle to find God's power when all the time it is well within our reach.

> Dear Bill:
>
> I have been trying for days to write you a letter. In fact, I have written pages and pages. I have unsuccessfully tried to shorten my letter to you and I have unsuccessfully attempted to find the words to express what I want to tell you. So I am starting over one more time. The last few times we have talked, I have felt frustrated and even angry that I can't seem to catch what you are trying to tell me. This time, I decided I was going to find it. After listening to several tapes of various retreats you have led, and reading the Big Book and *Compulsive Overeater*, I think I have finally found it!
>
> My insight came as I was watching my three-year-old son in the swimming pool the other day. He was wearing a life jacket but kept crying out to me that he didn't know how to swim. I told him that he didn't have to swim, he only needed to relax and let the life jacket hold him up. To illustrate my point to him, I slipped the life jacket on and showed him that it would even hold *me* up. But my son still would not believe that the life jacket

would keep him above the water. So he continued to thrash around. In his struggle, water got in his face and, for a moment, even over his head. He never *did* enjoy the pool that day. He never allowed himself to relax. Later, he just sat on the side of the pool and watched the other children play.

Watching my son struggle with his life jacket that day helped me realize that I have been so busy through the years fighting another kind of "life jacket"—God's power within me. It's hard for me to accept this fact because I have trusted God on some levels throughout my life, and I nominally gave my will and my life over to Him when I was a child. But I failed to let my commitment and my understanding of God grow with me when I became an adult. When I came to OA, I trusted God to remove my compulsion to overeat and it has been lifted. I haven't had a desire to eat between meals in over three years. Meals are a different story, but I have maintained a 65 pound weight loss without a food plan, so God's removal of the compulsion has remained. I don't know why it's harder turning over my "growing up" to Him. I've tried so long through man's rules and my own self-styled and often grandiose interpretations; I think it's time I went to the source. God loved me so much that He even came here to earth to show me how the "life jacket" works. All I have to do for it to be mine is to simply accept it. I have done that in the most ultimate internal sense, but I have trouble *practicing* it in all my affairs. The life jacket, once asked for and accepted, is there for me if only I can learn to relax and appreciate it, and quit trying to "swim" on my own.

I also learned this week that helping someone else is probably the best thing to do when those old urges to try on my own come back. I've had a big

humility lesson this week, too. In fact, I've had a
wonderful week! I know I still have a long way to
go toward maturity and my natural tendency is to
"work on it," which amounts to thrashing around,
pretending I can swim. My other natural tendency
is depression—in effect, sitting on the side of the
pool, watching the world go by. I need help to go
on from there. I did want to share with you what I
have learned. I hope I don't rest at this level too
long before making more progress, but I think I will
trust God's timetable this time.

Sincerely,

J.

Like my friend who wrote this letter, I think I finally
understand the source of God's power within me: it is
not something "out there" that I must seek and find. I
spent so much of my life looking outside myself for
answers that I completely lost sight of the fact that the
answers were *within me*. For years, I was convinced
that I had to seek and find things "out there" in order
to find joy and happiness. Now I'm amazed at the
authentic joy and happiness I experience through even
the most simple and common experiences of daily life.
This is not to say that I don't have problems or unhappy times, or that I don't feel anxious and
frightened. Of course I do! All of these feelings—good
and bad—are realistic in our lives and that is what
makes them so precious to me now. It follows, then,
that whatever superficial, transitory joy or happiness I
used to get from a doughnut, a sweet roll, or a forbidden extra portion of food is insignificant when com-
pared with the joy and happiness I now experience
from realities in my life: my family, my integrity, my

friendships, and my garden. The wellness, sanity, and appreciation of reality I have so completely fill my life now that concerns about the contents or calories of one food or another seem completely irrelevant.

I used to be so busy reacting to the past that I never gave myself an opportunity to experience the joys of the *present*. Now I derive so much pleasure from my existence, my relationship with the world around me, and the people in it. Why wouldn't I want to perpetuate that pleasurable feeling by practicing what the Program says to practice? I live within these Twelve Steps, not to obtain the reward of thinness, but to really understand that weight and food are not terribly important in an otherwise fulfilling life. We cannot experience love and hate at the same time; we cannot experience oneness with God and worry about what we're going to have for breakfast; we cannot be happy and unhappy simultaneously. These things are just incompatible.

No longer do I feel the need to punish and reward myself with denial, binges, weight loss, and weight gain. Instead of these old cyclical patterns, natural happiness and unhappiness are simply there for me to choose. Now I find that I consciously choose happiness more often. And the result is that my behavior based on these choices produces *more* happiness for me, not less happiness as eating and drinking did. This is really the key to our problem: for most of us, unhappiness was all there *was*. For years, we felt that happiness just wasn't worth the price of opening ourselves up, exposing ourselves, facing life as it really is. I thought I just wanted to lose weight, so I tried OA. But when I joined,

I had no idea of the revolution of feeling that would erupt within me as I began to really understand and work the Program. Who among us would have knowingly embarked upon this road in those early insane days?

The Third Step does not represent the act of avoiding something in order to let it go. I don't think we let go of a problem by avoiding it, ignoring it, or struggling with it. *We let go of a problem by grasping the power of the solution.* Some people say, "I'm 'letting go' of my problem because I write down my food in the morning, or I call it in." Now I just can't see how these activities constitute "letting go" of the problem. On the contrary, these actions are motivated by self-will and they make the problem seem more significant and powerful than it really is! Letting go means being able to reach inside oneself for a self-awareness that is based on freedom from obsessiveness and compulsive behavior.

The Third Step is introspective; it leads us to look at ourselves. The Steps should not represent a barrier to recovery or an ordeal we must come through with flying colors. I don't think that God rewards us for overcoming the "obstacles" of the Twelve Steps. Instead, the Twelve Steps represent a positive process that strips away the wreckage of the past to reveal our natural selves. I take the Twelve Step journey not because God is going to reward me for doing so, but because it will lead me to achieve my inalienable right, my birthright. As human beings, we have the freedom to choose. But when we deny that innate freedom to choose, we lose ourselves and eventually we suffer the consequences. Freedom to choose is having the ability to look at ourselves and say: "I have chosen this path. I can choose evil. God has given me that power. I would rather choose evil than nothing, but if I can choose evil, I can also choose *life*. I can choose the living death I've had before, or I can choose Heaven *within* myself." It is more than just saying, "I believe"; it's *experiencing* the belief. It is epitomizing God in our conduct, in all our affairs. Our task is to reflect and echo the light and spirit of God within us.

The incentive to work the remaining Steps is so much stronger when we begin to see the Third Step clearly. No wonder people hesitate to write inventories—who wants to do that when the only promise on the horizon is that "this is the way it works." That promise is not enough. But when we know that in partnership with God we can take charge of our lives, then the promises become much more significant. It's no wonder we can't make amends without clearly understanding and accepting this Third Step—why would we want to make amends when our primary motivation for doing so is the desire to be thin or achieve some number on a scale, or to be "happy," or to simply work the Program? With God's power, I can *choose* to be in charge of my life again—my food intake, my relationships, my career, my finances, my reactions to people and circumstances. With a clear understanding of God and His power, I make amends in order to find the real me, and to see myself as I'm supposed to be, with the ability to express God's power. What a difference! When we understand these things, we are motivated not by rewards and punishments, but by the desire to achieve what is natural to us. *Wellness is natural. God's power is natural. Compulsiveness is unnatural.* How much clearer the meaning of the Program is to me now, how much more understandable. Who wouldn't want that kind of God? That is how I have come to understand Him.

I know that I want to feel and that I want my choices to be mature, productive, and healthy. I want to capture—not as a remarkable occurrence, but as a common occurrence—my experiences with my own children. I want to feel the joy they feel. The very fact that I can *experience* my own change is, to me, the epitome of spirituality. Now I finally can allow myself to be *unhappy*, too. If my children are upset, or sick, I'm unhappy; if things don't work out the way I would like them to, I'm unhappy. I still get angry sometimes, but now I express my anger by *saying* that I'm angry, rather than by swallowing the anger or expressing it with violent behavior as I did in the past. I now express my anger verbally ("I am angry!" or "That makes me angry!") and sometimes I express it quite forcefully. *But I no longer expect other people to change in response to my anger.* My verbal expressions of anger are no longer followed by violence, or threats, or withdrawal from people, or unexpressed expectations that other people must change their behavior because I am angry. Where did this basic behavioral change in me come from? It came from me and from God's power within me. And these changes are natural to all of us.

Yes, there *is* insanity in this world. But it's also true that there are many sane and mature people in this world, and I have made a conscious decision that *I*

132

want to be one of them. I don't want to spend my time at OA meetings just because I feel good when I'm there. I want to spend my time at OA meetings because I also feel good when I'm *not* at those meetings. I want to continue to grow and mature. Because I've had a glimpse now of what sanity is like, I know I cannot return to where I was in the past. Now I can really say that I've experienced the joys of God's word and those natural joys far surpass anything ever supplied to me by food.

The Twelve Steps *

Adapted for compulsive overeaters

Step One
We admitted we were powerless over our food compulsion—that our lives had become unmanageable.

Step Two
Came to believe that a Power greater than ourselves could restore us to sanity.

Step Three
Made a decision to turn our will and our lives over to the care of God, as we understood Him.

Step Four
Made a searching and fearless moral inventory of ourselves.

Step Five
Admitted to God, to ourselves, and to another human being the exact nature of our wrongs.

Step Six
Were entirely ready to have God remove all these defects of character.

Step Seven
Humbly asked Him to remove our shortcomings.

Step Eight
Made a list of all persons we had harmed, and became willing to make amends to them all.

Step Nine
Made direct amends to such people wherever possible, except when to do so would injure them or others.

Step Ten
Continued to take personal inventory and when we were wrong, promptly admitted it.

Step Eleven
Sought through prayer and meditation to improve our conscious contact with God, as we understood Him, praying only for knowledge of His will for us and the power to carry that out.

Step Twelve
Having had a spiritual awakening as the result of these steps, we tried to carry this message to other compulsive eaters, and to practice these principles in all our affairs.

* The Twelve Steps reprinted for adaptation by permission of AA World Services, Inc. © 1939.

The interpretations which follow are those of the author, not those of AA, and are neither endorsed nor opposed by AA.

Chapter 13

Turning It Over

...we can spend the rest of our lives think-
ing about what a terribly unfair world this
is and trying to make it fair, or we can say:
"Yes, this is an unfair world. And from this
unfairness, I will grow not by tilting at
windmills, or by living in the past or in a
fantasy world of the future, but by getting
in touch with God's power within me and
giving of myself."

Writing an inventory can help a person see how compulsive behavior first became necessary in his or her
life. Writing an inventory can also help a person see
how he or she *continues* to make compulsive behavior
necessary and what he or she has to do to clear away
the wreckage of the past. When we talk about inventory and clearing away the wreckage of the past, remember that *we* are the wreckage of the past. We
cannot change the past. But *we can* change *today,*
and today will be the past tomorrow.

"Turning it over" is basically *our awareness of God*
within us. We turn our lives over to God not with the
expectation that He is going to make us happy, but in
order to grasp *what has always been there.* God is not
going to reward us by making us happy; He has

already given us everything we need to be happy. When we talk about getting in touch with the power of God within us, we are talking about *achieving oneness* with God, not about "writing this down and eating that." How do we know this? Each person in the Big Book shares, through his or her individual story, the way he or she established a relationship with God. This is the decision I made: "I want to establish a relationship with God. The Twelve Steps help me recognize that I can tear away the barriers erected through years of twisted learning. In order to establish this oneness with God, I only need to get rid of whatever I learned in the past that now denies me oneness with Him."

I always feel uncomfortable when I hear people refer to a natural catastrophe as "an act of God." I just don't believe that God says, "Now I'm going to stage an earthquake and kill thousands of people in the process." I also don't believe that God interferes to *stop* natural disasters. And if God doesn't interfere with natural disasters like earthquakes and tornadoes, why would He bother to interfere with my eating behavior? Is He going to say, "I'm going to take away Bill's appetite because he did a Twelve Step call?" No. By doing a Twelve Step call, I've taken positive action to break through the barriers that have kept me from grasping what God gave me *in the first place*.

I really don't know whether or not there's special meaning in the pain we go through in our lives. I certainly can see and feel what has happened in my life, but a more important thing is how I *respond* to the pain in my life. This is exactly what an inventory is really all about—it gives us the opportunity to see the pain in our lives and how we respond to it. When I began to understand the inventory process in this way, I was no longer uncomfortable with it. My response to life is to *recover* and, in that sense, my response to life is a rebirth, a restoration of sanity. If you want to recover, *then do it.* If you choose not to recover that is simply your choice; it is not bad or wrong. But don't fall into the trap of saying, "I can't do it; I can't help myself anymore." The fact is, *you can choose.* You have the power you need if you want to have it. And if you want that power, all you have to do is get rid of the things that stand between you and that power. Choose life. How can a person *not* write an inventory if he or she goes through the Twelve Steps this way? I continue to write inventories so that I can continue to grow. Every now and then, I sit down and do a Tenth Step. I feel an almost overwhelming sense of wellness and happiness when I consciously choose life.

The question is not why you eat compulsively, but what are you going to do about it? Perhaps life has dealt you a terrible blow. Wouldn't it be wonderful if everyone had a perfect body, robust health, ideal eating habits, perfect parents, a wonderful job, and all the material things they work so hard to acquire? Why isn't life perfect for each and every one of us? *Because it isn't.* Life *is* unfair and yet we have a choice: we can spend the rest of our lives thinking about what a terribly unfair world this is and trying to *make* it fair, or we can say: "Yes, this is an unfair world. And from this unfairness, I will grow not by tilting at windmills, or by living in the past or in a fantasy world of the future, but by getting in touch with God's power within me and giving of myself. What I really want is a feeling and I can get that feeling by being in touch with, being a part of, and expressing God-ness within me." *Perhaps we should think of God as a verb, not only a noun; we do God.*

"All right, I've bared myself," someone might say after writing an inventory. "I've disclosed myself. I've seen all the unfairness in my life, and the pain, and how I got that way, and how I hurt myself and other people, and I see all these defects of character, and this is *me*." At this point we might say to God, "These are the things that I ask you to remove." But we don't say: "Now, God, I'm a good person. You heard me; I'm on Step Nine. Get rid of my defects—just take them away." If letting go and letting God meant just reciting the Third Step and committing it to memory, we could say, "Here God, do this for me." Life would be so simple in that case; it would be a simple—and rather meaningless—exercise in which God rewards us for saying the right prayer and denies us for not saying the right prayer.

I don't like to hear people say, "I lost 200 pounds, but I didn't do it; God did it." I disagree—and I often communicate that by saying to those people: "God didn't lose it; *you did*! God didn't take the weight off you any more than He put it on you in the first place. *You* went through the loss and gain of every ounce and the pain of putting weight on and taking it off." My weight came off and stayed off because I said: "Live this life, Bill; forget the weight. Just enjoy life. Serve God by being the best you can be," not because

I said, "Bill, you have to eat this way, and if you don't, you're going to be fat and nobody will like you." When I learned to really *live* this way—enjoying life and serving God—*my weight came off and stayed off.* Why? *Because compulsive overeating and obesity were no longer necessary in my life.* Food no longer represented a way for me to find happiness and fulfillment. I learned to find happiness and fulfillment in just *living.*

We stop eating compulsively when compulsive eating behavior is no longer necessary in our lives. Compulsive eating will automatically disappear from our lives when we get from *living* what we once thought we got from sedating ourselves with food. When we experience more fulfillment for a longer period of time by living and growing, we are not going to worry about our next meal, the material things that we think we should have, or what people think of us. The feeling of joy I have when I'm growing or when I'm out sharing with someone far surpasses the joy I felt from compulsive eating, compulsive sex, or spending, or power, or ego, or anything else. Nothing can match the wellness that I feel at those moments when I'm growing and sharing. This is why I say that having had a glimpse of sanity, the temporary joys of insanity became unnecessary in my life.

These revelations of mine aren't all that exciting, I know. They don't have the appeal of a story in which someone tells wildly humorous anecdotes while relating the dramatic details of his or her 200-pound weight loss. But drama and grandiosity are not what the Program is about. The important thing is sharing our recovery, how we got there, what it is, and how it feels—*regardless* of its dramatic appeal. There is joy in giving of ourselves just to give of ourselves, not so that others will tell us we're wonderful. Where does this sense of feeling good about ourselves come from? I doubt that anyone can explain the phenomenon. I understand it only as an expression of God and His existence within me. If I can see that, express that, and grow from that, then I have responded well.

Turning it over is a long process. As a matter of fact, turning it over is a *lifelong process*. It will go on forever, and along the way we will goof, we will experience unhappiness, and at times we will even deny God's power within us. So what? No one promised us perfection. The question is, what will you do when a problem arises in your life? Wallow in it? Avoid it? Sedate yourself by eating compulsively? Berate yourself? Blame someone else? Request another sponsor? Go to another Program? Or will you simply say, "I had a problem today—now on to tomorrow"? Don't spend time worrying if you occasionally find that you're again focusing on negative thoughts and behaviors. This will happen now and then. You will focus on the negative for a time, that is all. How serious is this in the overall scheme of things? If you find that you have binged, or slipped, or relapsed, the issue should not be *why* you did it, but *what are you going to do about it now*? Are you going to beat yourself or let yourself get stuck in your failure and relapse further? Or are you going to respond to this temporary setback by growing and maturing? I say the "children's hour" is over and it's time for us to pack up our toys—the excuses and fears and rationalizations of the past—and walk confidently into adulthood.

- ○ *Do we dare strip away the hypocrisy, mysticism, and fear from the God of our childhood whom we still sometimes feel the need to placate by saying the right prayer in just the right way?*

- ○ *Do we dare say that God is the power that makes us feel a certain way? Then do we utilize that power in a responsible, mature manner as our* right *instead of pleading, cajoling, and placating for it?*

The problem is not how to lose weight. The problem is how to live non-obsessively. *Our work at this stage is introspective; we grow from here.* If one of us can do it, then all of us can do it. If I can go through the process of change, *you* can go through the process of change, too. If I can achieve happiness and a sense of order in my life, *you* can achieve happiness and a sense of order in your life, too. *Turning it over* is the awareness of the power within us to do these things.

The Twelve Steps *

Adapted for compulsive overeaters

Step One
We admitted we were powerless over our food compulsion—that our lives had become unmanageable.

Step Two
Came to believe that a Power greater than ourselves could restore us to sanity.

Step Three
Made a decision to turn our will and our lives over to the care of God, as we understood Him.

Step Four
Made a searching and fearless moral inventory of ourselves.

Step Five
Admitted to God, to ourselves, and to another human being the exact nature of our wrongs.

Step Six
Were entirely ready to have God remove all these defects of character.

Step Seven
Humbly asked Him to remove our shortcomings.

Step Eight
Made a list of all persons we had harmed, and became willing to make amends to them all.

Step Nine
Made direct amends to such people wherever possible, except when to do so would injure them or others.

Step Ten
Continued to take personal inventory and when we were wrong, promptly admitted it.

Step Eleven
Sought through prayer and meditation to improve our conscious contact with God, as we understood Him, praying only for knowledge of His will for us and the power to carry that out.

Step Twelve
Having had a spiritual awakening as the result of these steps, we tried to carry this message to other compulsive eaters, and to practice these principles in all our affairs.

* The Twelve Steps reprinted for adaptation by permission of AA World Services, Inc. © 1939.

The interpretations which follow are those of the author, not those of AA, and are neither endorsed nor opposed by AA.

Chapter 14

"Will Power"

*...it is only when we are relieved of our
fear of the results that we have a choice.*

For years I thought that my will was essentially *bad*
and that with some "magic" program, activities, and
words, I could get rid of my will and the problems it
seemed to create in my life. I also thought that once I
had gotten rid of *my* will, then *God's* will would somehow automatically take over, putting words in my
mouth and making sure that I always did the right
thing at the right time. But hard as I tried to deny my
own will for the will of God, I never was able to get rid
of *me*. So I just sort of sat back and waited for God's
will to replace my own, all the time trying to distinguish
His will from my will. Now I understand that we cannot
know God's will until we understand self-will.

Many of us try to distinguish self-will from God's will
with some loose subjective standard of whether or not
a decision we make is right or wrong. God's will is
always right for us, yet this rightness has nothing to do
with the results. If you told me that you wanted to
move to a new house in another part of town and
asked me if I thought it was God's will for you, I'd
probably tell you to look closely at your motivation. In
other words, why do you really want to move? To

have more space? To live closer to your workplace? To live near a lake? To avoid something? To escape from something? To pursue something that is based on fantasy? Let's say you want to move because you sense that your neighbors don't like you. In that case, you would not be exercising God's will, your freedom to choose. Instead you would be moving in order to avoid the feelings you have about your neighbor's reaction to you. Simply stated, *God's will is power generated from a foundation of free choice.* It is not imposed or compulsive, nor is it a reaction to or avoidance of something real or imagined. I take a good look at my motives for doing something when I want to know if I'm exercising my freedom of choice.

Suppose you want to move because you have a chance to buy a house in a location you like and you can realistically afford to do so. Let's say, also, that the new house is closer to the home of friends you enjoy spending time with and closer to your workplace. Each of these motivating factors is rational and based on freedom of choice. On the other hand, if you wanted to move in order to get away from someone or something, or in moving you were taking on a mortgage that you couldn't realistically handle, or you were moving to keep pace with your brother-in-law, then the motivation would not be based on the freedom of choice. Let's say that you *do* move based on rational considerations (being close to work, being able to afford the mortgage, living close to friends), then just two months later, life changes dramatically: your boss announces plans to move your office back to the area you formerly lived in; you find you need to spend a

144

large sum of money for improvements on the new home you purchased; and the friends you moved close to are transferred out of state. Now the final results of your move perhaps didn't turn out the way you wanted them to, but it's motivation—not the ultimate results—that we're talking about here.

I believe that when God created the universe and the people in it, He determined that things should be orderly. He set everything up; we have everything we need. There is a power called God that exists everywhere and creates everything, then lets it be. But I believe that God has put some limitations on Himself; I have to believe that in order to live a meaningful life. If I believe He will always intercede, then I can find no purpose in life. I can see no purpose in a life in which there is consistent divine intervention by God. He has given us all the power and opportunity we need to be well and we take it from there. Unless we understand this, we might tend to think of a negative result as an indication that our original choice was "self-will run riot" because it turned out wrong. Now that I understand this, I'm not really as concerned about results. Just by exercising God's power, I get to feel well *regardless* of the results. Think about it: if we were punished for bad deeds and essentially restricted to good deeds, there would be no freedom of choice to exercise. It follows, then, that God does not punish us for exercising the freedom of choice that He has given us. If He did, then we'd be doing things so as not to be punished, not because they are right, rational, or appropriate. The ultimate result of our choices will *always* be wellness if we choose His power.

Herein lies the key to our program: *it is only when we are relieved of our fear of the results that we have a choice.* If we make a certain choice to avoid punishment or to be rewarded, then we are motivated by fear or greed and our choices are not free ones in tune with God's will for us. But there is real harmony when our choice is made in tune with the natural forces of God within us. For example, when we willingly make a choice—not out of guilt, fear, or anger—we feel most well and most connected with the natural power of God within us.

Each one of us essentially stands alone with God. Even though we are supported by our fellowship and by people in our lives who care about us, we ultimately make decisions *on our own.* Sometimes it seems so much easier to be crazy and blame others. How simple it is to say, "My mother made me do that," or "My father did this to me," or "I'm afraid of that," or "I'm nervous about this." It's even easier to say, "I can't help it; I'm powerless," and then go around *proving* it. A tougher but more effective alternative is to say, "I am powerful. I have God's power and I have to exercise it every moment of my life. I have to decide to go here or there, to say the words or not, to stand or sit, to move or not move, or to do or not do something. Every action in my life represents a decision I have to make. And I make each decision with faith and trust in God's power within me, not based on a reaction to past experience."

We really stand alone in the sense that it is up to each one of us—in our own unique way—to choose God's power initially, and to continue choosing His power. Quite frankly, I was afraid of this autonomy when I first experienced it, yet it's a lot less frightening than the fears and threats and problems based on fantasy that dominated my life for so many years. And my fears of autonomy are really much easier to deal with than the fears I created about my mother and father, or my wife, or my neighbor, or my partner, or the person driving the car next to me. When I really exercise God's power, I become less fearful and less motivated to react out of real or imagined fear. The results get better and better.

One of the questions I'm frequently asked is the following: "How can I distinguish God's will from my will?" *My answer is that it is all God's will.* God's will is for us to *have* a will, and for us to choose, and for us to be happy. I think that God has given us a wonderfully simple way to determine whether something is right for us or not: if it is right for us, it makes us feel good; if it is not right for us, it makes us feel bad. For years, I had those simple indicators confused: in my insanity, I thought that something was right if it made me feel bad, but that if it made me feel good, then it was probably *not* right. I now believe that God's will is most evident in actions that are based on real, rational considerations and are an excercise in the God-given power of choice.

The first three Steps represent the formation of a new belief system, a new system of trust. Having that base sets us in motion to change, and our momentum carries us forward. These Steps are perfectly set out so that we can conceptualize them, work them, then internalize them in our lives. When I understood the appropriate attitude and foundation of the first three Steps, my mind began to clear. Now my *eye* and my focus are on recovery, not on the fantasized past or the unknown and perhaps frightening future.

The most important thing to consider is not "What is God's will?" The most important thing to consider is that we have the power to *do* God's will and that the deepest wisdom we can attain is the knowledge that service is ultimately God's destiny for man. I believe that *service* is the answer to the question in Psalms 116:12: *"How can I repay unto the Lord all his bountiful dealings with me?"* Steps One through Three are conceptual in nature and we need not consciously go through them each day as we do the Action Steps (Four through Nine.) Remember, the Big Book says that through spiritual experiences, "Ideas, emotions, and attitudes which were once the guiding forces...of...lives...are suddenly cast to one side, and a completely new set of conceptions and motives begin to dominate them" (p. 27). This is what we're talking about here, conceptions and viable beliefs. Motives are the reasons we do what we do, based upon those beliefs. The Big Book tells us that there are basically only two sins: interfering with one's own growth and interfering with the growth of another person. We need to remember this as we exercise our freedom of choice.

I'm convinced that people who don't write inventories have never really gone through the first three Steps, because understanding this concept of God and the power behind it makes it impossible to sit still. If I know that God's power is within me and the result of the exercise of that power is wellness, then why would

I want to continue being crazy? We don't have to eat or react to people, places, or things in order to feel well—feeling well is our *birthright*. We don't have to do anything in order to feel well as long as we give up the things that have produced and sustained our compulsive behavior. Who wouldn't want to get rid of these barriers that are blocking us from God's power and our overall wellness?

The Third Step either becomes part of us or it doesn't—it's that simple. Reading the Twelve Steps every day and focusing on the Third Step is not going to do the work for us. The Third Step either becomes part of our belief system or it doesn't. But if it *does* become part of our lives, then we are eager to complete the next steps of action in order to rid ourselves of the barriers that keep us from realizing God's power within us. And when the barriers are gone and we reach Step Nine, then we are recovering. At that point, we have the opportunity to proceed with life by freely choosing God's power, not by irrational thinking or a lock step reaction to fear.

The Big Book introduces us to the Action Steps: "Next we launched out on a course of vigorous action, the first Step of which is a personal housecleaning, which many of us had never attempted" (pp. 63-64). Steps Four through Nine—the Action Steps—represent the first part of this "vigorous action." These are the Steps we take to remove the interference that has occurred in our lives. We are motivated to do this because now we know what God's power is; we see it operating in our lives and we want to get to it. By tuning into God we can start our new lives *now*. A recovered person is a reborn person beginning a new life; recovery is not determined by the number of meetings we attend or the amount of time we dedicate to abstinence. Recovery is not an end, a final goal, or the attainment of perfection, but a beginning—the start of a new journey.

The Big Book describes a key concept in our understanding and acceptance of the will of God: "Neither could we reduce our self-centeredness much by wishing or trying on our own power. We had to have God's help. This is the how and why of it. First of all, we had to quit playing God" (p. 62). Unfortunately, many of us interpret this passage to mean that we must completely abdicate our responsibility for making our own decisions and that we must never advise other people. On the contrary, what we need to do is quit *playing* God and become more in touch with the *will* of God.

The Big Book goes on to make the distinction between playing God and getting in touch with the will of God: "...playing God...didn't work. Next, we decided that hereafter in this drama of life, God was going to be our Director" (p. 62). I don't think this means in any way that God is going to manipulate us but that, instead, He is directing the overall *effect* of the outcome, not the choices and acts involved. He *wants* us to be well. God has already determined that he wants us to be well by giving us the tools we need to have that wellness. God directs us by giving us options rather than controlling things that happen to us.

The Big Book describes the results of getting in touch with God's power and our relationship to Him: "He is the Principal; we are His agents. He is the

Father, and we are His children. Most good ideas are simple, and this concept was the keystone of the new and triumphant arch through which we passed to freedom. When we sincerely took such a position, all sorts of remarkable things followed... As we felt new power flow in, as we enjoyed peace of mind, as we discovered we could face life successfully, as we became conscious of His presence, we began to lose our fear of today, tomorrow, or the hereafter. We were reborn" (pp. 62-63). Losing this fear is very significant because our lives have been governed by fear of both real and imagined events.

"Many of us said to our Maker, as we understood Him: 'God, I offer myself to Thee—to build with me and to do with me as Thou wilt'" (p. 63). We are asking God to give us the *courage* to be in touch with and carry out God's will. "Relieve me of the bondage of self, that I may better do Thy will. Take away my difficulties, that victory over them may bear witness to those I would help of Thy Power, Thy Love, and Thy way of life" (p. 63). This victory over difficulties is the attraction. How can we effectively represent ourselves to a newcomer if we are still caught up in our obsessive behavior and have not yet experienced victory over our difficulties?

"We thought well before taking this Step making sure we were ready; that we could at last abandon ourselves utterly to Him" (p. 63). Abandoning oneself is not done in the spirit of abdicating responsibility for self and passively waiting for God to express Himself. Some of us might think at first that our sponsors in the Program represent the voice of God telling us what to

151

do, or see, or be. But the truth is that other people cannot tell us what to do because other people don't know God's will for us. As we work the Program, we learn that we find God's will by tapping the power within us that has free choice as its foundation.

The Big Book says this about getting closer to God's power: "Though our decision was a vital and crucial step, it could have little permanent effect unless at once followed by a strenuous effort to face, and to be rid of, the things in ourselves which had been blocking us" (p. 64). Character defects such as guilt and fear and resentment prevented us from getting in touch with God's power within us.

"Our liquor (food, compulsive overeating) was but a symptom." (p. 64). Clearly, our compulsive eating behavior was, for us, a symptom of this block in our lives. This behavior was something we got into and did automatically so that we couldn't or wouldn't have to deal with God's power within us. *We were afraid.* In fact, we will continue to be afraid of giving up self-will for God's will unless we understand both. My understanding of God's will has destroyed the fears I had regarding God's power within me. It can be very frightening to stop playing God and to finally acknowledge and understand that *we have the ability to choose God's power.*

When we achieve sanity, we also acquire commensurate responsibilities. Behavior that I didn't even notice in myself a year ago now represents changes I want to make. Now I carefully consider my motivation when I want to do something and I say, "I want to change that behavior; I'm uncomfortable with it."

When I first came to OA, I was convinced that the only behavior I wanted to change was my compulsive overeating. Now I am much more likely to question my motives so I can best determine God's will for me.

Now, more than ever before, I have *glimpses* of perfection in my life. Now there are moments—sometimes even entire days—that seem almost perfect, yet nothing particularly dramatic happens on those days. I honestly don't know why I feel so well one day and another day I don't. But the moments of perfection in my life seem to be getting closer together now. I experience more of them. Things that used to bother me now bother me less. Food is a less important consideration in my life than it has ever been. Impressing people is much less important to me now. Making a lot of money, just for it's own sake, is a less important consideration now, too. I find that the old motives in my life are motives for me less and less now. Very simply, these life-transforming changes are the result of living in the Tenth, Eleventh, and Twelfth Steps.

The Twelve Steps *

Adapted for compulsive overeaters

Step One
We admitted we were powerless over our food compulsion—that our lives had become unmanageable.

Step Two
Came to believe that a Power greater than ourselves could restore us to sanity.

Step Three
Made a decision to turn our will and our lives over to the care of God, as we understood Him.

Step Four
Made a searching and fearless moral inventory of ourselves.

Step Five
Admitted to God, to ourselves, and to another human being the exact nature of our wrongs.

Step Six
Were entirely ready to have God remove all these defects of character.

Step Seven
Humbly asked Him to remove our shortcomings.

Step Eight
Made a list of all persons we had harmed, and became willing to make amends to them all.

Step Nine
Made direct amends to such people wherever possible, except when to do so would injure them or others.

Step Ten
Continued to take personal inventory and when we were wrong, promptly admitted it.

Step Eleven
Sought through prayer and meditation to improve our conscious contact with God, as we understood Him, praying only for knowledge of His will for us and the power to carry that out.

Step Twelve
Having had a spiritual awakening as the result of these steps, we tried to carry this message to other compulsive eaters, and to practice these principles in all our affairs.

* The Twelve Steps reprinted for adaptation by permission of AA World Services, Inc. © 1939.

The interpretations which follow are those of the author, not those of AA, and are neither endorsed nor opposed by AA.

Chapter 15

Tearing Down the Wall

...we are here to clear away how the past affects the present.

Compulsive people want to control everything and everybody. In fact, we want to control our own pain to the extent that we'd prefer to hurt *ourselves* before someone else has a chance to hurt us. But we learn in the Program that other people are not "out to get us." And we also learn that other people don't even *notice* how fat or thin we are unless we want to be noticed or we somehow cause them pain. We are not just what we look like. What we are is *everything* about us, and that of course includes our physical appearance. Now, I don't mean to say that people shouldn't be thin if they want to be thin, or that abstinence is wrong. If thinness and abstinence represent things that you want, that is fine. But we need to put things like thinness and abstinence in proper perspective in our lives for they are not the *sole indicators* of sanity. A rational approach to food and eating is *only* that—a rational approach to food and eating, nothing more and nothing less. And even though rational eating and a rational response to food are important elements in a sane and healthy life, so are rational dressing, rational working, and rational relationships. For some reason, though, we continue to delude ourselves that if we eat properly, everything else in our lives will be just fine. But eating rationally is only the *beginning*.

We are victims of our history; we are the effect but not the cause. If we allow ourselves to be held captive by the effects of past experience, how can we ever achieve God's power? In order to achieve His power, the effects of our experience must be recognized and owned. We write inventory for the purpose of finding out about ourselves and how we came to be the way we are. We do this so that we can tear down the wall of lies, myths, deceptions, and delusions that we have built and get in touch with a journey to the power of God. When we do this we will never again have to say, "I am powerless, and my life is unmanageable." And when we do this, we get to see a number of revealing things: how we became powerless in the first place, how our lives became unmanageable, and how we are still relying on old behaviors and reactions long after they are useful to us. This is why detail is not terribly important to the inventory. The primary purpose of the inventory is to identify the present effect of past events. In fact, if a person learns nothing from writing an inventory except the present effect in his or her life of past events, the process has still served its purpose. We take a look at these past events so that we will have the opportunity to see them as clearly as possible, to know and own the effects they created, and to understand that it is unnecessary to continue to react to them now.

As a preparation for writing the Fourth Step inventory, I often suggest to people that they might wish to write what is called a "prenatal inventory"—a simple story that is essentially a fantasy, but perhaps loosely based on the circumstances of their life and experience. This prenatal inventory is a harmless, non-threatening way to familiarize people with the process of writing the Fourth Step inventory. Through the years, I have found that the prenatal inventory is a good way for newcomers to start thinking about themselves and their lives. I simply ask the person to write a story of approximately a page in length in which they describe, in the first person, their creation, what it's like in their mother's womb, and the birth process itself. The story that evolves in this prenatal inventory might go something like this: "I was created in a moment of passion between my parents. Now I'm starting to grow; my arms and legs are beginning to develop. My mother finds out that she is pregnant and she is very happy about it. My father is a little worried about my impending birth because his job security isn't great. My parents already have a girl child, so they both want a son very much." The person writing the prenatal inventory then goes on to describe what he or she feels about being created and being born and what he or she believes are the thoughts of his or her mother and father and anyone else in the family who might have an opinion about the birth of this baby. After a person completes this prenatal inventory, we sit down together and go through it looking for a "life script" or "life message." Even with this simple story exercise, we can often see principles, directions, and assumptions that have somehow been communicated to that person and that he or she subsequently has carried out in every aspect of life.

After we have reviewed the prenatal inventory, I then ask the person to write the Fourth Step inventory if he or she feels ready to do so. If for some reason a person does not choose to write the inventory, that is completely his or her own decision. I have found, though, that most of the people I sponsor who have gone through the first three Steps seem not only willing, but *eager* to write an inventory at this point. Some of the people I sponsor ask me to stay with them for the three to four hours it takes to write the Fourth Step inventory; other people I sponsor choose to write their inventory without having me present.

There is no carefully prescribed or perfect way to write an inventory. If you want to write one, then do it; if you don't choose to write one, then don't do it. You can write your inventory in any way that is meaningful to you. You can write using the Big Book as a guide. You can write from an inventory guide. The choice is yours. It is important to write an inventory; it is much less important *how* you write an inventory. A fairly common method is as follows: take a piece of paper and divide it into three columns with a wider column in the middle. Label the left-hand column *"Person,"* the middle column *"Event,"* and the right-hand column *"Effect."* The inventory is then divided into five sections based on chronological age groupings that represent basic growth stages: (1) birth through five years of age; (2) ages six through twelve; (3) ages thirteen through nineteen; (4) ages twenty through twenty-nine; (5) ages thirty through the present.

The growth stage of birth through five years of age represents the formative years. To a great extent, who we are is determined in this first growth stage. Ages six through twelve are what I call the "traumatic years"; these years represent the growth stage during which we form our most vivid memories. These memories compound the events of our earlier, formative years. Ages thirteen through nineteen represent the growth stage in which, ideally, we begin to mature. This is the period in our inventory that most often shows us how and why we did or did not develop and mature. Ages twenty through twenty-nine represent the early-adult stage, the period of time in which many of us get married, establish our careers, and begin to practice adulthood.

A portion of the first section of an inventory (birth through five years of age) might look something like this:

Person	Event	Effect
Mother	Didn't breast-feed me	Jealousy because she *did* breast-feed my sister
Father	Always working; never home	Anger and resentment

Note that the Fifth Step suggests only a recounting of the "nature" of our wrongs rather than specific details. I don't think that the inventory should be a detailed description of every event in our lives that we happen to recall. The inventory is not an autobiography, nor does it require that we be specific about every event of our lives or the details of our past behavior. In writing inventories, we *classify* the events in our lives rather than specifying each event that occurred. An example from my own inventory: my mother beat me, but I need not specify each and every incidence of abuse. For purposes of writing an inventory, it is enough just to indicate that *my mother beat me*. On the other hand, an isolated, one-time incident that you perceive has significance in your life should be included in your inventory. If a person includes in his or her inventory a single event that occurred ("Uncle Joe molested me"), then that event is important to that person's life. Generally, though, we are not looking for each and every memorable event that has happened to us. The inventory is about the person, the event, and the effect *in general rather than specific terms* so that we will understand how the event affects our life in the here and now rather than getting lost in details of the past.

In describing the Fourth Step inventory, the Big Book stresses the importance of not avoiding things and making sure that we discuss everything. I believe this means that writing an inventory is about clearing away the "nature" of things, the barriers; it is not about recapturing every memorable event in our lives. *For purposes of the inventory*, the fact that a person was molested by an uncle is now less significant than the way in which that event affects his or her life *now*. We are not here to try and change the past, because nothing can be done about that. Instead, we are here to clear away *how the past affects the present*. We are here to explore how we have used and continue to use events of the past as barriers between ourselves and

God's power. We are here to explore how we react to our the fear of the past as if it *were* the present.

We write an inventory to help us get to Steps Six, Seven, Eight, and Nine. The purpose of inventory is to see your character defects *now*, not your character defects when you were five years old. We write about past growth stages to help us see how some of our character defects developed and took hold in our lives. If you write about your mother in your inventory and see that you still have resentment about something that happened when you were five years old, then you will get to see that you are still hanging on to that resentment. If you said to me, "Well, I've gotten over that; I don't have any resentment," I would ask why you included that event in your inventory. Why would someone include in an inventory something that happened at three or four years old if it wasn't still prominent in that person's mind?

An inventory usually runs about two or three pages in length for each section. Adults over the age of twenty-nine have five sections (age groups) to cover, so we're talking about a total of ten or fifteen pages, that's all. They are sharing the inventory with *themselves*—owning it—an important step in the process of understanding how the past affects the present. I say to them: "Look at this. This is you. This effect first occurred when you were three or eight or twelve years old. The event that triggered the effect is not happening anymore, but the effect continues on in your life from day to day. The effects of an event that happened twenty, twenty-five years ago are still controlling you and controlling your life to a great extent. Until you stop reacting to those events, you cannot go on." Our goal here is to clear this effect away and the only way we can clear it away is by first seeing it, then owning it.

A person might say, "Uncle Joe molested me when I was twelve years old, but he isn't molesting me *now*, so why am I still reacting to men in gray overcoats and brown hats? Why am I still fearful, or compensating, or feeling guilty or resentful?" When someone tells me that he or she is uncomfortable with this deliberate process of clearing away the effects of the past, my response to that person is: "What does your discomfort have to do with what we are trying to accomplish now? What you are probably uncomfortable with now is the effect of something that happened years ago. Nobody said we must be comfortable to accomplish this effectively. In fact, I think the more uncomfortable we are, the more likely it is that growth is occurring. Growth is painful." Then I might say: "Let's look at your occupation; let's look at your relationship with your spouse; let's look at how you react to your parents *now*. Maybe you would like to begin to do those things differently." If the person is uncomfortable with that suggestion, my response is still, "So what? Maybe you can go home and tell your husband how you feel. Maybe you can go home and say to him 'You aren't going to control me any longer.'" If the person says he or she would be uncomfortable doing that, I point out that the discomfort probably is not related to speaking out or being open about feelings. Instead, the discomfort is probably related to a fear that is really a reaction to old experiences. I might say, "Your fear here is not of your husband's reaction itself, but how you will *feel* about his reaction."

I was having a discussion about present effects of past experiences with a woman I sponsor and she said, "Last week, I started to say something and my husband yelled and screamed." I said to her: "So, what does that mean? Your husband yelled and screamed. That really has nothing more to do with *you* than it has to do with *me*. Just because you share a house with a man who yells and screams doesn't mean that you need to feel fearful or guilty. Now I don't condone yelling and screaming, but if someone has not abused or threatened you in the here and now, why in the world should you be afraid of his yelling and screaming? Why should an adult *ever* be afraid of someone who yells and screams? That behavior is the other person's problem, not yours." Personally, I don't like yelling and screaming and I know exactly why: from early childhood on, I associated yelling and screaming with physical abuse from my mother, and that physical abuse was, of course, frightening to me. I know where my reaction comes from, but that knowledge doesn't mean that I no longer have the reaction. The difference now is that my reaction to yelling and screaming is not fear but action—when someone yells and screams, I get away from that person by choice, not out of fear. When I hear someone yell and scream, I no longer assume that they're going to follow up by physically abusing me. I haven't been beaten by my mother since I was a child and my mother is now deceased. So for me to react to my mother's abuse of me when I was a child by reacting in fear to yelling and screaming *now* is useless and irrational at this point in my life.

When people share their inventories with me, I always make it a point to listen only. As a sponsor, I'm not there to play psychiatrist or counselor and I'm not there to point out whether I think they are "good" or "bad" people. I'm there to listen to them and encourage them to work on the inventory. Occasionally I'll point out patterns in things they are saying or avoiding, but I am not there to *probe*. Whatever they say is fine with me. As sponsors, we are overstepping our bounds if *we do* probe or lead people to enagage in dialogue with us about their inventories. The role of a sponsor is to *be there and listen*. That is all. We guide others not with dialogue, but with supportive listening and with the example of our lives.

Someone who shares an inventory with me shares it with himself/herself and, in the process, comes to *own* it. At that point, I might suggest that the person read the inventory silently in a special communication with God. Once that is done, it is done forever. A man I sponsor hadn't written an inventory after five or six active weeks in the Program, so I said to him, "You know, it's been five or six weeks now. You often speak about the pain of your past experiences, so I'm wondering why you haven't written an inventory yet in order to get a good look at that pain. It certainly is your choice whether or not you write an inventory, but if your experiences were so painful for you, an inventory might be helpful." In response to my question, he said to me: "Bill, will you be angry with me if I *don't* write an inventory? Will you still like me if I don't write an inventory?" I told him that of course I wouldn't be angry with him and of course I'd still like him as a person, even if he didn't write an inventory. I don't allow myself to like a person more or less because he or she has or hasn't done what I've suggested or because he or she has lost or gained weight. I like fat people and I like thin people. If I like someone, I like that person and that is all there is to it.

Another purpose of writing an inventory is to make a list of amends that we wish to make to other people. We write inventories not to chastise ourselves, or to remind ourselves about how terrible we are, or to reflect on the mistakes our parents made. Sometimes we forget that writing an inventory is only one-twelfth of the Program. We might just zip through those heavy steps—Steps One, Two and Three—without any problem. Then Step Four seems such an incredible barrier to us. Sometimes we make the easiest things hardest and the hardest things easiest. Writing an inventory is not a burden if it is understood.

Steps One, Two, and Three are "heavy" steps. In this book, I have shared just a bit of the process that I went through in working these steps. I was overwhelmed when things finally began to come together for me as I worked them. But it frightened me when I realized that *this is it*: this is my whole life. I wanted Santa Claus to come; I wanted someone to save me. I wanted to believe that somehow God knew that my whole life was terrible, so He was going to rescue me with some wondrous miracle. Then I would appreciate life more. But nothing like that is going to happen. *This is it*; this is life. Look at what we have. Look how beautiful this world is, how miraculous we are, the miracle of how we human beings develop. We have the ability to negate or affirm everything.

Writing an inventory initiates the process of tearing down a wall built of lies, myths, delusions, and deceptions. We tear that wall down brick by brick, defect by defect, amend by amend, until we are left naked, much like a child reborn.

The Twelve Steps *

Adapted for compulsive overeaters

Step One
We admitted we were powerless over our food compulsion—that our lives had become unmanageable.

Step Two
Came to believe that a Power greater than ourselves could restore us to sanity.

Step Three
Made a decision to turn our will and our lives over to the care of God, as we understood Him.

Step Four
Made a searching and fearless moral inventory of ourselves.

Step Five
Admitted to God, to ourselves, and to another human being the exact nature of our wrongs.

Step Six
Were entirely ready to have God remove all these defects of character.

Step Seven
Humbly asked Him to remove our shortcomings.

Step Eight
Made a list of all persons we had harmed, and became willing to make amends to them all.

Step Nine
Made direct amends to such people wherever possible, except when to do so would injure them or others.

Step Ten
Continued to take personal inventory and when we were wrong, promptly admitted it.

Step Eleven
Sought through prayer and meditation to improve our conscious contact with God, as we understood Him, praying only for knowledge of His will for us and the power to carry that out.

Step Twelve
Having had a spiritual awakening as the result of these steps, we tried to carry this message to other compulsive eaters, and to practice these principles in all our affairs.

* The Twelve Steps reprinted for adaptation by permission of AA World Services, Inc. © 1939.

The interpretations which follow are those of the author, not those of AA, and are neither endorsed nor opposed by AA.

Chapter 16

Building Character

...the Sixth Step gives us the opportunity to identify and develop our natural character traits.

Why can't we be more tolerant when it comes to living the Program? Why do we label ourselves and others as bad, or wrong, or complete failures in the Program because of an occasional binge, slip, or relapse? Why is it that once we learn the Program we expect to practice it perfectly, with no mistakes, no slips, no accidental return to our old "language"?

I use the following scenario to illustrate the importance of patience and tolerance in working the Program: let's say that, for one reason or another, you find yourself in the the middle of rural China and nobody there speaks a *word* of English. How would you cope with the situation? As a resourceful person, you would no doubt try to learn the Chinese language. Almost immediately you would begin to pick up a few words or phrases, but you would still be *thinking* in English. At first you would also find that you were automatically uttering a few words in English, only to remember that you were not being understood. Now think about it—if out of sheer force of habit you still spoke English now and then while in rural China,

169

would you be tolerant of yourself? *Of course you would be.* Furthermore, do you think the Chinese people would be tolerant of you, a foreigner in their country who still occasionally uttered words unknown to them? *I think it's reasonable to say they would be.* Of course, the Chinese people might seem confused and they might fail to respond to you when you accidentally spoke to them in English. But at that point you would realize that you had forgotten to speak Chinese, so you'd probably find the Chinese word for what you were trying to say and add it to your vocabulary. As time went on, you would learn more of the Chinese vocabulary through this kind of trial and error communication with the natives, and gradually you would become more proficient in speaking and even conceptualizing the Chinese language. But even then, you would occasionally slip, automatically uttering an English word or phrase. At this point, I'm willing to bet that you would feel it was perfectly acceptable to make an occasional mistake and slip back into your native English. You might even say to yourself: "Of course it's permissible to make a mistake now and then. I haven't learned Chinese yet; it takes time." Granted, use of the English language would not work in this situation, but that doesn't mean that English is *bad*.

And so it is for those of us in the OA Program who are struggling to learn a new "language"—we have learned something in our past that just doesn't work in our present situation. Continuing to be what we were doesn't work anymore, but that doesn't make us *bad people*. What does work is for us to be what we are now. I pose the question again: why are we not tolerant of ourselves and others as we learn our new "language," our new way of life in OA? We *all* relapse at times, if not with compulsive eating behavior, then with some other character defect we are trying to eliminate from our lives.

I think that many of us actually create *more* problems and more stress for ourselves because we think of character defects as feelings rather than behaviors. But character defects are simply things that we do, that is all. They are the learned behaviors we perform, certain ways we have learned to act out our thoughts and feelings. *I think of character defects as learned behavior that has outlived its usefulness.* Character defects represent the behavior we want to change.

Take a piece of paper and on the right-hand side, write down the character defects that come from your inventory. Making this list is the Sixth Step. When you have completed this list of character defects, make sure that you acknowledge and accept the fact that these defects were necessary activities that you engaged in to survive at some point in your life. Remember that whatever it was you did, *you perceived that it was absolutely necessary to your survival at the time.* As we really begin to look within ourselves, we will be able to see that we were taught to be the way we are. We also might discover that we turned out exactly as we were supposed to turn out, given the way we were programmed. It is important to remember, however, that what we learned through past experience probably doesn't apply to us any longer. We have a new life and we are changing; we are becoming different people. We begin to see that, for example, the feelings of resentment we developed based on things that happened to us when we were very young children took root in our lives. Perhaps as adults we have even *created* new situations that help us keep the resentment alive.

Fear of losing control—I believe this one character defect is fundamental to all other character defects. But even this defect is masked and complicated in many different ways and, as a result, we may not be able to identify it. In fact, many of our character defects are difficult to identify. For example, jealousy is often really resentment; resentment can be a form of anger; guilt is sometimes an expression of fear. Think about it: what is a fear reaction for someone at the age of five may evolve into anger at the age of twelve to cover up the fear, then guilt at the age of twenty. It somehow seems appropriate and socially acceptable for children to be frightened or angry. But as adults, we believe that fear and anger are somehow inappropriate for us, so we cover up those responses with guilt.

Suppose your learned behavior is lying. I would say to you, "Do you *really* want to get rid of lying?" And you might respond: "Yes, I want to get rid of lying. It's a character defect. I can see where it came from. I learned to do it to protect myself. As a child, I believed it was necessary to my survival." A young child may indeed learn that lying is necessary to his or her survival in order to deal with embarrassment, fears, and threats that he or she imagines or experiences *as a child*. But the point here is that what we perceived as necessary behavior when we were children is no longer necessary to us as adults. In this case, lying behavior has outlived its usefulness. Similarly, character defects (learned behaviors) such as compulsive eating, drinking, gambling, manipulation, greed, jealousy, and resentment are wrong not in the sense that we will be punished for them; *they are wrong in the sense that they have outlived their usefulness.*

Before I really understood and worked the Sixth Step, I lied even when there was absolutely no reason to do so. In those days, lying was a learned behavior for me. I learned to lie at a time in my life when I thought I *needed* to lie in order to survive; then I continued to lie. Lying gradually became very important in my life. Like so many compulsive people, I couldn't stand confrontation and when faced with even the *possibility* of something unpleasant happening, I would automatically say to myself, Do whatever you have to do in order to get out of this. No confrontation. Whatever you do, don't confront the problem. Avoid the problem, even if it means that you have to *lie* to do so. Seeing the uselessness of my old learned behaviors now relieves me of an incredible burden: for most of my life, I experienced such tremendous feelings of guilt because of my character defects and I saw myself as a *bad person* because of my behavior. But my guilt disappeared when I began to understand that my character defects developed *because I believed they were necessary to my survival* and that, furthermore, I was *powerless* over them. I finally realized there was no reason to feel guilt or shame for my past behavior. I began to look at myself differently and said, "Well, I can see where these behaviors have outlived their usefulness in my life and now I am willing to get rid of them, even though it will be uncomfortable and occasionally I'll revert to the old behaviors."

Character defects don't go away simply because we want them to go away or because we start working on them. New character defects develop and old defects we think we have conquered resurface. Or, defects we never even *thought* about may suddenly appear. When we begin to wonder about these new, old, and continuing defects and how and where they originated, we need to remember that Steps Six and Seven represent a lifelong endeavor taken care of by the continuing personal inventory of Step Ten.

The Big Book says the following about ridding ourselves of character defects: "When ready, we say something like this: 'My Creator, I am now willing that you should have all of me, good and bad. I pray that you now remove from me every single defect of character which stands in the way of my usefulness to you and my fellows. Grant me strength, as I go out from here, to do your bidding. Amen'" (p. 76). Does this mean that we just repeat that prayer, then sit back and watch our character defects disappear from our lives forever? Of course not. When I first began working the Sixth Step, I said that prayer, but the character defects remained. Time after time I tried to *make* my defects go away, and time after time I failed. We can work endlessly, but there is no way we can *make* the character defects go away. In fact, there is only one thing we *can* do: through the power of God within us, we can work on developing natural character traits like honesty, trust, patience, and joy. Then, as we concentrate our efforts on new behavior, old behavior actually ceases to be useful to us.

We cannot get rid of behavior that has been developing for years by simply wishing or praying it away, for *these are steps of action.* We take our list of character defects and for every defect, we find a corresponding natural character trait to develop. We say to ourselves, Am I willing to do these new things? Developing these character traits is new behavior. And instituting new behavior in our lives is unquestionably a frightening and less-than-perfect process. But we find that as we concentrate on our natural character *traits,* our character defects gradually become less useful in our lives and they may even disappear *entirely.* I felt great relief when I finally stopped concentrating on my defects and started concentrating on my natural character traits. I couldn't fail or be concerned about imperfection while concentrating on my natural character traits because I had never really been aware of these traits in the first place! It is obvious to me now that I still have many of my character defects. God doesn't just reach inside me and remove them as I once thought He should do. Instead, He has given me the power, and I have learned to reach for and grasp that power. As I develop my natural character traits, I begin to feel well again. And, as a further result, I develop insight and knowledge and awareness *that has always been there.* The big difference now is that because I already feel well, I don't have to do these things in order to protect myself from guilt, fear, or resentment.

The Fifth Step gives us the opportunity to examine the nature of our wrongs and the Sixth Step gives us the opportunity to identify and develop our natural character traits. What we are praying to God for here is that He will give us strength, courage, and determination to *change*. This is the kind of prayer that is answered. As you prepare for change in your own life, it might be a good idea to ask yourself this question: Am I really willing to give up the old behaviors? There will be many consequences if I do. I have led a certain kind of lifestyle based, at least in part, on my learned behaviors. I must face the fact that as a result of the changes I make in my life, I might also change relationships in significant ways—I could lose friends and I could even lose my present job. Am I really willing to give up these things if that should become necessary in the process of change?

There is a Bible story in which Jesus encounters a crippled man while on one of his journeys. The man asks to be healed and Jesus says to him, "Do you really want to be healed?" The man says, "Of course I want to be healed. Just look at me, I'm broken and lame." Jesus again asks the crippled man, "Do you *really* want to be healed?" The reaffirmation that Jesus asked for is worth remembering as we set about to replace our character defects with natural character traits. I can tell you from experience that it is not enough to want desperately or pray fervently to get rid of character defects. If we think that these changes are going to come about by sitting back and *wishing* for them, we will be sadly disappointed. It doesn't work that way at all. The next time you are experiencing jealousy (or any other character defect), try this: instead of saying to yourself, Oh, I'm not supposed to be this way, ignore the jealousy and concentrate, instead, on developing your natural character traits of acceptance and trust. This conscious process of substituting natural character traits for character defects puts us in touch with our natural selves. Being in touch with our natural selves makes us feel well and that, I believe, *is God's will for us.*

The Twelve Steps *

Adapted for compulsive overeaters

Step One
We admitted we were powerless over our food compulsion—that our lives had become unmanageable.

Step Two
Came to believe that a Power greater than ourselves could restore us to sanity.

Step Three
Made a decision to turn our will and our lives over to the care of God, as we understood Him.

Step Four
Made a searching and fearless moral inventory of ourselves.

Step Five
Admitted to God, to ourselves, and to another human being the exact nature of our wrongs.

Step Six
Were entirely ready to have God remove all these defects of character.

Step Seven
Humbly asked Him to remove our shortcomings.

Step Eight
Made a list of all persons we had harmed, and became willing to make amends to them all.

Step Nine
Made direct amends to such people wherever possible, except when to do so would injure them or others.

Step Ten
Continued to take personal inventory and when we were wrong, promptly admitted it.

Step Eleven
Sought through prayer and meditation to improve our conscious contact with God, as we understood Him, praying only for knowledge of His will for us and the power to carry that out.

Step Twelve
Having had a spiritual awakening as the result of these steps, we tried to carry this message to other compulsive eaters, and to practice these principles in all our affairs.

* The Twelve Steps reprinted for adaptation by permission of AA World Services, Inc. © 1939.

The interpretations which follow are those of the author, not those of AA, and are neither endorsed nor opposed by AA.

Chapter 17

Amends: Pathway to Freedom

Learning to do what we have to do without being dependent on ~ another person's reaction makes us autonomous, independent, and truly free from bondage.

During my years in OA, I have discovered something about people who have been in the Program for a long time yet continue to have essentially the same problems they had when they joined—there's a good chance they haven't completed the Ninth Step. In other words, they have not completed their amends. Of course, some people with long histories of doing harm to others may never have the *time* to complete their amends. Others may find it impossible to locate all the people they wish to make amends to. Failure to complete this step may indeed involve situations that cannot be influenced or controlled by the individual seeking to make amends. For this reason, I maintain that an attitude of sincere *willingness* is the most important element in completing the Ninth Step. We make amends not necessarily to feel better, but to right wrongs, break down barriers of fear and ignorance, and rid ourselves of the heavy burden of guilt. Sometimes I feel good about making amends and sometimes I don't. Some people appreciate the fact that I make amends to them, and other people act as if they would rather forget about the past and the memories that my amends may conjure up.

Steps Eight and Nine deal with amends from the inventory completed in Step Four. We take a piece of paper and on the right side draw three little columns labeled *A, B, and C.* We label the left side of the page "Amends." Using information from our inventory, we list in the "Amends" column every person we think we have harmed:

- ○ *Column A* should include every person who is not listed in Column B or C.

- ○ *Column B* should include people you are unable to locate, but to whom you are *willing* to make amends should you find them.

- ○ *Column C* should include people who are no longer living, or people who you are otherwise unable to make amends to, for to do so would harm them or another person.

I always carry my *B* list with me because I never know when I might encounter someone I've lost contact with yet want to make amends to. It is almost always preferable to make amends *in person.* As I see it, one of the primary objectives in making amends is to dispel the myth that to do so is humiliating. Talking face to face with a person is more immediate than writing to that person. But if a personal meeting is not possible, I think a phone call is the next best method. Letter-writing is probably the *least* effective method of making amends, but sometimes it represents the only option available. Regarding people in the C Column, I recommend thinking and talking about these people and then saying to yourself, If I could, would I make amends to these people? *If you can honestly answer that you would willingly do so, I think that is sufficient.* In making amends we need not look at the past and say, "What an awful person I was."

We need to learn that God gives us all the power we need to change. The only sin is continuing to do whatever is unnatural for us long after we know it ceases to be necessary in our lives. We would *never* get on with our lives in the Program if we waited until we had completely and successfully accomplished Step Nine. I know many people who, like myself, probably never will finish making their amends to others. I continue to find new amends to make for things that develop in my life and there are people I'd like to make amends to whom I've never been able to find. But even though I have unfinished business in this area, I can still move on with my Program and my life because of my *willingness* to make these amends.

When I'm ready to make amends to someone, I simply say, "I want to make amends to you." If the person I am speaking to is aware of my Program, there is no need to describe the concept further. If, however, the person is *not* aware of my Program, I just say, "I find it necessary for me to make amends to the people I have harmed. You are one of those people, and I want to make amends to you." If I have actually *taken* something from that person in the past, I tell the person at this point that I want to replace it. It's really much easier to make amends when we do so without the defensive, guilt-ridden stance that fails to separate the person from the behavior. Instead of hanging my head and saying, "Listen, I want you to excuse me. I'm a terrible person. I stole from you when I was eight years old," I can look anybody in the *eye* because I know that what I did in the past was what I *learned* to do; it was all that I knew at the time. I don't spend my time chastising myself for past behavior. My past behavior may have been objectionable by most standards, but it was all that I knew and now I can easily separate that behavior from *me*. My unacceptable behavior in the past didn't make me a bad person then and it doesn't make me a bad person now.

If there is any chance whatsoever that by making amends you will harm another person or persons, it is essential to get their consent before you proceed. In making amends, it is important to remember that *your peace of mind is not to be gained at the expense of another person.* For example, let's say that someone has had an affair with a married person and feels that he or she needs to make amends to the husband or wife of that person. In this case, the individual who wishes to make amends must first get proper consent by telling the spouse directly involved in the affair of the need he/she is feeling to make amends to his/her wife/husband. An assurance must also be made at this point that the amends will not be made if to do so would harm either person. Another example of the considerations that must be made prior to actually making amends: let's assume that making amends to an employer may result in your being fired and that, furthermore, this loss of income would adversely affect the security of your family. In this situation, your family should be consulted regarding the risks related to this action. If it's agreeable to them that you take the risk by making amends, then do it. If, however, making amends to your employer involves risks that members of your family are unwilling to subject themselves to, then you may be forced to make your amends anonymously. *It is important, however, to take an anonymous approach only to avoid hurting others, never to avoid dealing with consequences yourself.*

Despite the fact that we do not make amends when to do so would harm others, neither do we make amends to *please* people. We make amends primarily to rid ourselves of displeasure and to replace that feeling with feelings and behaviors that are natural to us. If you find yourself in a situation in which you are making amends only to please another person and to experience his or her *reactions* to you, then you are making amends for the wrong reasons and you may actually be better off not making them at all. When amends are made without the proper attitude, they simply will not work. I believe that the lessons we learn from making amends are even more important than actually correcting the wrongs we have committed. For example, learning to face another person honestly, yet not get caught up in his or her reaction to our amends is a simple lesson that can transform our lives. Through the process of making amends, we learn how to confront people and talk to them and really *experience* their reaction to us—even when they are upset with us—without feeling the need to react to *them*. Learning to do what we have to do without being dependent on another person's reaction makes us autonomous, independent, and truly free from bondage.

When we work the Program, positive new things begin to happen in our lives *automatically*. We become more honest with ourselves and others and we begin to really *face* our problems. For example, we may discover that we're responding to a phone call or a piece of correspondence *immediately*, rather than procrastinating about it because there is a chance that the call or letter might be unpleasant. We also begin to respond to *people* differently. As always, other people are bound to be unhappy with us from time to time, but we are no longer upset about this fact, nor do we try to change it or avoid it. As our response to people begins to change, others might say things like, "You are changing and I don't like what is happening to you." Now we can comfortably respond to them by saying, "Thank you; I understand." While speaking at a retreat not long ago, I encountered a very argumentative person. During my presentation, she stood up and really spouted off at me. I encouraged her to express herself and never interrupted her. When she was finished, I simply acknowledged her and what she had said by saying "OK." I said nothing more, then continued on with my presentation. When my presentation ended, a woman came up to me and said, "You know, you really handled that interruption well." I told her that I didn't really know what else I could have done. The woman looked me in the eye and said, "Bill, I remember a time when you would have argued with a person who interrupted you like that and you would have fought to have the last word, but this time all you said was 'OK.'" Had I changed? I think so, and for the better.

"Painstaking"—I think the use of this word in the Big Book is very appropriate. When you think about it, most of our growth comes not from *avoiding* pain but from feeling pain, going through it, then going on with our lives. My biggest problems now are not the problems that plagued me in the past. For years, I thought that the fundamental problems in my life were the people around me and my own character defects. Of course, now I know that those problems were never really significant in my life. The real problem all the time was that *I avoided confrontation at any cost.* I didn't want to have to deal with life as it really was, so I created strawmen, phony problems, situations that would make me feel safe by helping me to avoid *real problems.* But as I began to develop and grow in the Program, I saw clearly that I had avoided not only real problems but *reality itself.* For years, I simply refused to confront any kind of reality that I thought might be upsetting to me. (I wouldn't even open letters that had an official look.) During this time, I carefully avoided *anyone* who wanted to see me if I thought there was any chance whatsoever that our encounter might be unpleasant. But as I began to work the Program and the Steps, I came to see that through this process of avoidance, *I had complicated and magnified both real and imagined problems.* It was as if I consistently chose to deal with the problem in my fantasy rather than to confront it, deal with it, and get on with my life. Solving a problem was actually *frightening* to me, for it left me with more time and energy to confront *myself.* I would say, "I have a problem with my children...my wife...my job...my car." I used virtually *anything* to avoid confronting and resolving a problem. Now I know that resolving a problem means to recognize it, accept it, solve it, and go on, or to accept the fact that the problem *cannot* be solved. It really *is* as simple as that. But for years I didn't see it that way at all. Instead, I made sure that I always had a problem to live with *in order to avoid myself*.

While talking with a therapist once, I finally opened up to him about my tendency to leave problems unresolved. He said to me: "Bill, how could you *possibly* have carried this burden around for so long?" At that point, I finally realized the tremendous burden I had taken on by not resolving either real or imagined problems. For example, I would postpone relatively simple car repairs for weeks, all the time wondering when and where my car would finally break down completely. I remember one time when I discovered that my car radiator was leaking. Instead of solving the problem right away by taking the car to the service station for repairs, I chose to keep the problem alive by saying over and over to myself: "I just don't have time to fix the radiator." As long as I had to deal with my car, I wouldn't have to deal with *Bill*. So instead of arranging to have the radiator repaired, I'd stop at a gas station every hour or two just to add water to the defective radiator. Leaving this kind of problem unresolved actually gave me a degree of comfort. When I look back on it, I realize that I used this kind of dodge in every area of my life. As long as I had to deal with my car (or countless other things), I wouldn't have to deal with *Bill*. In the long run, when a problem was solved, it sort of left me with the hollow feeling of *now what?*

Nowhere in the Big Book does it say we are going to stop our compulsive behavior or that we have to be perfect in order to fully realize the promises. Instead, the Big Book says that the promises "are being fulfilled among us—sometimes quickly, sometimes slowly" (p.84). Those times when we're impatient and we want the promises *now* are the times we must remind ourselves that the promises "will always materialize if we work for them" (p.84). I think that the "work" referred to here is the Twelve Steps. The promises are not a reward but a breakthrough that frees us from the barriers of ignorance and fear. What evolves from the promises is a new person who is beginning, slowly but surely, to grow and mature. And, in this process, the desire to eat compulsively suddenly disappears.

The Twelve Steps *

Adapted for compulsive overeaters

Step One
We admitted we were powerless over our food compulsion—that our lives had become unmanageable.

Step Two
Came to believe that a Power greater than ourselves could restore us to sanity.

Step Three
Made a decision to turn our will and our lives over to the care of God, as we understood Him.

Step Four
Made a searching and fearless moral inventory of ourselves.

Step Five
Admitted to God, to ourselves, and to another human being the exact nature of our wrongs.

Step Six
Were entirely ready to have God remove all these defects of character.

Step Seven
Humbly asked Him to remove our shortcomings.

Step Eight
Made a list of all persons we had harmed, and became willing to make amends to them all.

Step Nine
Made direct amends to such people wherever possible, except when to do so would injure them or others.

Step Ten
Continued to take personal inventory and when we were wrong, promptly admitted it.

Step Eleven
Sought through prayer and meditation to improve our conscious contact with God, as we understood Him, praying only for knowledge of His will for us and the power to carry that out.

Step Twelve
Having had a spiritual awakening as the result of these steps, we tried to carry this message to other compulsive eaters, and to practice these principles in all our affairs.

* The Twelve Steps reprinted for adaptation by permission of AA World Services, Inc. © 1939.

The interpretations which follow are those of the author, not those of AA, and are neither endorsed nor opposed by AA.

Chapter 18

I Am Recovered

A person is recovered when he or she has gone through the Ninth Step and is living each day in the Tenth, Eleventh, and Twelfth Steps—the living Steps—and goes on from there.

Some people don't want to recover from compulsive behavior because they know recovery means giving up the insanity that has come to be so much a part of their lives. They just don't want to give up what has become a blanket excuse for their crazy behavior. I don't want the insanity and I don't want the state of mind or body that accompanied my insanity. *Because I want recovery, I have recovery.* I think that God gives every one of us the tools we need in order to have well-balanced, healthy lives. It's just that somewhere along the way, we stopped listening to Him and began to put other things *first.*

The OA Program offers us the opportunity to get our lives and priorities back in order. The recovery we reach after completing the first nine steps represents not the achievement of a goal, but the fresh beginning of a new life. If happiness, wellness, and the freedom to choose are the things we want from this Program, then we *begin* to get these things by working the Steps.

And as we begin to experience that happiness, wellness, and freedom to choose—*that is the recovery.* A person is recovered when he or she has gone through the Ninth Step and is living each day in the Tenth, Eleventh, and Twelfth Steps—the living Steps—and goes on from there.

How do we start our new lives in recovery? At first we make mistakes because of our inexperience, but as time goes on we gain more experience in recovery and we develop a better sense of ourselves. Indeed, some people become so experienced and adept in working the Program that it becomes fully integrated with their lives. For these people there is no longer a Program, they *become* the Program; for these people there are no longer any Steps to concentrate on, they *live* the Steps every day of their lives. That's really what we're here for—to work toward the goal of internalizing our Program so that it becomes one with who we are.

What about *weight* and recovery? Let's say that within the first two or three weeks in the Program, a newcomer has completed the Ninth Step, and is living in the Tenth, Eleventh, and Twelfth Steps, but hasn't lost much weight. Has that person recovered? Yes, I think that he or she *has.* Just as losing weight may not *necessarily* mean that a person has recovered, in some cases the only thing standing between a recovered person and weight loss is *time.* For one person that element of time may be just a few weeks or months, but for another person that element of time may be a couple of years. An individual may have eliminated compulsive eating behavior from his or her life, but the specific amount of weight he or she loses and the rate at which the weight is lost are variables beyond the control of that individual. When we really work the Program, we find we are on *God's* timetable, not on some superficially imposed weight-loss timetable. Two people of the same age and weight can come into the Program at exactly the same point in time and eat the same foods, yet they will lose weight at different rates.

Many of us become impatient with God's will for us. We want to give His timetable a little nudge, so we attempt to regain control with righteous self-will—we diet. And our strategy seems to work because we subsequently lose weight! I maintain, however, that we deny ourselves the full potential of the Program when we perceive weight loss as our primary goal and resort to self-will in order to achieve that goal. If we feel the need to prove something, or if we feel uncomfortable because we're not losing weight as quickly as we'd like to, then the real issue to focus on is our own daily work with the Program: where am I cutting corners? Do I have additional amends to make? Do I need to learn to be more patient with myself? In my opinion, people who struggle to have perfect abstinence actually *interfere* with miracles. They just don't trust; don't believe it is going to happen. And so they listen for other voices and, unfortunately, there are *scores* of other voices.

In looking at the elements of recovery, I think it's probably best to focus on the promises as explained in the Big Book. Note that the Big Book does not say that the alcoholic will not have had a drink for a long time (or, in our case, that the compulsive overeater will have dieted or lost a specific amount of weight.) Instead, the Big Book says: "We will intuitively know how to handle situations which used to baffle us. We will suddenly realize that God is doing for us what we could not do for ourselves." (These promises) "...are being fulfilled among us—sometimes quickly, sometimes slowly. They will always materialize if we work for them" (p.84). I maintain that "working" for those promises does not mean dieting. If we are patient with ourselves, and if we are in the Program to find pleasure and enjoyment in our lives—to learn to be whole and well—then the results of our work will come without having to use elaborate strategies of self-denial.

Many of us seem to have an expectation that if we work the Program we will never again experience pain, suffering, discomfort, frustration, anxiety, or depression. Believe me, I wish I could say that the Program guarantees a glorious, trouble-free existence, but we all know that just isn't so. Through this Program, we give ourselves *permission to be wrong.* As with anything that is new to us, we live in the Program less perfectly in the beginning, then somewhat more perfectly as time goes on. We get better and better. Yet, we still stumble and relapse at times. Some of us relapse into old behaviors of compulsive overeating and some of us relapse in other areas of our lives.

As an excuse for reverting to old behaviors, some people might say, "We are never perfect; the Program says we can never be perfect." Now that statement isn't completely accurate, particularly when it's used as justification for not working the Program and living the Steps. What the Big Book actually says about perfection is this: "No one among us has been able to maintain anything like perfect adherence to these principles.

We are not saints. The point is that we are willing to grow along spiritual lines. The principles we have set down are guides to progress. We claim spiritual progress rather than spiritual perfection" (p.60). When we find ourselves having to resort to rigid plans of eating, reporting, and self-denial in order to protect ourselves from compulsive behaviors, what we're really saying is that we cannot avoid the temptation and we have to work very, very hard. But if a healthy new attitude toward food, a protection, has been given us as the Big Book says, "...without any thought or effort on our part" (p.85), then why in the world do we need to struggle and exercise so much control and self-will? If we don't have an attitude of trust, the world is going to pass us by. "We have not even sworn off," the Big Book says. "Instead, the problem has been removed" (p.85). I think that "the problem" referred to here is the lack of power. What we are saying, in essence, is this: "I don't have the power to maintain." Recovery is the return of sanity and sanity is not perfection but, rather, the ability to live with imperfection.

The Big Book says the following about the protection we are granted as we work the Program: "We will seldom be interested in liquor [food.] If tempted, we recoil from it as from a hot flame" (p.84). The Big Book does *not* say that we will never be interested in food, or that we will never eat compulsively again. The Big Book does say that, "We react sanely and normally, and we will find that this has happened automatically. We will see that our new attitude toward liquor [food] has been given us without any thought or effort on our part. It just comes!" (p.84-5). I think

193

that this new, healthier attitude was actually given to us long ago. And the only thing we really have to do to regain that attitude is to break down the barriers we have erected and reach out for it. The Big Book says the following about this new attitude: "That is the miracle of it. We are not fighting it, neither are we avoiding temptation. We feel as though we had been placed in a position of neutrality—safe and protected. ...That is how we react so long as we keep in fit spiritual condition" (p.85). So long, I might add, as we keep maturing by living the Steps.

The Big Book adds this caveat: "It is easy to let up on the spiritual program of action and rest on our laurels" (p.85). I agree. We accept the Program and we discover that we have this new source of spiritual guidance that brings wonderful changes into our lives. Then suddenly something happens and our compulsive behavior returns in full force; perhaps old habits return and we start eating compulsively again. This kind of slip should indicate to us that we have somehow allowed our spiritual program to lose immediacy and momentum in our lives. As we consider our lives and our progress at this point, we might think to ourselves that we're working all the Steps, doing all the right things. But we don't really know this for a *fact*. The real reason for our relapse/slip may be so deep within us that it is difficult, if not impossible, to identify. Those times when we have nothing tangible to blame our compulsive behavior on are the times we tend to give the Program a nudge of self-will. We go back to our old habits and grasp at cures for the *symptoms*, rather than confronting reasons for our relapse/slip.

The Big Book reminds us that if we *do* let up on the spiritual program of action, "We are headed for trouble ...for alcohol [compulsive eating] is a subtle foe. We are not cured of alcoholism [compulsive eating]. What we really have is a daily reprieve contingent on the maintenance of our spiritual condition" (p.85).

We absolutely *have* to keep on going on in order to grow emotionally. After a period of time in recovery, many people *do* experience a return of old behaviors. This relapse may involve a failure to make amends or an imbalance between giving and taking, most often with the emphasis on taking. At times like this, it can be very difficult to convince people (or for them to convince themselves) that they are not giving enough. In response to the suggestion that they may not be giving enough, a person might say: *"But I go to meetings. I sponsor people."* My response would be this: "How long have you been doing those things?" "I've always done that," they might say. Then I ask, "Well, is there *growth* in continuing to do the same things you've always done? Are you sponsoring new people? Do you continue to reach out? Are you dealing with this Program as if your life depended upon it? Are you still excited and vibrant in the Program and internalizing it in your daily life?"

After fifteen years in OA, I am *more* involved in the Program, not less involved. I now go to fewer meetings than I did when I first came to the Program because then I was compulsive about going to meetings. Even though I don't attend a lot of meetings anymore, OA is in my life all the time. In fact, *every* day I'm in contact with people in the Program—someone I sponsor, my own sponsor, perhaps someone who calls me or sends me a letter. And I continue to start new meetings and sponsor new people. We cannot simply tread water in this Program; we must continue to grow and nurture our own involvement.

Like everyone else, I sometimes become complacent in the Program. I realize now that each time this happens, I receive some kind of warning that tells me I must continue to look within myself. Fortunately, most of us seem to get these signs when we first begin to get complacent—perhaps our appetite returns, or we find ourselves cheating a bit, telling little white lies to justify our behavior, or we become irritable and defensive. At that point, it's too easy to say, "I've got a handle on it; I'm taking care of it; I'm going to think about it and pray." I wish I could tell you that these pat little phrases are enough to revitalize us in the Program, but unfortunately they're not. It is important to remember that reaching for God's power within us is a never-ending process. Sometimes I feel so tired and I wonder when I'll reach the point where I can relax, coast, take a few days off, and just be the crazy person I used to be. But I know the answer to the underlying question before I even ask it. I'm just not willing to pay the price in order to return to old behaviors. I regard the Tenth Step as a step of continuous action and growth. When you think about it, the Tenth Step is really a daily practice of the first nine steps.

Through the years, I've discovered that defensiveness on my part is a very good indication that I'm becoming complacent in the Program. In other words, I *know* there is a problem each time I find myself protesting too quickly when someone says to me, "Bill, I think you are...," (for example, abrupt, self-centered, judgmental). But when I feel defensive in reaction to something that is said about me, I try to slow down and catch myself *before I respond*. I'll take a few minutes and reach inside myself by thinking carefully about the comment that was made. Then I tell myself that while this person may not be right, he or she might be leading me to something I need to look at in myself.

Sometimes I think that we learn more about ourselves from our enemies than we do from our friends. Even though my enemies have a negative perception of me, I can learn a great deal about myself through them. My friends, on the other hand, tend to accept me as I am and they are willing to overlook some of my character defects. I find it helpful to approach those people who are not my friends and seek out their perceptions of me. When asked for their opinion of me they might, for example, tell me that I'm selfish and manipulative. I then have the opportunity to carefully examine their perception of me and consider whether or not there might be some element of truth to it. At that point, I might share the perception with my *friends* and ask for feedback from them. Or I might go to my sponsor for an honest observation. She is always there for me and even though I don't always agree with her assessments, she gives me yet another opportunity to receive some honest feedback. I make it a point never to reject my sponsor's feedback immediately. I always listen to her and think carefully about whatever she says, then I meditate and/or write about it. After those activities and considerations, I am ready to accept or reject her observations. Fortunately, my sponsor accepts me whether or not she accepts my opinions or my behavior. Her motto is "Win with the stickers." To her way of thinking, people who have been working the Program for a long period of time must have something good going for them.

I compare recovery to holding water in my hand—I can feel it and it's refreshing, but it's not tangible in the sense that I can hold on to it or even really grasp it. I guess you could say that in some ways, I'm fortunate that I have not binged on food since the day I joined OA. On the other hand, maybe I would have been luckier had I binged on food rather than bingeing on subtler, less tangible things like negative feelings and patterns of self-defeating behavior. When my obsessive craving for food returns (and it does), that's an important sign for me to look within myself and then go on. As I was paying my bill in a restaurant not long ago, I noticed a box of chocolate doughnuts displayed next to the cash register. I picked up the box, looked rather longingly at the doughnuts inside and immediately began to plot my strategy: I could come back later when nobody I know would be around, buy these doughnuts and have them all to myself without anyone ever finding out. Then I quickly caught myself and thought, What are you doing, Bill? Fifteen years in OA and you're *still* thinking this way? There must be *something* going on. I never *did* find out exactly what was going on with me that day; sometimes we don't. Furthermore, what *is* going on at times like this isn't nearly as important as our openness and willingness to explore our feelings. So after that incident in the restaurant, I wrote a brief inventory about my experience, then looked at it and shared it. And in the process of doing these things, the food cravings I felt earlier that day disappeared.

I hear variations of this story from many people: "Everything was going so well for me when all of a sudden these feelings returned, and I felt like eating compulsively again. What should I do so that I won't eat?" I tell people I don't know what they should do at times like that, *and I don't.* There is no sure-fire defense against compulsive overeating. If I try to help people by offering them advice about mind-games and other strategies to help them stave off a binge, I'm contributing to the problem and actually doing a *disservice* by offering a temporary and superficial solution. It really *is* better for a person to fall on his or her face again rather than to focus energy on a short-term cure. Failure can be an integral part of the process of maturing in the Program. And if the compulsive eating behavior is caused by some unresolved anxiety, then failing may actually help to *force the issue* so that the underlying problem is finally addressed and dealt with in an appropriate way.

The OA Program is designed to help us become the kind of people for whom compulsive behavior is not necessary. OA is not a social group or diet club; OA is a way of life. Just because we don't exemplify the Program to perfection all the time doesn't mean that recovery is not working in our lives. A person stays in the Program because he or she chooses to be in it and chooses to progress. I believe that if a person eats compulsively today, it is not because of what happened

199

today but because of what *didn't* happen yesterday, or last month, or even last year. I believe that a person eats compulsively today because one day he or she slipped, managed to get by with the slip and then concluded: "Oh well, I didn't go to a meeting tonight and nothing terrible happened." I'm sure that people have excellent excuses for not attending meetings or working the Program *at the time*. Then, later on, these same people wonder why their appetites unexpectedly return. They'll think to themselves, I'm doing so well; I'm sponsoring eighteen people and going to all the meetings. Then when they look back in time and see that two months earlier, they just let up, they suddenly realize that this earlier lapse is manifesting itself in the form of a "sudden" return of compulsive eating behavior.

Many of us still have the desire to eat compulsively at times. People who successfully work through the feeling are the ones who say, "I want to eat and I'm not going to." Those who are *less* successful in working through the feeling might say: "I want to eat and that must mean I have done something wrong; I must be bad. Where did I go wrong? I've got to do it. I can't help myself. Beat me. Show me how bad I am. Show me what a mistake I've made." When we are recovered, we react to what life *is*, and life is most certainly *not* a protected environment. It is not realistic to protect ourselves to the point that, for example, we refuse to go to restaurants. I go to Italian restaurants all the time and when I'm there, I eat what I *choose* to eat. Now, everyone else in the restaurant may be eating pizza and spaghetti, but that is *their* food, not mine. On many occasions, I've been in an Italian restaurant and ordered only a salad, or maybe just a couple of meatballs. I do the best that I can with my choices, but I don't protect myself to the extent that I completely close down options. How do you suppose so-called "normal" people deal with tempting foods they cannot eat for one reason or another? Normal people make their way by saying things like, "I have a medical problem and for that reason I don't eat certain things." They *don't* resort to saying things such as, "Oh, I can't go. I have high blood pressure and can't eat salt, so I can't go to the movies because movies mean salted popcorn." Recovering alcoholics don't necessarily stop going to places where alcohol is sold. The reason they can go ahead and do this is because they have *learned* to react sanely and normally. They simply say, "That is alcohol, and I don't drink it." In my case, I have a problem with sweets. I get fat when I eat them and I don't want to be fat. That is all there is to it. With that kind of attitude, I can be around any kind of food and not feel guilty or defensive or abnormal for choosing not to eat it.

The Eleventh Step is the Step in which we keep in touch with God's power within us. Keeping in touch with God this way requires that we look inside ourselves to determine what is natural for us and what makes us feel good. Let's say that you're trying to decide whether or not to take a day off work and you ask yourself the following question: *"Should I take a break from work today and pursue some leisure-time activity, or should I go to work because I have some important projects and deadlines to attend to."*

201

Furthermore, let's say that you can be happy with either choice. The important issue, then, is not the activity you ultimately choose, but the *motives behind the choice*. Are you taking a day off work in order to enjoy yourself and make yourself feel good? Or, are you taking a day off in order to protect yourself, or otherwise avoid or deny something that you need to confront there?

When the motives for doing or not doing something are in touch with God's will for us—what I call the *naturalness* of us—the end result is going to be satisfactory. Now that doesn't mean that we're necessarily going to get the money, the job, the new relationship, or a lower number on the scale. Being in touch with God's will and acting on it simply means that we're going to *feel* well. I'd hazard a guess that most people want to lose weight because they want to feel good. In that case, one of the most important things to do is to stop *worrying* about the weight, because worry erodes good feelings. When a person uses his or her energy to work at feeling good rather than to worry, then excess weight is more likely to disappear because it no longer serves a purpose in that person's life. When a person is *already* feeling good, there is little need to use food to generate a temporary and superficial sense of well-being.

The Twelve Steps *

Adapted for compulsive overeaters

Step One
We admitted we were powerless over our food compulsion—that our lives had become unmanageable.

Step Two
Came to believe that a Power greater than ourselves could restore us to sanity.

Step Three
Made a decision to turn our will and our lives over to the care of God, as we understood Him.

Step Four
Made a searching and fearless moral inventory of ourselves.

Step Five
Admitted to God, to ourselves, and to another human being the exact nature of our wrongs.

Step Six
Were entirely ready to have God remove all these defects of character.

Step Seven
Humbly asked Him to remove our shortcomings.

Step Eight
Made a list of all persons we had harmed, and became willing to make amends to them all.

Step Nine
Made direct amends to such people wherever possible, except when to do so would injure them or others.

Step Ten
Continued to take personal inventory and when we were wrong, promptly admitted it.

Step Eleven
Sought through prayer and meditation to improve our conscious contact with God, as we understood Him, praying only for knowledge of His will for us and the power to carry that out.

Step Twelve
Having had a spiritual awakening as the result of these steps, we tried to carry this message to other compulsive eaters, and to practice these principles in all our affairs.

* The Twelve Steps reprinted for adaptation by permission of AA World Services, Inc. © 1939.

The interpretations which follow are those of the author, not those of AA, and are neither endorsed nor opposed by AA.

Chapter 19

The Power of Prayer

As long as we seek external efforts to make us feel good, we are victims. God's power is not designed to make us feel well; God's power is designed to give us the ability to be well.

When I first came to OA, I found the Eleventh Step very difficult to practice because I didn't understand much about God, and I *certainly* didn't understand much about prayer. At that time in my life, I thought of prayer as merely an exercise of ritual, so I was caught up in superficial concerns about the mere *act* of praying. Should I get down on my knees? Should I stand up? Are there right prayers and wrong prayers? Are there good prayers and bad prayers? Are there good times and bad times to pray?

Now I understand that the Eleventh Step represents the power of God that exists within me. I have come to understand this vitally important Step not as a ritual, but as a daily opportunity for me to reach within myself for strength and power from God. And in the process of reaching within myself, I grow. Situations that used to *seem* absolutely catastrophic to me don't seem nearly as bad anymore, yet nothing has really changed. I still experience unpleasant situations and unhappy times, but the difference is this: now I respond to these adversities by reaching inside myself and growing. Life may be terrible at times, but how we respond to it is significant *both as a question and as an answer.* Do we gather our strength from God and move through adversity, or do we try to do all of the work ourselves, tread water, and eventually drown?

The story of Jacob in The Book of Genesis clearly illustrates two very different attitudes toward prayer held by the same man at different times in his life. As a young man, Jacob betrayed his brother Esau; Esau then threated to kill Jacob in retaliation. At his mother's urging and in self-defense, Jacob subsequently traveled hundreds of miles away from his home to live with his uncle. As he journeyed to his uncle's home, Jacob came to a river and there he first prayed about his situation and attempted to bargain with God. As a frightened young man, Jacob thought he could make promises to God—bribe Him, in fact—in order to insure a better, safer life for himself. In his prayer, Jacob essentially told God he would do anything—attend religious services, pray regularly, be truthful—if God would only guarantee his well-being. Years later, Jacob returned from his uncle's home to the home of his birth in order to meet again with Esau, the brother who had threatened his life many years before. Jacob was now a very successful man with a wonderful family of his own, great wealth, and a mature faith. As an older and wiser Jacob prepared to meet Esau again, he no longer tried to make a deal with God, nor did he try to bribe Him. In effect, Jacob simply acknowledged that God had already given him so much and that he was turning to Him now *simply because he needed Him*. Now Jacob hadn't somehow become superhuman in the ensuing years. In fact, Jacob was still frightened at the prospect of facing Esau again. But this time, he knew for a fact that he absolutely could not meet the challenges ahead of him without the help of God. Despite his success and maturity, Jacob knew that he couldn't handle the confrontation with his brother alone, and that he would need strength and courage from God. In praying to prepare for his meeting with Esau, Jacob did not ask God to punish Esau, to take away his possessions, or even to remove the pain of the past. Instead, Jacob simply asked God to give him the courage and strength he would need to handle whatever he might encounter when he arrived home again.

Like the young Jacob, we could pray to God that He will make our lives free from problems, *but that just won't happen*. We could ask God to keep us free from illness, but that won't happen either. We can't very well ask God for a guarantee that trials and tragedies will only happen to others and not to us. Adults who pray for miracles usually don't get the kind of miracles they ask for any more than children who pray for toys, good grades, or friends get those tangible things through prayer. But like the older and wiser Jacob, when people pray for courage, strength, and the insight to focus on what they *have* instead of what they *don't* have, they usually find that their prayers are somehow answered. Even in the most devastating circumstances, we can find the ability to survive and go on with our lives. Like Jacob, if we face our fears and

207

pray for help, we can summon up more courage and strength than we ever imagined possible. In our desperation, we can open our hearts to God in prayer. The response to that kind of prayer will be a golden opportunity to renew our bond with God and His strength within us. This renewed strength will help us go on with our lives no matter *how* impossible things seem to be at the time. Isn't that an example of an answered prayer? Simply stated, a prayer for strength, courage, and faith is much more likely to be answered than a prayer asking God to make us thin.

No doubt about it, life is difficult and seemingly unfair for *all* of us at times. I spent years in painful insanity and additional years desperately attempting to recover. Now I've spent years in recovery and my life is still far from perfect. The questions that have haunted me for years continue to surface periodically. Why am I still unhappy at times? Why do I still have problems? Why do I still have the ominous feeling at times that my life is about to fall apart? Why do I feel that some problems are insurmountable? Why isn't everything just wonderful? It is this process of looking within myself, through prayer, that enables me to go on even though I still have questions and doubts. I continue to encounter adversity in life, but *I have learned to go on in the face of that adversity.*

The Book of Job illustrates some classic questions and answers pertaining to man's relationship with God. Job was a good and righteous man who had a deep faith in God. He was also many times blessed with a large and loyal family and substantial wealth. And then Job lost it all—his family, his property, his health, and his wealth. Virtually everything that he thought made life worthwhile was taken from him in a rapid succession of misfortunes. In response to his overwhelming losses, and assuming that God always punishes evil and rewards good, Job's friends began to question his faith and his honorability. Not long ago, my daughter was working on a school project relating to the Book of Job, so we had an opportunity to discuss the story together. I asked her how she felt about Job's friends questioning his faith the way they did—relating his misfortunes to sins they felt he must have committed. My daughter said, "I don't really know if his friends were right or wrong, but they seem bad to me because they're blaming Job for his troubles." When I first read the story of Job, I felt the same way as my daughter did. I can remember thinking that those so-called "friends" of Job's who questioned his faith during his crisis were evil and mean-spirited. But now I have a different understanding and a less judgmental view of Job's friends. Quite simply, they came to Job in his time of trouble; they were there when Job needed people. Now, perhaps these people were judgmental and said the wrong words and made the wrong assumptions. In their own imperfect ways, however, I think they were still messengers from God. Their responsibility to Job was just to *be* there for him, not to serve or flatter or patronize him. Right or wrong, they asked questions and ultimately those questions led Job to look carefully at himself and his God. What better friend is there than one who gives us the opportunity to find answers for ourselves? At various points during his overwhelming trials, Job asked God why he was being punished so unfairly. In essence, God led Job to ask himself *not why, but what am I going to do about it?*

I believe that instead of answering questions *for* us, God gives us opportunities to respond to questions. One of the greatest gifts God can give us is the opportunity to respond to adversity. In times of trouble we can go on in our love for Him and grow in the power He gave us, or we can walk around in a living death. Compulsive overeating is just one of the adversities that we have encountered in our lives. We can face that adversity, acknowledge the problem, and go on from there, or we can die. The question really becomes this: how do we answer each adversity as we encounter it? Do we try to answer it by learning long or short-term methods of control or denial, or do we *grow* from the adversity? Each time we give up and say, "Poor me. Look what happens to me. Look at this problem I have," we are actively denying God's *absolute* power within us—the power to go on, to choose not to dwell on our adversity or blame others for our misfortunes. God created us and then He gave us freedom to make choices. I find it helpful to think of God saying this to me: "Here you are. You can choose the road to life or the road to death. Choose life or choose death." The choice to go on is ours. Only by reaching within ourselves can we find the power and will of God. As long as we seek external efforts to make us feel good, we are victims. God's power is not designed to make us feel well; God's power is designed to give us the ability to be well.

Life's adversities come from all directions: the family

breadwinner loses his or her job; a wife or husband becomes a compulsive overeater; children make some bad decisions; parents attempt to control the lives of adult children. With each adversity we can respond by going on, or we can opt to lose a little more of our lives by reacting, analyzing, ruminating, and trying to answer the questions ourselves. Then, instead of going along with life and joining in the passing parade, we backtrack and move against the natural flow of things. Sometimes we fight terribly hard just to hold our ground and prove to ourselves that everyone *else* is wrong. We want other people and things to change to accomodate *us*. We want the weather or our community or country to change; we want other people and situations to change instead of us. The real question is not what are you going to do about *it* now, but what are you going to do about *you* now?

The Twelve Steps *

Adapted for compulsive overeaters

Step One
We admitted we were powerless over our food compulsion—that our lives had become unmanageable.

Step Two
Came to believe that a Power greater than ourselves could restore us to sanity.

Step Three
Made a decision to turn our will and our lives over to the care of God, as we understood Him.

Step Four
Made a searching and fearless moral inventory of ourselves.

Step Five
Admitted to God, to ourselves, and to another human being the exact nature of our wrongs.

Step Six
Were entirely ready to have God remove all these defects of character.

Step Seven
Humbly asked Him to remove our shortcomings.

Step Eight
Made a list of all persons we had harmed, and became willing to make amends to them all.

Step Nine
Made direct amends to such people wherever possible, except when to do so would injure them or others.

Step Ten
Continued to take personal inventory and when we were wrong, promptly admitted it.

Step Eleven
Sought through prayer and meditation to improve our conscious contact with God, as we understood Him, praying only for knowledge of His will for us and the power to carry that out.

Step Twelve
Having had a spiritual awakening as the result of these steps, we tried to carry this message to other compulsive eaters, and to practice these principles in all our affairs.

* The Twelve Steps reprinted for adaptation by permission of AA World Services, Inc. © 1939.

The interpretations which follow are those of the author, not those of AA, and are neither endorsed nor opposed by AA.

Chapter 20

There Is a Tomorrow

Our "disease" may be progressive, but so is our recovery.

The Twelfth Step encourages us to share and give of ourselves. When you think about it, the *only* thing we really have to give to others is ourselves. But we need to give of ourselves in the spirit of *being* there for each other, not in order to accumulate "credits" toward some anticipated reward from God. I just don't think He works in that way. I'm not going to rate extra blessings from God because I regularly share with fellow OA members or because I'm writing this book. Instead, I think He has *already* rewarded me by giving me life and the freedom to choose my own way as I move through and grow in my life. I believe that each and every one of us is on this earth to experience His reward.

We are here for a Twelve Step Program of recovery based on the power of God. The Program itself really has nothing at all to do with what, where, or how a person eats. Nowhere in the Big Book does the Program hold out a promise to help the alcoholic stop drinking. The Twelve Steps that guide both the OA and AA Programs lead us to believe that we can achieve God's power if we really *live* the Steps. And

213

when we achieve that power, we find that compulsive behaviors are not necessary in our lives anymore. The Big Book points out that the Program works for "us" and if we want to try it, we are encouraged to do so. On the other hand, if a person does not want the Program, it simply won't work for him or her.

Like so many people, I first came to OA with a desire to solve some problems in my life. But it was difficult for me to determine exactly what I wanted from the Program because I hadn't even *identified* the problems I wanted to solve. While I understood the concept of recovery, I was not certain about what it was I would be trying to recover *from* in the Program. I wasn't alone in this confusion about my goals—I would guess that every person who joins OA at least *perceives* that he or she has a problem and, furthermore, many people are confused or unclear about the specific nature of their problem. Real or perceived problems may manifest themselves in compulsive eating behavior. In my case, I think I was unhappy not because of my weight, but because I had been *programmed* to be unhappy. Following that line of thinking, then, compulsive overeating would appear to be the *result* of my unhappiness. I think many of us actually *use* compulsive eating and the problems associated with being overweight and out of control to somehow justify the fact that we feel so miserable about ourselves. When I joined OA, I just assumed I was unhappy with my physical self. As a newcomer to the Program, I believed with all my heart that if I achieved a certain weight-loss goal—realistic or not—I would feel better about myself. Of course that belief was a delusion, and like

214

most delusions, it helped me to avoid reality.

Soon after joining OA, I lost a significant amount of weight—long before I even understood the Program. Like many people new to the Program, I went through what is sometimes called the "Honeymoon Period" in OA. Now I don't mean to discount the positive aspects of that wonderful period of time. I was absolutely *euphoric*! My life suddenly seemed clearer to me; everything had new purpose and meaning. And the best thing was, the price I had to pay for this new lease on life seemed to be such a small one—attend OA meetings and share with others. In return, OA gave me new friends, a place to go, and things to do. For those first few years, it appeared that the quality of my life *was* better; I was on a perpetual high. During that time I lost weight steadily and kept it off for more than three years! And I achieved these things without actually working the Program. I really *didn't* have much of a program during that time. All I did was rush around, desperately trying to be all things to all people in OA.

When I finally turned to the Big Book after three years of keeping my weight off—and missing the point of the Program almost entirely—I couldn't understand how I had managed to maintain my weight loss. Then, as I really *studied* the Big Book, I knew the answer: driven by my ego, I had quickly grasped the Program's opportunities to share with and serve others. In reality, I was serving only that ego of mine, not myself (or anyone else in the Program, for that matter.) But ironically, in the process of feeding my ego by running around, speaking, and sponsoring people, I *was* doing things that kept me involved with the Program. In spite of my motives, I was working the Program in many ways while I was speaking and sharing with others. During that time, I was involved on a daily basis with activities and I never refused to make a Twelve Step call. It all boiled down to this: anyone in OA could call me at any time of the day or night and I would put aside my most important work priorities and even the needs of my family in order to satisfy my ego that someone needed my help. So I was there at all times, for all people, and for all purposes, even though my *motives* were wrong. I think that my total involvement with others was the *only reason* I managed to maintain my weight loss during those three years. Eventually, though, if I hadn't moved past my ego and into the real Program with the right motivation, I would certainly have regained the weight. Three years into the Program, I realized that I would have to change my motivation in order to maintain my weight loss. *I knew then that I really had to get into the Big Book.*

Our "disease" may be progressive, but so is our recovery. It gets better and better and expands more and more into other areas of our lives. This is not to say that there aren't crazy days in recovery; there are. Even with the Program there will be moments—sometimes significant periods of time—when we revert to old feelings and behaviors. We will continue to experience both depression and anxiety. Our lives will still seem to fall apart from time to time, and periodically we will eat compulsively. The difference now is, so what? Big deal! With the Program as our guide, there is more to life than recounting our slips and punishing ourselves for relapses. There *is* a tomorrow. Tomorrow used to hold the potential for fear and guilt. With the Program, tomorrow can hold the promise of new opportunities.

The Twelve Steps *

Adapted for compulsive overeaters

Step One
We admitted we were powerless over our food compulsion—that our lives had become unmanageable.

Step Two
Came to believe that a Power greater than ourselves could restore us to sanity.

Step Three
Made a decision to turn our will and our lives over to the care of God, as we understood Him.

Step Four
Made a searching and fearless moral inventory of ourselves.

Step Five
Admitted to God, to ourselves, and to another human being the exact nature of our wrongs.

Step Six
Were entirely ready to have God remove all these defects of character.

Step Seven
Humbly asked Him to remove our shortcomings.

Step Eight
Made a list of all persons we had harmed, and became willing to make amends to them all.

Step Nine
Made direct amends to such people wherever possible, except when to do so would injure them or others.

Step Ten
Continued to take personal inventory and when we were wrong, promptly admitted it.

Step Eleven
Sought through prayer and meditation to improve our conscious contact with God, as we understood Him, praying only for knowledge of His will for us and the power to carry that out.

Step Twelve
Having had a spiritual awakening as the result of these steps, we tried to carry this message to other compulsive eaters, and to practice these principles in all our affairs.

* The Twelve Steps reprinted for adaptation by permission of AA World Services, Inc. © 1939.

The interpretations which follow are those of the author, not those of AA, and are neither endorsed nor opposed by AA.

Chapter 21

The Message

...the messenger is the message.

The Twelfth Step says that we have *"had a spiritual awakening as the result of these steps."* Note, however, that the Twelfth Step *does not say that we have lost weight.* The Twelve Steps and the Program address much more than specific compulsive behaviors; they address the issue of how we react to the opportunity of living in God's world. Do we grasp it or do we turn our backs on it? I believe that the *"spiritual awakening"* we have had *"as a result of these steps"* prepares us to be happy, joyous, and free to make choices in this life.

The alcoholics who organized AA and developed the Twelve Step Program tell us that in the process of living the Program, we develop a special relationship with other people. We move on and *grow* in the Program by carrying the message to other people. After several years in the Program, it's very clear to me that the messenger is the message. As we carry the message to others, what we say and do are really secondary to what we *are*—particularly in light of what we were before. We are not here to teach others how to lose weight. Instead, we are here to illustrate how we live without compulsive overeating. Working at Intergroup or starting a meeting represents the *process, not the message.* The message is you and how you respond to life: why are you starting the meeting? What are you giving? Are you sharing sanity? Are you sharing wellness? Do you express it? Have you reached the source of power? Do you know how to live with adversity? When you leave an OA meeting and return to your home or your job and encounter anger, resentment, or frustration there, how do you deal with it now that you have the Program and work the Steps?

The primary purpose of sharing is not to solve problems for other people but just to be there and listen. In fact, "Be There and Listen" is my motto as a sponsor. If we do only those two things, we will be effective sponsors. As I see it, there are only two rules that govern my sponsorship of people in OA: I will not discuss the food they eat or don't eat, nor will I indicate to people that they have any obligation whatsoever to call me. *I am not a parent, policeman, warden, or watchdog for the people I sponsor.* Our sponsor/ member relationship is based not on a parent/child model, but on a model of equality and a mutual need to learn from and share with each other. I make it clear to the people I sponsor that they are welcome to contact me at any time, but that it is completely their choice—not mine—whether or not they call me on a regular basis. I assure the people I sponsor that I will always be there for them, no matter what they do. But I don't feel that it's appropriate for me to judge the people I sponsor; I'm not working with them as a sponsor in order to proclaim when, how, and why they are missing the mark, misunderstanding the Program, or behaving inappropriately.

I always try to keep the following concept in mind when I'm sharing with others: the key to this sharing is not what I give to others, but how I grow and learn from them, and how I see myself through their eyes, their friendship, and their love. The Big Book says this about sharing with a newcomer: "Outline the program of action, explaining how you made a self-appraisal, how you straightened out your past and why you are now endeavoring to be helpful to him. It is important for him to realize that your attempt to pass this on to him plays a vital part in your own recovery. Actually, he may be helping you more than you are helping him" (p.94).

Those of us who share the Program with others ultimately carry the message to our communities, to our friends, to our families, and to the workplace. Believe me, I know this kind of "messenger service" can be very difficult. Certainly it's discouraging to deal with a mother who is not the kind of mother you would like her to be, or a neighbor who will never be the kind of neighbor you hoped he would be for you. But then, perhaps you are not the ideal child or neighbor for *them* either. We can carry the message in a number of seemingly mundane ways every day of our lives. For example, I might let that driver in the other car pull ahead of me as I merge into a single lane of traffic; I might encourage somebody to move ahead of me in the supermarket check-out line because he or she is apparently in a hurry; I might overlook something another person does or says that usually would elicit an angry response from me. It's not always easy to do these things, I know. But think of the subtle good feelings we can pass along to others; we can set in motion a chain of positive responses. Now it's highly unlikely that anyone will applaud us for doing these things and, in fact, there's a very good chance that nobody will even *notice* these gestures. The important thing, however, is that *we* will know that we have worked out our defensiveness, impatience, and anger without saying a word. While these things are not as dramatic as group applause for a 20-pound weight loss, they do represent a maturing process that will ultimately contribute much more to your Program and your life than the loss of body weight alone.

I emphasize again that as messengers we *are* the message, and the truth is that we almost never deliver the message perfectly. And we will be more effective messengers for some people than for others. But as we carry the message, we can always look at Step One and say to ourselves: "I've moved. I'm not the way I was; I've acknowledged my powerlessness over food and I am a little better. I have more hope; I have more opportunity; I have more information, and I can go on. I may not do it all the time, but here and there I begin to change. Slowly and steadily, I begin to mature." I don't know anyone in this world who does anything perfectly all the time. It is not too late for any of us. God has created us with the capacity for growth and change and both resources are always within our reach. Note that the Twelfth Step says "...we practice these principles in all our affairs," not that we "do" or "live" or "adhere" to these principles. Do you know anybody who *practices perfectly*? At first I was very hard on myself when I discovered that I was reverting to old ways of thinking and old behavior. But I started being kinder to myself when someone pointed out to me that if it were essential to do things perfectly in order to work the Program, then the Big Book would *say* that and challenge me to strive for perfection.

For years, I worried about what it might be that God wanted of me. Should I lose weight? Should I abstain from flour and sugar? What is God's will for me? Then, when I first came to the Program, I worried about how to share with others appropriately: what kind of service should I do? When should I share? How should I carry the message? Now I know that the answer to these questions is really very simple. This memorable little verse beautifully sums up what I feel in my heart God wants for each and every one of us:

> "It hath been told thee oh man, what is good and what the Lord does require of thee. Only to do justly, to love mercy and to walk humbly with thy God."
>
> (Micah 6:8)

PERSONAL STORIES OF
MAINTAINED RECOVERY

Doris's Story

When I felt that I wasn't good enough,
when I felt that other people didn't like me,
and when I found myself wallowing in self-
pity—those are the times I set myself up to
binge.

The concept of "changing old ideas" was always very difficult for me to understand because I could not accept the fact that I had "old ideas" to change. Why would I "ask for the courage to change..." if I was *already* perfect? I felt certain there was nothing wrong with me, so I wondered why *other* people couldn't see and do things as I did. These are the attitudes I came to Overeaters Anonymous with over twenty years ago. I was a spiritual misfit—egotistical, controlling, judgmental, and convinced that everyone *else* was out of step, not me. I had all the answers and I was convinced there was no God. As I used to say, only half-jokingly, "There can't be a God; there can't be two of us."

The first "old idea" of mine I had to deal with was that change could and should happen immediately. In the past twenty years, I have come to believe that *growth is continual change*, that change doesn't happen overnight, that growth takes time, and that wounds heal slowly, but with time *wounds do heal*. I have learned that I must have patience and that I've got a lifetime in which to change. Another "old idea" of mine was that weight and food were my problems. I failed repeatedly in my attempts to lose weight. I would begin a new weight-loss diet, pill, or fast on a Monday morning. Then when I first began to experience the discomfort of withdrawal—and not understanding that—I would say, "Oh, the hell with it," and that would be the end of yet another diet. I got to the point where I consistently chose to soothe my feelings with a giant chocolate bar, rather than confront whatever was bothering me. I have since learned that guilt, resentment, anger, jealousy, procrastination, laziness, and envy were my problems, not weight and food.

I also had some "old ideas" about God that I had to change. I used to wonder what He could possibly have to do with my weight problem. I thought that God was only for those little old men and women in the synagogue who prayed and asked for forgiveness. I was much too sophisticated for *that*. Growing up, I got the distinct impression that God was a judgmental and vindictive record-keeper who punished thoughts and behavior. As a child I was terrified of God, so I learned to block out all feelings about Him. How would I change that "old idea"? I "Made a decision to turn my life and my will over to the care of God, as I understood Him." I did this by making the decision to embrace the Overeaters Anonymous Program totally and unconditionally, with each of its Steps and promises. As I said before, growth takes time. When the Third Step says "Made a decision...", no time limit is implied. The Program is suggested and no one rushes you. *Take your time, but do it.*

Today, I believe that I am created in God's image, that God is love, and that I am no longer alone. I have a partner in God and as in all good partnerships, I must have the willingness to take a certain amount of responsibility and do my share. Never before in my life have I felt that God loved me or that I was even *worthy* of His love. When I felt that I wasn't good enough, when I felt that other people didn't like me, and when I found myself wallowing in self-pity—those are the times I set myself up to binge. But now I feel good about myself and worthy of God's love and the love of others. I have had a series of "spiritual awakenings": a change in my attitude, learning to love and trust, and learning to carry out the Twelve Steps in my daily contacts with family members and friends.

I've also changed my old ideas about *love*. I was married for forty years to one man—a kind, nurturing, understanding, loving man. (He would have to have all those attributes to survive forty years with me, a practicing compulsive overeater whose life was unmanageable.) I honestly believed I knew the meaning of love; now I realize I did the best I could. I see now that I didn't fully know how profound, deep, and unconditional love is. How could I love someone else *unconditionally* when I couldn't even accept and love *myself*? As it says in the Big Book, "...you cannot transmit something you haven't got" (p. 164). My "old idea" was, how could *anybody* love a critical, arrogant, self-centered person? I know today that I am a loving and giving person created in God's image. Love is an integral part of my life and I see it working in my improved relationships with other people. When I say,

229

"Go with love," I mean responding to anger and rage with love instead of *reacting* to anger and rage. With love, it works. We have Twelve positive Steps that replace negativism, which is a strong barrier to love.

What about my "old ideas" regarding control? My growth has been slower in this area. The need to control is strongly ingrained in me, so I will need more time to improve. I've had to learn to let go of "running the show," and thereby allow others the privilege of serving. Another "old idea" of mine was that *other people* had to validate me. My sponsor insists that I am perfect. He says I was born perfect, but subsequently bought "old ideas" from other people. I accepted and carried these "old ideas" along with negative thoughts and character defects until the Program told me that I could clear away the wreckage of my past by making "a searching and fearless moral inventory" of myself. Now I know that the only person responsible for my validation is *me*. Other "old ideas" that I am changing are my perfectionism, my feeling that I know everything, my failure to say I'm sorry for my inappropriate behavior, and wearing emotional "masks"—one for friends, one for my husband, one for my family, one for me. No longer do I need to put *someone else* down in order to feel good about *myself*, nor do I have the need to fix everything and everybody.

I have lost close to 125 pounds and while this is important, what is *more* important to me is that I have also learned to love unconditionally, to give strength and sustenance, and to live a joyous, comfortable life.

All these wonderful things I have learned are the gifts of Twelve blessed Steps.

Curt's Story

I wanted to be fully justified in my self-hatred, so I worked hard to kill off anything in me that resembled goodness or decency.

When I was a child, I loved sugar so much that sometimes I poured it directly from the jar into my mouth. As I was doing this one time, I remember my mother walking into the kitchen and saying with some alarm in her voice, "*What on earth are you doing?!*" Feeling a little guilty for my bad manners, I simply told her that I was eating sugar. "Yes, I know you are," she responded. "But why are you eating it from the jar?" I answered my mother truthfully: "Because I love it and it tastes good." Now, am I supposed to look back on this childhood habit as proof that I was a "crazy compulsive overeater" even then? I don't think so. Doing that, I think, would just be another way of calling myself by that old name of "bad."

Belief in my essential "badness" affected me for most of my life. This perception of myself was a distortion I was guided by and actually *perpetuated* for more than thirty-five years. At some point relatively late in the game, I began to see that no matter what behavior I engaged in for immediate gratification—compulsive sex, compulsive eating, compulsive spending, or just an obsessive need to be right—in the end, I always got to feel bad about myself. Was I *bad* for eating? Knowing what I now do about my past and the kind of anxiety, fear, and hopelessness I mistakenly identified myself with, I think it's reasonable and understandable that I did seek and *find* relief in food. It was the one resource around that was available to me on a consistent basis. I once saw a sign in an AA meeting room that read "Not Guilty." I understand that concept; it doesn't mean not responsible or not accountable. It means *not bad.*

By the time I turned thirty, I had amassed a great deal of evidence against myself. I had mastered techniques that helped me consistently *prove* my unworthiness to myself. After all, who but someone *bad* could have done what I did? I'm the one who bit, kicked, and threw the cat around. I'm the one who was abusive to my mother and father for years. I'm the one who ate uncontrollably, stole from others, and betrayed the trust of a close friend. I have learned that I am not a bad person, regardless of my past behavior. Instead, I behaved badly in the past *because I wasn't in my right mind.* And that's what I needed to come to, my right mind. I was at war with myself and with everyone else. Is it any wonder I sought relief in food? I was never calm, never relaxed, never at peace with myself. I had no sense of purpose or well-being.

Now I think I know what it is to be in my right mind. I have gained a *measure* of self-acceptance and acceptance of others. I also have learned to think sanely and clearly, and to channel my energies constructively. Now I am more in touch with my own goodness, the goodness of others, and the basic goodness of life. I can see that the way of life the Program leads me to fosters my personal growth and self-realization. The more I come under the influence of my own soul, or higher self, the freer my mind is of distortion. And to the extent that my mind is free of distortion, I find that I am free from the destructive thoughts and feelings that once ruled my life. This change did not occur overnight, nor did it come as a result of my *initial* experience in OA.

When I went to my first OA meeting, I was in turmoil and had a willingness to do something about it. At about the same time, I developed a habit of eating, then throwing up. Throwing up, like eating, brought me relief and in some way seemed to give expression to my internal rage. This habit ultimately served my negative perception of myself. (Doing something like this that violates the laws of nature practically *guarantees* that we get to feel bad about ourselves.) With this behavior, I could expand my vision to include a sense of *evil*. And, since I had never heard of anyone else engaged in this kind of perversity, I also could now think of myself as a *freak*. More accurately, though, I guess I had always felt this way about myself. Now I just had more proof.

So it was that I first came to OA—unhappy, engaged in a struggle with food, possessing a shameful secret, and not yet aware of how much I really *hated* myself. The people standing in the front of the room at those OA meetings really impressed me. They could laugh and joke, and they conveyed to me a real sense of the group's camaraderie. They *looked* like winners and it was obvious they were winning the battle with food and weight. As my efforts to follow a food plan failed, and as my unhappiness with everything else in my life intensified, I had to consider seeking help. I dreaded doing that. Swallowing my pride and feeling quite fearful, I asked a man in the Program whom I respected if he would help me. He said he would and suggested that we go out for coffee together after a meeting. This man then spent three hours with me. Looking back on it, those three hours with him represented my first experience with the kind of sharing that is so crucial to recovery. Here was this man, a stranger, spending so much time with me and really *giving* of himself. And I was *receiving* love because he was there with me, really listening to me, and accepting me just as I was. I was so grateful for that opportunity. Still, the focus of our conversation about "working the program" centered on controlling my behavior with food. He talked to me about the importance of "writing it down" and "calling it in" and "turning it over" and "calling your sponsor."

At this point, neither of us understood that the real source of my problem with food—and with everything else in my life—was in my *mind* and that the answer to my problem required *a change of mind.* No one I had talked to seemed to know that I needed to be restored to sanity. No one I had talked to explained the real nature of my problem, or that living the Program could solve that problem and free me from the distortions of my mind that kept me so enslaved. No one I had talked to seemed to realize that I was completely dominated by powerful negative myths about myself and my life.

If there was one thing I was lacking during my early days in OA, it was the ability to exercise the power of choice when it came to food. I can tell you, though, that I also lacked the ability to exercise choice in every other area of my life as well. I wondered what was wrong with me: why couldn't I get myself to stick with what had been presented to me as a solution? Was I weak-willed, insincere, unwilling to do my share, pay the price, go to any lengths? There were times I had no will whatsoever, except to eat or to argue. And then, when I really *wanted* to stop this compulsive behavior, I was unable to do so. Hard as I tried, it seemed to me that I just wasn't destined to become "good" like the winners. Of course, this just reinforced what my mind had been telling me all along—that I was *bad*. No matter what I did, I could not rid myself of my unhappiness. I felt unable to cope with the realities of adult life.

The turmoil I felt at home, at work, and in relationships continued to intensify. My crazy eating behavior seemed to have increased threefold. It was obvious that the only way I knew how to function was harmful to me and to other people as well. I felt increasingly more isolated and depressed. From time to time, a scenario would come into my mind that symbolized my deepening despair: I'd be walking along and suddenly I'd notice the sunset. But this majestic expression of life and hope for a new day only brought confusion with it, because it reinforced what seemed like an *unbridgeable* gap in the natural beauty of the earth and the emptiness and despair that governed my life. Undeserving as I felt, I asked myself over and over again what I had done to deserve such suffering. Was I being punished by God? Other people didn't deserve this suffering, so why did *I* deserve it? I just couldn't understand. Was I *that bad*? I was so immersed in negative thoughts and feelings that I couldn't see beyond them.

I finally concluded that being involved in OA was an unnecessary form of "torture" that I would be better off without. This was not an easy conclusion to come to because, miserable as I was in OA, I *did* feel I belonged there. Nevertheless, I believed that I had experienced too much torment and the only way to get relief was to leave OA. At this point, a friend of mine suggested that I go with her to an OA retreat. She said that a man from California with a different perspective on the OA Program would be speaking there. I figured I deserved a weekend in the country. I knew I was leaving OA anyway, so I figured I had nothing to lose.

Five minutes after this man began sharing himself at the OA retreat, several things began to dawn on me simultaneously: what he said made sense to me and, furthermore, he seemed to be a living example of what he talked about. Almost instantly I understood why I had failed for so many years. I had been working so hard to exercise the very ability that I was completely out of touch with—the power to control and discipline my behavior with food. I knew that I desperately needed that power back, but I didn't know what to *do* to get it back. I knew that not having the power to make choices was not a normal condition. It was a distortion of what it is to be a human being. That just made sense. I also understood that if I could somehow be restored to sanity, I would function the way sane people function. I began to see the Steps as a "vehicle for change," a process that could restore me to my right mind, freeing me from negativity and self-hatred and giving me the opportunity to become the person I was meant to be. This man's sharing had a sobering effect on me. It helped me realize that I was out of touch with my natural self, and that I was suffering from a thought distortion that made me identify myself with darkness, contempt, and despair. Intuitively, I understood that my life would move from chaos to joy, purpose, and fulfillment if only I could get in touch— and stay in touch—with my natural self. For the first time I could see that if I became sane, I *couldn't* remain crazy when it came to eating.

It was clear to me from this man's story that he had known his own personal hell. It was also clear to me that this man was no longer living in that hell. What I saw in him was *freedom* and how it looks in a person who has found it. His demeanor radiated that freedom and his sharing communicated to me a life that was vital, sane, and productive. I understood that what I was seeing in him were qualities of heart and mind that make a human being fully alive: warmth, humor, calmness, self-acceptance, common sense, the ability to both give and receive love, a sense of being at home in the world, and feelings of self-worth. And yet this man had been in the same prison I was in. He was now sharing how he had gotten out of that prison: he had found a way of living that had brought him a measure of happiness as well as a measure of freedom from his compulsive behavior with food. This was something I had not been able to do for myself. I couldn't even *count* the number of times I swore that I would "never, ever, ever again" allow myself to sink this low for this kind of existence was "too much, too painful, too unbearable." Each time I said it, I meant *every* word with all the strength and sincerity of my being. But then just *five minutes later*, I'd begin another losing battle with compulsive behavior. I couldn't stop myself. Hadn't I meant what I said? I had, but I just didn't have the power people have when they are in their right minds. That kind of power seemed to be missing in me.

Being so out of harmony with my natural life had cut me off from God's power within me to choose life and to live it with sanity and wholeness. And now I could see that there was a path that would lead me home again to my true and natural self. I began to see the possiblities: the gap between the beauty of sunsets and my despair *could* be bridged. I wasn't positive I could do it, but I saw that this man had done it; that meant that *it could be done.* This realization "ruined my life" in a sense, because the old excuses no longer worked—*now I knew there was a way out.* Of course, to my mind, this man made it because he was special. He succeeded because he had the right qualities. I was convinced, of course, that I was lacking the necessary qualities of courage, strength, and commitment to succeed. There I was with new understanding of the *possiblities*, yet still singing my old "bad" song, still perceiving myself as unloveable, undeserving, cowardly, and incapable. But I went home from that retreat with new information that made sense to me. I proceeded to put into practice what I'd heard, and I immersed myself in the Big Book, *Twelve Steps and Twelve Traditions*, and *Compulsive Overeater*. Practicing the concepts brought me periods of abstinence and the overall sense that I was making progress in every area of my life. I went to many, many OA meetings just to find people I could share with afterwards. I consciously tried to "be there" for others. I was beginning to feel better about myself and found some freedom from compulsive overeating behavior.

But I was still an emotional wreck much of the time. And I continued to revert to my old behaviors: anger, acting on my need to be right, compulsive overeating, and self-pity. I just couldn't seem to get past a certain point of progress. One week I'd be fine, the next week I'd be compulsive again about food and my emotions. After three months, this feeling of being "stuck" really started to get to me. After ten months of practicing the concepts of the Program, it looked as if I would never make it. It seemed as though I just couldn't *sustain* a willingness to go on. I got lost in my disappointment and finally said "the hell with it all" and isolated myself more completely than ever before.

I spent the next six months living under the cover of darkness. I saw daylight only if dawn came as I was heading home from the local coffee shop with newspaper and detective novel in hand. I quit my job and instead spent my days eating, sleeping, reading, watching television, listening to the radio, and going to movies. I neglected my physical health and care. I stopped going to meetings and saw no one. I unplugged the phone and used it only to let my mother know that I was still living. I really just *went away*. I stopped binge-eating and throwing up only because there came a time when I felt that if I continued doing this, I would do some permanent damage to my body. Sometimes when I was throwing up, it almost felt like I was going to rip a nerve out of my brain or spinal cord. One day when I was feeling extremely anxious about the harm I was doing to my body, I just kept on eating and throwing up. In some ways, I think I actually *wanted* to do some permanent damage to my body. I just didn't give a damn anymore. *I didn't care that I didn't care.* I wanted to die and even prayed to God for death. I wanted endless sleep so much and managed to keep myself sedated with food and medication. Sometimes I'd pray to be healed, and other times I'd deny God and His power. I even had suicidal thoughts at times, which was something new for me. I knew, however, that I was too much of a coward to actually take my own life. My biggest problem was that I kept waking up, because waking up meant I would feel, and feeling led to misery. I was so self-absorbed, so full of self-pity and sorrow. Worst of all, I just didn't want to experience *anything* anymore.

Occasionally my isolation would be interrupted by a phone call that signaled I'd accidentally forgotten to pull the plug again after calling my mother. Often these calls were from someone in OA who said they needed some support from me. In response to their need, I would come out of my self-absorption—sometimes with very little effort—and be with them the best way I knew how. Then, after our conservation ended, I would be very angry that this kind of spontaneous response was still living in me. "How self-defeating," I

thought, "for me to interfere with my image of myself."
*I wanted to be fully justified in my self-hatred, so I
worked hard to kill off anything in me that resembled
goodness or decency.*

One day, for some unknown reason, I found myself
getting dressed to go out at two o'clock in the afternoon—an hour of the day much too early for me to
be functioning. When I stepped outside, I was alarmed
that I couldn't remember *why* I had gotten up and
dressed so early or *where* I was going. Of course this
disturbed me, and the disturbance grew into a realization that I was not only lost in the moment, I was
completely and totally *lost in the world.* An alarm went
off inside me and I was overcome with a sense of
panic. My head was spinning. I felt I was hopelessly
caught up in something powerful and destructive that
I had no control over whatsoever. I was scared. I sat
down, held my head, and kept saying, "Oh God, don't
let this happen. Please, I can't handle this." The feeling
I had was different from unhappiness or despair; this
was *sheer terror.* I knew I was too fearful to kill myself,
yet I knew I couldn't go on this way. I could not tolerate
it. I knew I could not live like this. I had to get out.
Feeling this panic, I became willing to do anything I
had to do in order to find freedom. Looking back, I
can see that this was my spirit breaking through as the
will to live; this was my spirit asserting itself long after
I thought it had died. I finally realized that it was time
to get help and, believe me, this time I *moved.* This
time I knew I'd have to do some things I had managed
to pass over the first time around in the Program.

I knew *I needed to really see and accept myself the*

way I was. I didn't have to *like* what I saw, but I knew I had to see it and accept it without judgment. I would go back and do Steps Four through Nine, which I had somehow managed to avoid during my previous involvement with the Program. I also knew I'd have to do something about finding a sponsor. This time, I'd have to swallow my pride, shame, and embarrassment, and at least *begin* to let other people really get to know me. Clearly, it was my pain and my spirit breaking through that finally moved me forward. I remembered something a friend had shared with me about her experience in the Program. She told me that when she became committed to going through the Steps, she made up her mind to do just that—no matter what. She decided that if she ate complusively along the way, that wasn't going to stop her from going through the Steps. She was willing to trust that the solution to her eating problem *was in the recovery process* and that her energies belonged there. I took heart from my friend's observation. I could see for the first time that the *process of recovery* could break my compulsiveness.

After I had focused my energies on the recovery process for several months, the kind of craziness I had known for so long was *gone.* I just kept on working the Program, even though I sometimes ate complusively along the way. So what? I was choosing life, and that is all that mattered. When I *did* eat, I did so less destructively, and then just kept right on with my recovery process. I am very grateful for that new sense of momentum because with all the self-hatred I still felt, it was a terrible struggle to stop berating myself for eating. I didn't fool myself into thinking that I was no longer eating compulsively. I *knew* I was. But what mattered most was that I continued to put my energies into the Program, and had the willingness and the power to overcome my problem. Along the way, I had the opportunity to have someone get to know me. I risked that because I knew it was time to grow. Afterwards, I felt I had turned another important corner on the road to really connecting with others and accepting myself.

These days I don't *always* have to be prodded and challenged by pain, but most times I still do. But now there is a new orientation alive in me that has also influenced my motivation. I want to be in harmony with my highest self, with the best in me. I want to relate to life according to a sense of what is right and wrong, sane and true. I want to be in right relationship to others. I want to grow in this direction because this kind of growth represents, to me, life as it is supposed to be—life characterized by love, sanity, and well-being.

What has become of me? I have not become a perfect person. I make mistakes all the time, and yet now I know I'm not *bad* because of that. When I do things I *know* are wrong, I now take responsibility for my actions, clean up the damage that might remain from what I've done, and go on from there. I am less interested than ever before in my old perception of myself as "bad." I know reality too well now to allow myself to be stuck for long in myths and distortions.

Like everyone else, I probably have much more pain to encounter in my life. (Our lives, I have noticed, are never completely free from that.) But I don't have to *run away* from pain anymore, either. I have choices now and I have the *power* to choose. As I continue to grow in my connection with the Higher Power of my understanding and as I continue to act in accordance with what I *see*, I find that I have a sense of purpose and well-being. I feel good about myself far more often than I did before. I believe that I will continue to overcome inner obstacles, and that I will continue to find the courage to take the next step, then the next. I find I have the strength to live. I know that being alive gives me the opportunity to share and contribute, and that is a gift beyond all others. There is really nothing like it.

I am recovered because I stand at the beginning of my new life with tools for living that are available to me if I choose to use them. I am often calm and relaxed and able to think and act sanely. I know what it is to experience peace and harmony, love and joy. And I *know* that my life has meaning. I experience God both within me and outside of me. And I know that the power of love and good will is greater than the power of negativity and separation. I also believe that if *I* can recover, *anyone* can recover.

Rose's Story

*My life was backwards: I loved things and
used people.*

I was raised in a middle-class family and participated
in traditional childhood activities, but there always
seemed to be something radically different about me.
As a young child, I was involved in a variety of activities: Sunday School, scouts, dance classes, and
drama classes, but somehow I always resisted the
mold. Even though I joined these groups and performed very well in some of them, it seemed there was
always a schism between my attitude and the attitudes
of my contemporaries. I hesitate to use the word
"friends" when I speak about my childhood, because
I didn't have many. The children who *did* consent to
play with me often did so because I bribed them with
a promise that they could play with my dolls or use my
art supplies. I never felt acceptable or appealing to
others just for being *me*. As a child, I never even *had*
a best friend, a fact which was very painful for me. I
was invited to birthday parties, but I always suspected
that I had been asked only for the gift I would bring.

As a young girl, I was big for my age—tall and
plump. When the neighborhood boys weren't using
me in baseball or football games (I was a good athlete),
they rejected me and teased me about my size. I
became very aggressive in response to this rejection
and teasing. In elementary school, I expressed my

247

aggressiveness by participating in "gang warfare" on the playground—a game we called "chess." Our conflicts proceeded in a very orderly fashion and we moved according to our titles. I was always the queen in this game, because I threatened anyone who opposed me. I enjoyed the power. I decided that if I couldn't join them, I might as well beat them.

When I was twelve, the first major trauma in my life occurred—my sixteen-year-old sister died of a cerebral hemorrhage. My family was devastated; we literally fell apart. Though my parents stayed together, I could tell that they were no longer communicating with each other. My father went into a deep depression and my mother somehow hung on in solitude. My brother was eight years old at the time, and he didn't express an awareness of what was happening; he just went on in his own quiet way. At the time, I was just passing into puberty. I jumped into the challenge of adolescence in a blindfolded swandive. I began running around aimlessly, never really aware of what I was looking for. By the time I was fifteen, I thought I had found what I was looking for in food and drugs. My task each day was to alter whatever state I was in when I awoke in the morning. I became accustomed to living as if I were on a merry-go-round filled with sensations that first enlivened, then deadened, my body, mind, and spirit.

At the age of sixteen, I was a hippie—complete with boots, beads, and sunglasses. I was also using drugs. When I was seventeen, I was arrested for selling an ounce of marijuana and sentenced to ten months in a state hospital. Even though I had already been incarcerated for short periods of time, I was scared to death.

Prior to this, my longest stay in an institution had been sixty days in a juvenile facility. This time I was placed in a locked psychiatric ward for *ten months*. Beginning on my first night in the hospital and continuing throughout my stay, I'd start screaming in my sleep at midnight—like clockwork—stopping only when I was too exhausted to continue. My screaming sometimes lasted for ten minutes. I was upset by this new behavior, but I covered up my distress by using tranquilizers I managed to get from other patients. This experience was devastating because it taught me not to trust. I learned not to trust my parents, because they had turned me in to the police in the first place. I learned not to trust institutions, because I suffered so much in this facility. I also learned not to trust *myself*, because I realized that I was responsible for what had happened to me.

As bad as the state hospital experience was for me, it was there that I finally confronted and eliminated one self-destructive behavior: self-multilation. Beginning when I was a young teenager, each time a boy rejected me, I would scratch his name on my arm with a razor blade. I assumed I was the only person who engaged in this kind of behavior. But at the state hospital this kind of self-mutilation was practically a group sport. Some of the patients even had contests to see who could mutilate themselves most. After seeing such displays of insane self-abuse played out before me, cutting myself was never quite the same again. I finally gave it up completely.

After I left the state hospital, I lived with two different sets of foster parents. The first family I lived with had many problems of its own. I was very rebellious and was always in trouble there, so I was placed with another family. The second home I lived in was better in many ways. But then one morning my foster father climbed into bed with me. Though he did not try to have sex with me, his behavior made me very angry. Shortly after that incident, I was unjustly blamed for accusing him of sleeping with his secretary. I felt that this was a diversionary tactic designed to destroy my credibility, just in case I ever told anyone about his behavior with me. In response to these events, I stormed out of the house and away from this family in a hurt rage. After that, I drifted in and out of a variety of living situations.

Life, for me, became a revolving door of institutions. The diagnosis upon my admission alternated between drug abuse, depression, and suicide attempts. Each stay lasted for thirty to sixty days. I'd spend that time talking to the psychiatrist, participating in sheltered activities, or flirting with male patients. At the end of each hospital stay, I'd ask myself what I was going to do with the rest of my life. My response? I'd immediately get high and find my way back into a state of mind that would lead to yet another hospitalization.

By the age of twenty-two, I was a burned out, suicidal, 205-pound drug addict. It was during my twentieth hospital stay that I decided *enough really was enough*. I decided to end it all for *real* this time. Even though I was on the hospital's suicide-watch and was closely monitored, I managed to isolate myself in a bathroom. Then, while I stood on a trash can, I wrapped the bandage that had been on my wrist around my neck and the shower-head pipe. I pulled against the rope, feeling the tension gradually easing out of my life's breath. But then, I confronted the truth: *I realized I really couldn't kill myself!* I really didn't want to die; I just couldn't stand living with the *pain* I was in. Having made a decision that I didn't want to die, I had to get myself out of the mess I was in at that moment. The only solution was to make a lot of noise so that I'd be heard by someone who could rescue me. I banged the trash can loudly with my foot, a nurse came in, and pandemonium broke loose. I was immediately shot full of some psychotropic drug and locked in a seclusion room. (I later found out that the shower-head pipe was designed to break away under *any* weight. If I had gone ahead with my plan, I would have merely ended up as a big fat heap on the floor with a shower pipe necklace.)

After that incident, my doctor immediately arranged to have me committed to the same state hospital I'd been committed to following my arrest for selling drugs. I was *terrified* at the prospect of returning to what I had come to politely refer to as the "snake pit." I was *signed* in by two consenting psychiatrists, *sealed* with a court order, and was waiting to be *delivered*. It was only through the grace of God that I was spared the misery of being sent off to the state hospital again. I was released and started a course of treatment that included a supervised diet, daily visits to an outpatient treatment center, and weekly visits to a psychiatrist. At the end of six months, my behavior and my body had improved immensely. I had lost 75 pounds, had a respectable job, and was also working as a live-in

251

counselor in a home for girls. I fell in love with a nice man who was a counselor.

I sailed along on a "smooth sea" for about six months. I've since learned that I had enough resources at that time to *get* my life together, but not enough to *keep* my life together. I've always been quite successful in my attempts to *get* better, but much less successful in my attempts to *stay* better. It was only a matter of time before my new resolve cracked and I started binge-eating. I convinced myself that only death was worse than fat, so I decided I'd have to resort to drastic measures to curb my bingeing. (I didn't go so far as to control my eating.) Instead, I found that if I forced myself to vomit after a binge, I could immediately counteract the effects. I later discovered that laxatives also seemed to make food "go away" faster, so I put myself on "laxative therapy." My life was getting more and more out of control. As I saw it then, getting married was the only viable solution to my problems. I hoped that this dramatic new enterprise would somehow make life better for me. Wrong again!

To this day, I feel remorse for the way I used and abused my husband. He really loved me and I really used him. I realize now that I lived with him for my own convenience; I was *married* to drugs and food. *My life was backwards: I loved things and used people.* Not surprisingly, our relationship disintegrated within a year. By that time, I was addicted to narcotics and desperately in need of drug treatment. I was shipped off to a treatment center, but lasted there only a few weeks. I returned home and decided to find answers on my own. During my brief marriage, I had become accustomed to spending a lot of money. In one year of marriage, I compulsively spent thousands of dollars buying anything and everything I wanted. There I was at the end of my marriage—a woman with expensive tastes and very few marketable skills. Or so I thought. But then, a friend of mine who made costumes for dancers told me that I could make money dancing in bars. *That was the beginning of the end for me.* After three years of this kind of work, I deteriorated in many ways and eventually saw only three options for my life: insanity, death, or recovery. Whatever moral fiber I had when I entered this new world of dancing in bars disintegrated to the point that I was hustling, prostituting, bingeing, and vomiting my life away. I hated myself, and I abused myself in many ways. Instead of carving my arm with a razor blade as I had done earlier in my life, I channeled my self-hatred and anger into drugging, bingeing, vomiting, and loving abusive men.

One day I knew I just couldn't take it any longer. I had reached the end of my rope. I withdrew completely and hid in my room at home. I stopped taking drugs and began a destructive cycle of bingeing and purging. I assumed that if I would just stop using drugs, then everything would be fine again. *I was so wrong.* I sank into a deep depression. It was then that I faced my second moment of truth. I needed help, the kind of help that would generate and support radical changes in my thinking. I called my old counselor. She told me they understood, she wanted to help, and that I should come back.

I thank God that I chose recovery, even though it's been a slow, joyful/painful process. The last five years have been a long journey over some difficult terrain, but I'm fortunate in that I've had a trusted guide—a loving God who expresses Himself in my life. His greatest gifts to me have been the Twelve Steps of Alcoholics Anonymous, the adaptation of these Steps for Overeaters Anonymous, and the fellowship of both OA and AA. There have been many triumphs and setbacks along the road to recovery. My drug addiction was lifted first. Even though I was still vomiting and abusing laxatives, I was on the road to recovery. *The Big Book emphasizes progress, not perfection.* I had to use a very liberal interpretation of that concept in order to survive. It took me another three years before I was able to live my life a day at a time without vomiting or abusing laxatives. Then, in my fourth year of recovery, I suffered a relapse. As I look back, I think that I relapsed because I neglected to use the Program in dealing with the pain I felt when a relationship in my life ended.

I have come to learn that ALL of the process is recovery—the good times as well as the bad times. If I'm truly on the road to recovery, the times I stumble and fall allow me to fortify my humility. These defeats help me see what does and doesn't work for me. As I experience my powerlessness and the pain of fighting it, I can reach out to the One who has all power. *That one is God!* Self-will can so easily become what the Big Book calls "*self-will run riot.*" Through the pain of acknowledging my inadequacies, I have learned that the power I need is available from my Creator.

I believe that life teaches rather than punishes. I thank God for my life, exactly as it is. I know that I could not live out any other person's story, just as I know that no one else could live out mine. I have developed an understanding and compassion for other people's pain. I no longer sit in judgment of anyone, for I know that *there but for the grace of God go I.* I no longer feel the sense of separation from other people that made it possible for me to judge them. I forgive my past because I know it was just the prelude to the person I am now, and I thank God for that person. I have come to know a new way of living. I have undergone the profound personality change described in the Big Book. And though I still see myself as an adult with adolescent dilemmas, I know that I am traveling the road of recovery one day at a time.

MaryEllen's Story

*My real addiction was to the pain of feeling
bad about myself.*

I began using food to dull my feelings at about the age
of twelve. I didn't like adolescence, so I didn't *do*
adolescence. I grew up in a family in which alcoholism
was prevalent and compulsive overeating was a way
of life. I don't remember ever having been told not to
eat something because it wasn't good for me. Very
early on, I learned that if an item of food was available
and I wanted it, *I could eat it.* Even with this kind of
freedom, I began to lie about eating. I also learned to
enjoy eating in private. I married at a very young age
and by the time I was twenty-two, I had two babies,
my marriage had broken up, and I was working in
order to support myself and my children. I attended
school while I was working full time and raised my
children by myself.

The inventory process affords me the opportunity to
better understand myself, past and present. Recently I
learned that for the past twenty-four years, I have been
trying to live up to my father's last words to me to
"take care of everything" for him when he died. After
my father's death, I assumed responsibility for my extended family, in addition to my immediate family.
With all of these responsibilities, I was smiling on the
outside but filled with buried resentment I didn't even

257

know was *there*. I was already taking diet pills to control my weight and when my family responsibilities increased, I just increased my pill intake so that I could function non-stop. I gradually became addicted to the feelings of euphoria and stamina that I got from the amphetamines. For the next fourteen years, I was a junkie. The more I tried to accomplish, the less I measured up to my own impossibly high standards and the more I chastised myself. *My real addiction was to the pain of feeling bad about myself.* My life began to fall apart around me: I was fired from my job; I was unable to continue on in school; my behavior became more erratic; and my relationships grew more unhealthy. I attempted suicide several times and felt anger each time I failed. The last time I attempted to take my life I was very nearly successful. After that incident, I ended up in a mental hospital for a short period of time. I knew that isolation was beginning to have an hypnotic, almost sensual, attraction for me. When the effort involved in maintaining my uncompromisingly "perfect" facade became too great, I would go off by myself and rent a motel room. There I'd eat if I was out of diet pills, or talk to myself and write incessantly if I was taking diet pills. I would isolate for days at a time, each time trying to break my previous record for having no contact with the outside world. My fantasy world seemed real and it was certainly more attactive to me than the real world I was trying to escape.

After many years of this kind of living, my compulsive eating reached its peak. I hated the work I was doing. My mother was living with me and we didn't get along. At this time in my life, eating continuously was the only way I could control the frustration I felt, a deep frustration that made me want to scream constantly. I was forty years old and I thought I was forever trapped in the kind of life I had then. For most of the fourteen years I took drugs I was 25 pounds *underweight*, but now I was 120 pounds *overweight*. There seemed to be no relief in sight for me and again I was suicidal. Although the pain and self-hate I felt were now stronger than they were when I attempted suicide several years before, I didn't try it again simply because I knew God wouldn't let me die. I hated Him for that.

I attempted to control my weight in many ways: diet pills, hypnosis, health spas, exercise, diets, diet clubs, psychotherapy, anything that didn't involve a needle. *And everything worked!* I'd lose great amounts of weight, only to go crazy after a few months of rigid adherence to whatever plan I was following. *So I'd gain the weight back, and more!* I just couldn't understand it. My weight went up and down, yet my self-esteem was dependent on the numbers I saw on the bathroom scale. I returned to the weight club again and became a star there when I lost 60 pounds very quickly. But I knew *even then* something was wrong. I began to resent the restrictions imposed on me by the club, and I thought that *this time*, I certainly would be able to lose weight and keep it off on my own. I gained 30 pounds in a few months and became frightened that I was again heading for my top weight—and beyond. But now the most terrifying thing of all was my irrational thinking. Even in my confused state, I knew I was insane. I believed that no one loved me, and that the only way I could receive any validation was to pamper myself. So I isolated in my apartment with my dogs, my television, my books, and enormous supplies of heavily sugared food. I was in a downward spiral of depression which led to more eating, then still more depression. *I hit bottom.*

Then a friend suggested that we *both* try OA. I resisted the idea because I had been told that in OA people sat around talking about God. Being an agnostic, I said I didn't want to be involved with "a bunch of Bible-thumpers." Instead, I planned to return to the diet club, even though I knew from past experience that it was probably not the answer for me. I thought that if I lost the weight again, maybe some miracle would happen and *this time* I would be able to keep it off. (Secretly, I thought that there might be something morally defective about me because I couldn't control the way I ate.) Finally, having no other place to go—feeling completely defeated and terribly frightened—I agreed to attend an OA meeting *for the sake of my friend.* I have never felt as utterly hopeless and frightened as I felt on that first night I attended OA. But almost immediately I perceived that the people in that room had something I wanted, an indefinable poise and confidence that showed from their eyes as though they had little candles burning somewhere inside. My years of petulant anger at God melted away that night, and I walked out of that room with an understanding I had never had before—that a Higher Power could be an important part of my life!

I began to work the Program to the best of my ability and was thrilled with the physical and emotional changes occuring in me. I've always been a strong beginner, only to drift onto something else after awhile. But this time things were different: *I stayed with OA.* My first sponsor told me that my willingness was my greatest asset, and I should never let go of it. After a few months of working with this sponsor, certain circumstances made it impossible for her to continue to sponsor so many people and she dropped me. I told her that I understood the situation and, in a way, I *did.* But still I was angry with my sponsor for dropping me; my self-obsession told me that she dropped me because there was something *wrong with me.*

After a few months of going it alone in OA without a sponsor, I heard a man speak at a retreat. I was struck by some similarities in our backgrounds but, more than that, I was impressed with the "common sense" manner in which he discussed the Program. I saw in him what I wanted for myself: honesty, humor, and a calm acceptance of self. I wanted to ask him to be my sponsor, but I was afraid. I finally got my courage together and, shaking like a leaf, I asked this man if he would consider sponsoring me. He said that I could call him and together we would discuss the possibilities. After we talked, he agreed to sponsor me, and my life has changed under his guidance and encouragement in ways I never could have imagined. He is my friend; he is a person I can trust to tell me the truth all the time and a person who likes me and "tough loves" me regardless of what I do or don't do. He shares himself with me and allows me to see, firsthand, how he works his program in *his* life. Through the example my sponsor sets for me, I understand that all I can do is tell other people what I did and what works and doesn't work for me. If they want what I have, it is their responsibility to put the Program to work in their own lives. I find that sharing with other people on a daily basis is tremendously beneficial to me. The dynamics of this Program are such that when I give it away, I get to keep it.

After I had lost all of my excess weight—120 pounds—I began to have problems. Even though I understood and accepted the caveat that "Thin is not necessarily well," something deep inside me still told me that once I was thin, everything in my life would be perfect, including me. But even after I lost the weight, I experienced pain that was worse than any pain I'd experienced before I joined the Program. I was no longer sedated with food, and the rosy bubble I thought was OA had burst—*the honeymoon was over!* At that point, I understood that I had spent my first year in OA dieting and entertaining myself with numbers on the scale. With that diversion no longer available, I had to face myself and get busy really *working* the Program. I had to learn to work the Program *within my own mind* rather than focusing on attending meetings, performing service, and all the other things we can do in this Program that tend to prevent us from looking *within*. I said to God every day, "I don't understand this pain, but I stand here before you *ready to change*. Show me what you want from me and I'll do my best to comply." I made a decision at that point to really turn my life over to the care and protection of God, and to follow His direction. Things began to get better and somehow easier.

Today, I'm doing work that I love; I have returned

to school; my relationships improve as I work my Program in all my affairs; and I have love in my life to an extent I've never known. I now accept myself and I accept other people. Today I choose to be responsible for living my own life instead of avoiding myself by living in someone *else's* life. I still have bad moments, particularly when my feelings come with an intensity I'm unaccustomed to. (For years, I sedated myself to avoid my feelings.) Now I am feeling some things for the first time in my life. I still sit in judgment of myself and also of my feelings at times, forgetting the fact that feelings are not good or bad; they are just feelings. But now when I feel bad, I do what I've been taught; I acknowledge the feeling, write about it, talk to my sponsor or another OA person, and then get on with my life. Today I understand something I never knew before: God is *always* there for me and no matter what is causing my pain, *it will get better.* I also understand that pain can serve as the catalyst to help me change and grow. Today the prospect of change doesn't frighten me as it used to. The sharp line which used to separate my OA life and my "outside" life has become blurred; more and more, I find that I'm practicing the principles of the Program in *all* of my affairs and with *all* of the people in my life.

Recently I was asked to participate in a marathon and was given the opportunity to choose my topic from among several topics. The topics I chose—"Came To Believe" and "Into Action"—characterize my Program today. I feel a great sense of gratitude to the Program, to my sponsor, to my children and the rest of my family, to the OA fellowship, and to my friends. I am also grateful to myself for my *willingness* to change. More than anything, however, I am grateful to God for carrying me through the bad times when I would have destroyed myself and those around me but for Him, for bringing me to this life-giving program and not forsaking me, and for helping me to realize more each day the unlimited potential He has placed within me.

Rita's Story

...the truth was that I hadn't forgiven myself.

I was one of four daughters and always felt an obligation to be the son my father never had. I often fantasized that I was a celebrity and spent *hours* dreaming that someday someone would rescue me from my boring life and raise me to my rightful position of importance in the world. Despite my rich fantasy life, I was the center of attention in our home. I spent my youth trying to get out of doing work, but still expecting the *rewards* that come from hard work. I could talk my way out of any situation, but I was basically dishonest and didn't like myself.

I projected an image of being happy-go-lucky, independent, and confident, but I was really frightened, lonely, and miserable. *I hated life.* It seemed to me that other people were *living*, but I was just faking it, hoping all the time that no one would ever find out how miserable I really *was.* Being overweight had always been a problem for me. In the back of my mind was always the idea that when I achieved a normal weight, then everything in my life would miraculously change. Only *then* would I begin living—men would be attracted to me, I'd enjoy my job, buy pretty clothes, take dancing lessons, swim, and become a famous actress. I was always waiting for that magic day, but it never came and I continued to eat.

One summer I made a bet with friends that I could lose weight. So I began another diet, this time with more determination than ever before. To my surprise, though, the harder I tried to lose weight, *the more weight I gained.* I subsequently joined various weight-loss groups thinking each would be the answer, but each program I started ended in failure for me. Finally, I began forcing myself to throw up after my binges so that I wouldn't gain weight. After bingeing and vomiting one Sunday morning, I suddenly became very frightened. I knew I couldn't control what was happening to me and I remember asking for God's help. That was the day I called OA.

After joining OA, I went on a strict diet, lost a lot of weight quickly, *and was more miserable than ever.* I began bingeing again, only this time I felt that my situation was totally hopeless. There seemed to be nothing to live for. I went to OA meetings to get help, but no one there was able to help me. I asked sponsors how to work the Steps, but no one seemed to know what to do. I knew God had *something* to do with my problem and its solution, but I didn't think He could forgive me for the things I had done in the past. I convinced myself that God wouldn't want to have anything to do with me anyway, so I would just ignore Him.

Then, at an OA marathon, someone told me that God forgives us as soon as we ask Him to. It was then I knew *the truth was that I hadn't forgiven myself.* This same person also suggested that I should get to know my Higher Power. I began to ask God to just *be with me,* to hold my hand throughout the day so that I might have the courage to live. In time, I began to feel the nearness of God. Slowly, our relationship became stronger. I began to trust my new Friend, and a degree of peace entered my life for the very first time. *But my obsession with food continued.* Then, one day, I heard a woman in OA say that food was no longer a problem for her. I was shocked, but said to myself, Now, that's great for her, but it could never happen to me. I listened carefully to this woman as she explained how she had gotten well by just working the Steps. Oh, those mysterious Steps! I had read them hundreds of times, but never really *did* them. I was stuck at Step Four, that's for certain. Another year of my life passed and things got even more unbearable. I wanted to die, but was afraid to kill myself.

One weekend in 1979 I went to an OA convention in New York City. It was there I first realized that I had to work *all* of the Steps, and I was determined to do it that weekend. I had always thought that Step Four and Step Five would be very hard, but I discovered that when a person gets really desperate, he or she will do *anything* to get well. At that point, my weight didn't matter to me anymore, so I wrote an inventory and gave it away. For the first time I became *willing* to let God remove my character defects. I left the convention and wandered into a church. As I sat in that church, I prayed the Seventh Step Prayer, made a list of the people I'd harmed, and went home. From the moment I left the church that day, my life has changed. It was as if I had gone through life with a lamp shade on my head and now the lamp shade was *gone*, and at last I could see clearly. The world was beautiful and God was giving me an opportunity to start my life over again. He had also given me new guidance to live by. That was more than five years ago and since that time, I've continued to learn more about myself and what is really important in my life.

Every area of my life has improved. I used to be a dreamer who hated herself, her life, her body, and everyone around her. I am now a woman who loves life, people, herself, and, yes, even her body. I know there are no magic answers. I've heard it said that recovered people are like swans—they seem to be floating through life, but what you don't see is how hard they are working just to stay afloat. I live the Steps daily and sometimes life isn't just the way I want it to be, but that's okay. Now I am experiencing *life.* I feel joy and pain. I no longer feel that lonely ache I felt within me for so many years. It is gone. I know that God is with me always. My compulsion is gone. I am a swan. *I am recovered.*

Emily's Story

I realized that living according to the dictates of a measuring cup and scale or calories was a barrier, not a pathway, to recovery.

The power of example has been a valuable motivating force in my recovery. When you think about it, that's how AA began: Dr. Bob's glowing clarity and change in attitude hinted to Bill Wilson about another dimension that he never dreamed existed. More than two years after I walked into my first OA meeting, I finally met someone who offered me that same kind of clarity and loving acceptance. Until then, I had not met a person who I felt exemplified recovery through the Twelve Steps. Finally, here was a person not governed by fear and rigidity who had attempted to live as an example of God's power and, through that power, had experienced what I believe is the true promise of the Program—a spiritual awakening. This promise included his willingness to pass it on to me. I leapt at the chance and this is when my own recovery *really began*. I had reached a point where I was no longer willing to do what I had been doing for the first two and a half years of OA meetings. I was no longer willing to live a control-oriented life, victimized by my fears of being out of control and not getting what I needed. I was no longer willing to control my food intake by adhering to a food plan and reporting to a sponsor. I was miserable manipulating my life to get what I thought I needed. Furthermore, this manipulation of my environment and the people in it seemed increasingly alien to the real purpose of the OA Program.

All my life I had done things to be okay, to feel safe, to get what I needed. But somewhere along the line, I missed out on learning how to feel good about *myself*. Consequently I spent most of my time trying to justify, excuse, and cope with my basic unhappiness. Control became *crucial* to this effort. I grew up in an unstable environment and quickly learned that uncomfortable feelings were threatening to my stability. Feelings like anger, fear, and sadness were practically *taboo* in our family; I got the message that "good" people didn't feel these things. So I attempted to get iron clad control of my feelings and, in the process of doing that, I became numb. Occasionally, though, I'd fly into an uncontrolled rage, then feel truly villainous and alienated. I've since learned that trying to control feelings is an impossible goal.

Perfectionism was perhaps my strongest and most pervasive attempt at control. I believed that if I could just be the *best*, then the pieces of my life would all fall into place beautifully. The expectations and pressures that are so much a part of this delusion overwhelmed me; I thought I absolutely *had* to earn all A's in school to be acceptable. But when I earned the A average I aspired to, I was *still* miserable. I've since learned that whenever I do *anything* because I feel unacceptable and want to make myself acceptable by doing it, *I always end up feeling bad*. Perfectionism is a *design* for failure; the absolute perfection we strive for will always exceed our grasp. When I fell short of my own expectations, I always felt as if I had failed completely. I now realize that my real expectation was *feeling bad* because that was what I had been taught; that was all I knew. In this way, I succeeded *perfectly*. Life, for me, was an ongoing struggle to find happiness. I lived with the delusion that if I could just exert enough control to achieve desired results—good grades, enough friends, the "right" feelings—then I'd be successful. I rationalized that in the meantime, the reason I didn't feel good was because I had not yet achieved these results. I already had an excuse and eating became another one: I was unhappy because I was fat, and once I was "thin enough," everything would be fine.

Then OA came along and offered me a diet, a food sponsor, and a food plan to give me daily guidance. I was seduced into believing that weight loss was the answer for me; 45 pounds later, nothing about me had changed except my physical appearance. Sure, I was happy about having lost weight, but I would not call it a real and *secure* happiness. I had given a measuring cup and a scale the power to determine whether I would feel good or bad about myself. As I became more and more afraid of food, bingeing, and "being out of control," I also became increasingly rigid in my interpretation of the Program. About that time, I began to suffer from severe insomnia, and I experienced my first anxiety attack, followed by horrible mental obsessions. *Something had to change.*

Then I realized that there was *something* about the

Program I had never paid much attention to: the Twelve Steps. I was forced to return to the Steps because what I *was* doing no longer worked in a way that I wanted my life to work. When I became more open to the Twelve Steps, I met this person who really lived the Steps and passed his knowledge along to me. I eagerly accepted what he had to share. For me, the whole process of recovery started when I finally developed a concept of God that worked for me. My recovery continued when I decided to live on God's terms to the best of my ability and began to challenge my old ideas and actively demonstrate a willingness to change. I felt strongly that it was time to break my "addiction to unhappiness." *I realized that living according to the dictates of a measuring cup and scale or calories was a barrier, not a pathway, to recovery. These dictates only perpetuate the same kind of control that made me miserable, the same kind of control that the Twelve Steps say I must be willing to surrender.* I began to see food control as a direct contradiction of the First Step; how could I sincerely admit *powerlessness* over something while I continued to manipulate and control it? This approach had been a seductively comfortable one for me. Had I not gained new insights about these issues of manipulation and control, I probably would have continued to live with the delusion that once I achieved my "goal" weight, I would be happy. The Twelve Steps allowed me to see that I no longer had any use for that delusion in my life and I no longer had to do things to make myself acceptable. I have to be willing to accept myself, fat or thin, *regardless of what happens.* These are God's

terms. Now, my self-acceptance is less and less dependent upon specific achievements or meeting the
expectations others may have of me; instead, my self-
acceptance comes from the unconditional love and
acceptance of God. This knowledge represents the underlying truth in my recovery. Believe me, a great deal
of the pressure I felt in my life disappeared when I no
longer felt I had to do certain things in order to be
acceptable. I have learned to direct my energies toward
being a whole and healthy person rather than toward
sustaining my anxiety and frustration.

To me, recovery is simply a mature and responsible
expression of my humanness. I continue to make mistakes, have painful feelings, and act inappropriately.
But instead of beating myself when these things happen, I think about them as opportunities to expand my
awareness and *learn*. I am no longer a victim of my
life. What an incredible realization it is to see my *natural* perfection as a child of God and to see that there
is nothing to be afraid of. And when fear does come—
and it does—I am no longer *governed* by it as I was
in the past. There are so many feelings to experience,
so many avenues of humanness to travel. Recovery is
an adventure in discovery. My potential is limitless with
my newly discovered source of power, a source I know
is not "out there" somewhere, but inside of me. Compulsive behaviors no longer serve a purpose in my life.
I no longer have to eat in order to cope with bad
feelings about myself *because I don't have bad feelings
about myself anymore.*

Probably the most difficult thing I have ever done is
to stop writing the script for my life so that I will stop

attempting to control results. Just as someone else was a powerful example of recovery to me three years ago, I have become an example of recovery to other people. I have become a vehicle for that inspiration in all my affairs. It is my responsibility to share with others what I have learned. This Program has *everything* to do with an attitude change brought about through a working relationship with God based on the Twelve Steps and nothing at all to do with food or weight control. In fact, when I concentrate on changing my attitude, then my weight—the thing I had always perceived as my primary problem—takes care of itself. I have been restored to sanity and I am learning to accept my natural inheritance: happiness, joy, and freedom. Life's not such a big deal; *it's an adventure!*

Bob's Story

I had learned to switch compulsions from overeating to abstinence, but food was still my God.

The story of my recovery actually began on March 7, 1978. On that day I entered a hospital on the East Coast to participate in a five-and-a-half-month experimental program for weight-reduction. The doctors conducting the experiment had sought out relatively healthy obese people in order to study the physical effects of a 400-calorie diet. Since I was already looking for a place to be "locked up" so that I could stop eating compulsively, I willingly signed on as a participant in this program. My participation was actually the culmination of a seventeen-year struggle to lose weight and *keep it off*. I had been obese since the age of nine, and from the age of nineteen on, I consistently weighed over 300 pounds. I had successfully lost more than 100 pounds three separate times in my early adult life, only to regain all that weight *and more* just a few months after losing it. As my involvement in the hospital's experimental program began, I learned three facts about myself: my weight had ballooned to 380 pounds; I was now a borderline diabetic; and I had so much fat in my liver that the cells of that organ were actually *dying*. I was overwhelmed by feelings of fear and depression during my first few days at the hospital.

I kept thinking that now I was 200 pounds overweight and I would *never* be normal. I had lived in fear of diabetes for years, and now my fear was a reality. My aunt had recently died of cancer of the liver and now I was terrified to know of my own liver disease. Also, I found it very difficult to adjust to the conditions at the hospital. Several patients in my ward were terminally ill and participating in a cancer-research program. I felt an incredible sadness for them and was fearful about my own situation. My father had died in a cancer hospital eleven years before, and it seemed that I was just now feeling sadness about that experience for the very first time.

After I had been hospitalized for about two months, I began attending OA meetings in town. I had attended a few OA meetings near my home three years before, and remembered that those meetings had turned me off somewhat because the people there seemed so very rigid in their abstinence. But I also remembered the acceptance and love I felt from some of the members of that OA group. As a hospital patient, I desperately wanted that kind of contact again. When I first began attending OA meetings during my hospitalization, I did so mostly to get away from the hospital on Thursday evenings. I did not plan to make OA any kind of permanent part of my life. I attended meetings with this attitude for two months, but then I slowly began to change my mind about OA and my real *need* for it. About this same time, I learned that every person who had participated in the hospital's earlier experimental weight-reduction program had regained all the weight they had lost within six months after leaving the hospital. That discouraging news, along with the fact that people were telling me they were doing things through OA that they could never have done on their own, made me feel a strong and immediate need for the Program.

Ever since I decided to make OA an ongoing part of my life, I have tried to learn what works and *use* it because I realized that, for me, a return to compulsive overeating would very likely result in a life-threatening illness. So, as a new member of OA, I made a conscious effort to learn what was working for other people. I heard many people at OA talk about using a cup and a scale to measure their food, reporting the food they ate to a food sponsor, and going to OA meetings each and every day, if possible. I also heard talk of God at these meetings, but I didn't know how He worked—was it through the cup and scale, the reporting of food to sponsors, or the meetings? Despite some confusion at this point, I *did* work the program to the best of my ability and promptly lost 50 pounds.

At this point, I became somewhat well-known as an OA speaker. I'd go around telling great horror stories about my days as an overeater, emphasizing the many vivid memories I had of my five-and-a-half-month hospitalization. I have always had a powerful speaking voice and at a crucial point in my OA presentation, I would bellow out: "If you want to be successful in this Program, then abstinence must not only be the most important thing in your life without exception, it must be the *only* thing in your life that is important." Today I must state with humility that I was wrong about that. After eight months of so-called "maintenance," I began

277

to overeat again. Then I developed an allergy to lettuce, which was an important food item for my "abstinence." When I stopped eating lettuce, I began to overeat again. In just three months, I regained 50 pounds. *I had learned to switch compulsions from overeating to abstinence, but food was still my God.* Now I know that I did this because I had never really changed my thoughts or my feelings. In some ways, I was worse off at this point than I was before I *came* to OA. Prior to joining OA, I *knew* I was crazy. But after I joined OA, I actually thought I was getting better when, in reality, I was as obsessed with food as I had ever been. I now believe that treating compulsive eating disorders with a food plan and a food sponsor is like giving pain medication to someone with a brain tumor—the pain may temporarily subside or disappear, but the person will continue to be ill and may eventually *die* of the disease.

I came back to the OA Program the first Monday of November in 1979, and at that meeting I was struck by two things. First of all, the tremendous love and acceptance I felt from the group members shocked me and also made me feel wonderful. I had expected judgment and anger, but received unconditional love and acceptance instead. The second thing that struck me that evening *disturbed* me. The speaker, who was thin and appeared to be well, said that all of the answers were in the Big Book of Alcoholics Anonymous. I had never bought the book, nor was I particularly interested in it. But because of my feelings of desperation and fear that night, I *did* go out and buy the book. It was still a long time before I read the Big Book, but shortly after I finished it, I went on to read *Twelve Steps and Twelve Traditions* ("Twelve and Twelve"). I will never forget how shocked I was to learn that alcoholics don't call other people in the morning to tell them what they are going to eat and drink that day in order to avoid alcohol. (I had always assumed recovering alcoholics did that.) As an OA member, I had been told that the most important part of each day was calling someone else and reporting what I would eat that day so that I wouldn't binge or eat the wrong kind of food. I felt angry and betrayed when I began to realize that many things we did in the OA Program had no basis at all in the AA Program. At that point, I threw myself into trying to learn what AA people did to allow the Program to work for them and I started to question everything I had been taught in OA. Another important thing I learned in reading "Twelve and Twelve" was that an alcoholic's relationship with God is the most important thing in his or her life, *even more important than not drinking.* This concept was in stark contrast to what I had learned in OA—that an attitude of abstinence was, without exception, the most important thing in the life of a compulsive overeater. I also came to see that alcoholics expressed their relationship with God through unselfish and unending service to other alcoholics. Before I understood this, I had given service when it was convenient for me to do so, but I had never given service with the total dedication referred to in "Twelve and Twelve." I immediately began increasing my service to others with a new attitude and a new spirit of dedication.

In the fall of 1980 I attended a Big Book retreat. It

is truly impossible for me to put into words what I feel about that experience. I know for certain that God worked that weekend to provide me with information which I have since used to save my life. In the ten minutes we studied Chapter Two of the Big Book that weekend, ("There Is a Solution," pp. 17-29), I learned more than I had learned in my first *two years* in the OA Program. I had always thought that my "disease" was basically that physiologically my body was not normal when I ate sugar and I got fat from it. I also knew that when I *did* eat a little sugar, I was unable to stop. But I learned that my body physiology and my use of sugar were not my problems after all; *my real problem was that I had been aware of my difficulties with sugar for a long time yet I continued to eat it anyway.* I had always assumed that this kind of behavior was an indication of weak will power, but I have since learned that I have a very strong will. My will, however, is to eat and to be self-destructive. I had actually become addicted not to sugar or even to overeating; *I had become addicted to negativity.*

My problem was that during those seventeen years I believed I was bad, worthless, and unacceptable because I was fat, I had actually *become* bad, worthless, and unacceptable. I had become resentful, judgmental, manipulative, dishonest, and overbearing in order to cope with my self-hatred. During my first two years in OA, I had not in any way confronted *another* disease that affected me—my lack of self-acceptance. Until I read in the Big Book where Dr. Jung says that you are hopeless because "You have the mind of the chronic alcoholic" (p. 27), I hadn't realized that I was hopeless because of my *state of mind*, not because I continued to regain weight I had lost. I suddenly knew that the task before me was a tremendous one, and now I knew that my disease was much more serious and all-encompassing than I had realized. The reason I had failed so many times, even in the OA Program, was because I had concentrated on "dieting away" my character defects.

At this retreat, I also learned that the Twelve Steps are the *solution*. The Steps are what a person must *live* in order to accomplish the attitude change that is required to bring about a solution to the problem of compulsive overeating. I left the retreat that weekend with a tremendous sense of commitment to OA, not as a diet club *but as a way of life*. I began studying the Big Book and going through the Steps. The Third Step came to be a Step of trust for me. I learned to trust that I would be well if I allowed God's power to develop *within me*. This trust gave me the courage to go on to the other Steps and discover barriers I had put up that adversely affected my ability to live a fulfilling life.

Over the next two years, the hardest part of recovery was *unlearning* many things I had been taught. Of all the things I heard that first weekend at the retreat, the one concept that stuck with me most was this: no matter what I do to myself in the future in terms of compulsive overeating, it would be *worse* to chastise myself for my compulsive behavior because if I do that, I will only keep repeating the behavior. I used to think that when I overate, I should chastise myself because guilt would help me to eliminate my compulsive behavior. Now I understand that recovery begins when an individual is able to accept himself or herself and recognize that self-hatred is *at least* as much a part of this disease as the craving for food.

I spent twenty-seven years on my own and two years in the Program trying to achieve four things: normal weight and appearance; a good relationship with my mother instead of one characterized by the guilt I felt over her pain about my obesity; healthy relationships with people; and self-acceptance. I believed these four things would give me happiness. I had always failed in my attempts to achieve these things, so when I first failed in the OA Program, I gave up even thinking they were possible. In the past three years, I have stopped thinking about *making* such things happen and instead I have focused solely on *living* the Twelve Steps. My motive is to become a person who is able to be of service to God and the people around me. And during the past three years, the things I had always dreamed of achieving have become reality for me: I have successfully maintained a 175-pound weight loss; my relationship with my mother is much better than it was; I have healthier relationships with people because I focus on being the kind of person I will love and accept rather than focusing on what I think other people want me to be; and I have learned to accept *myself*. Most important to me, when I really look at myself these days, I feel peace and acceptance instead of the hate, fear, and disgust I used to feel.

In the past three years, OA has come to represent a quest—a journey of coming home to the person I was born to be, instead of the sick and insane person I had become. When I have any food problems now, I do a

Tenth, Eleventh, and/or Twelfth Step, and the problem disappears. Today I have learned to value the concepts of surrender, love, forgiveness, and acceptance. And to the degree that I live a life that reflects those qualities, I have sobriety and joy.

Gay's Story

Abstinence comes as a by-product of the Twelve Steps.

At the end of my first OA meeting nearly six years ago, I knew that after a long and painful search, I had finally and forever found home. I wanted to be thin and I wanted to stop feeling miserable, but I wanted to accomplish these things *and* continue to eat whatever and whenever I *wanted* to eat. I relapsed before my first year in the OA fellowship ended. And I believe I relapsed because I was concentrating on the OA "fellowship" instead of working the OA Program. I dieted, but I failed to really look at myself and I failed to work on my spiritual growth. During that first year in the Program, I was truly in a state of ignorance because I didn't even know what OA was about. For the next two years, I collapsed helplessly and hopelessly into a pattern of compulsive overeating. Then I entered into a phase that was quite foreign to me: I began saying things and behaving in ways I could not understand. I lied to anyone and everyone in order to protect the illness within me. I felt totally and completely diseased, *and I was.* It seemed to me that almost nothing remained of the basic goodness I once believed I had within me. *I was no longer someone I could trust.* When I looked in the mirror, I saw a monster—a Dr. Jekyll and Mr. Hyde. I didn't know *me* anymore.

I couldn't find myself beneath the layers of lies, fears, resentments, and self-pity.

My recovery came gradually. The first concrete evidence of it came through my willingness to present myself on a weekly basis to an inventory "Truth" group. Many of the people in this group had already been through the process outlined in Chapter Five of the Big Book ("How It Works", pp. 58-71). These people offered me unconditional love while they helped me confront both the realities of my problem and the things I would need to do in order to change. For the first time in my life, I admitted and accepted the fact that unless I sought help, I would be forever doomed. My ego was deflated and my pride was leveled, but I began doing what recovered people did: whenever somebody had the kind of recovery I wanted, I made it a point to find out just what they were doing, then I copied it to the best of my ability. It was a struggle to do this because it took time for the last germ of my illness to die.

I continued to binge for six months while I learned the Program. I share this information with people who have been taught to believe that they have to be abstinent *before* they can work the Steps. I don't think that's true. *Abstinence comes as a by-product of the Twelve Steps.* By working the Steps to the best of my ability and receiving support from my recovered friends during that six-month period of frustrated bingeing, the Program eventually prevailed over the problem. Then, because of the spiritual experience I had and the resulting change in my personality, it became *unnecessary* for me to eat compulsively; the problem was removed. I had been a person who was obsessed with food every waking moment of every day, but I have not had the desire to binge for more than two years now. I am as much in awe of this change as anyone else.

My recovery has been *filled with wonder.* I continue to learn daily lessons for living which are transforming me into the person I always wanted to be. Where there used to be only blind darkness and despair for me, I now have a new vision for myself. I share this solution with anyone who sincerely wants it. I share it in the same way it was shared with me. How can I do this? As a member of OA, it is my *obligation* to do this. As a member of OA, this sharing is also the key to my freedom from compulsive behavior. I will be forever grateful to the original members, their followers, and especially to the many important people who have come into my life through the Program. With stories of their own recoveries and their lives today, these people are gifting me with *living proof* of the message of the Program.

I wrote the preceeding story when I was in the third year of my recovery. It is now nearly four years later, and with God's grace and power, I will soon begin my seventh year of recovery from compulsive overeating. The realization of this continues to amaze me. It still seems like a miracle to me that I am no longer eating compulsively and that I have even lost the desire to eat compulsively. But I'd like to share my story as it is today and, at the same time, reflect on some thoughts I've had since the time I wrote that first story.

There's an apocryphal tale about Michelangelo that

I like because it expresses the way I feel about myself and the philosophy of recovery. Someone asked Michelangelo one day how he had carved and sculpted the statue of David. Michelangelo thought about it a few moments and then supposedly said something like this: "Well, you see, I took this defective block of marble that nobody else in town wanted and chipped away everything that was not David, and that allowed the *real David* to emerge." This is what the Program has done for me. Every inventory I have written, *every* moment I have spent soul-searching and developing personal honesty, *every* amend I have made, *every* way I have sought to know God better—each of these efforts has helped to chip away everything that is not me, allowing the *real me* to emerge.

My life is good today. Not all of my days are good, but that is life. *And that is real. I am learning to take risks and become more authentic.* And I have discovered a whole world out there filled with interesting things to do. I remember the days when I didn't have any interests other than food. Then, my life revolved around bingeing, getting more food, and figuring out when and where I would be able to binge again. I put all of my energies into these things and so it was a very lonely and empty existence. I've discovered something else: purpose. Now there is purpose to my life and I know that I can contribute to the world in my job, through my outside interests and activities, and with my family and friends and fellow compulsive overeaters. Now I love being alive and being part of the human race. I have choices and I can be whatever I want to be. *I am free!*

Victor's Story

...God is not just a specialist in alcoholism and compulsive overeating; He is a general practitioner.

I had my last drink of alcohol on October 15, 1971, and found Alcoholics Anonymous. I thought all my worries were over then, because there would be no more jails, fistfights, broken homes, and all that went with my life as a practicing alcoholic. At that time, I had no idea that I was also a compulsive overeater. Sure, I had a big belly, but I assumed it was the result of all that beer. I also assumed that my "beer belly" would just *disappear* after a few months of sobriety in the AA Program. But that was not to be, because the first thing those good people in AA gave me was orange juice with sugared syrup...to stop the shakes, of course. At AA meetings, I snacked on cookies, doughnuts, and candy. Then after the meetings, several of us would go to a nearby restaurant together and order banana splits, hot-fudge sundaes, or pie à la mode. So, instead of my "beer belly" disappearing as I expected it would, it started getting *bigger*. I began to worry. I went to an oldtimer in the AA Program and asked him what I should do about my weight. He smiled at me and just said, "Victor, you're sober, aren't you? Don't get involved with anything else right now. Don't drink, and be sure to go to plenty of meetings during your first year in AA."

By the time I had completed my eleventh month of abstinence from alcohol, I was 100 pounds heavier than I was when I first came to AA. About that time, I ran into a fellow member of AA who had been fat like me. I hadn't seen him for quite some time, and I was really shocked at his appearance! He had lost *all* of his excess weight and looked trim and healthy. The first thing I said to him was, "Bob, how in the world did you lose all that weight?" He said, "Vic, I belong to a national weight-loss organization and it's great. It's kind of like AA. A person pitches to you about how wonderful it is to be thin. They weigh you once a week. They give you a food plan you can live with and they sell you a little scale so that you can weigh your food. It really works." So I joined this national weight-loss organization in October 1972. I went to my first meeting and I was weighed there and given my goal weight. I bought a little food scale at the meeting and someone gave me a food plan I could live with. The next week, I went to my second meeting having had no problem with food that week and already weighing six pounds less! And so it went...I lost from four to six pounds each week. I reached my goal weight, then quickly lost four additional pounds. By then I was a "model" member of the organization and received tie pins, lapel buttons, and other tokens of my "success." I became a life member of this popular weight-loss organization.

Then it happened. When I reached my goal weight, I was given a food plan that included "one scoop of ice cream." I looked at this and went to the man in charge of the meeting and said, "*I have never had 'one scoop of ice cream' in my entire adult life! Pints and quarts and half-gallons maybe, but never just a single scoop."* He shook his head, laughed, and said, "Victor, we have taught you how to eat properly. Who is stronger, you or that scoop of ice cream?" I told him that I thought the scoop of ice cream was. He laughed again and said, "Of course not, Victor. *You* are stronger. You have won every award our organization offers." I believed him. (At this point, it had been over sixteen weeks since I'd had ice cream or *any* of the other foods I had binged on so often in the past.) You can probably *guess* what happened next: *my obsession with food came back stronger than ever.* In no time at all, I was back to eating compulsively. I quit going to the weekly meetings of this weight-loss organization because I was getting fat again and, frankly, I was ashamed of myself. I felt that I had let the organization down. And even at my AA meetings, I began to hear remarks like this: "Victor, aren't you gaining weight again? Aren't your clothes getting kind of tight?" For the next six years, I was back to my old routine: gaining weight, dieting without success, finally losing some weight, then gaining it all back again, and more. It was like a very unpleasant merry-go-round ride that never stopped. At the same time, I had abstained from alcohol for over six years. I was working with several AA "babies" (newcomers to the AA Program) and I no longer had problems with liquor, *but my eating was out of control.*

Then a man in my AA group told me that a neighbor of his was a member of Overeaters Anonymous and this neighbor had asked him to be her sponsor. I asked him, "Do you really think that's OK?" He said, "Sure, we help whoever wants our help." The next day he told me that this woman had asked if she could go for coffee with us after our meeting that night; she wanted to hear more about the AA Program. I said I'd be glad to meet her. And so this beautiful lady from OA started having coffee with us on a regular basis. She didn't say much; most of the time she just listened to the two of us from AA talk, and occasionally she'd ask a few questions. In our conversations we never talked about losing weight. Instead, we talked about how the AA Program works, the spiritual recovery in AA, the Twelve Steps, the Big Book, and Bill W., and Doctor Bob, the founders of AA. *But as the weeks went by, she was losing weight and I was getting fatter!* I was really confused. I kept asking myself, How can this woman use what *we* tell her about the AA Program and lose weight, *but I can't?* One night I said to her, "Kathy, whatever that 'overeating' problem is, I think I have it." She looked at me, smiled, and said, "Victor, I was hoping you would see that." A few days later, someone from my AA group called me and said, "Victor I have a copy of the fifteen questions that Overeaters Anonymous uses to determine whether or not a person is a compulsive overeater, *and I think that I am one.* And if *I'm* a compulsive overeater, then so are *you!* There is a meeting of OA close by. Will you come with me?" Being this man's sponsor in AA, what could I say but "yes"?

On February 13, 1978, I went to my first OA meeting. The only thing I knew about OA at that point was that they used the Big Book and they adapted the AA

Program in order to deal with the problem of compulsive overeating. I had one definite advantage over most newcomers in OA because I knew how *AA* worked. I had experienced the miracle of sobriety through the AA Program and so I went to this OA meeting with an open mind. I'll never forget that first meeting. I walked in with my friend from AA, and the first thing we saw was what appeared to be a room filled with fat people. My friend looked at me and I looked at him and he said, "Let's get out of here!" I said, "No, let's wait a while. Somebody here has *got* to know what to do. Let's sit down in the back of the room." We both felt a little better when we noticed a few thin people in the crowd. The speaker at the meeting that night was an alcoholic *and* a compulsive overeater. Through his presentation, he gave me the key I needed to unlock the mystery of how I could apply the principles of the AA Program to the problem of compulsive overeating. This is what the speaker said: "Tonight I have been sober in AA for fourteen years and I have nine years of abstinence in OA. If I lose my abstinence in OA, I will also lose my sobriety in AA because I cannot be sober in one program and slip around in the other. *I must have sobriety in all areas of my life.*"

The speaker's words hit me like a ton of bricks. I said to myself, "Of course, I have to look at food like I do alcohol." I then felt that beautiful spiritual experience—when the tremendous weight is lifted from you—the same feeling I had six years before when I first received and understood the message of AA. I remember smiling and relaxing, then turning to my AA friend and saying, "Greg, I've got the answer to this food business." He looked at me and said, "You're kidding. What did you hear tonight that I didn't?" I told him, but it didn't mean a thing to him. All he could see were the fat people in that room. So I said to him, "They told me in AA I would never have to drink alcohol again if I didn't want to. I believe that the same promise holds true for me with this problem: *I never have to eat compulsively again if I don't want to.*"

That first visit to an OA meeting was more than six years ago and I have successfully maintained my 75-pound weight loss during that time. But the most important thing for me is that *now my sobriety is complete.* I have come to believe that God is not just a specialist in alcoholism and compulsive overeating; He is a general practitioner. He will handle anything that I am willing to surrender to Him.

Jean's Story

...awareness is not enough.

I remember that even as a young child, I always had a craving for love or food or someone or something that would make me *feel good* and make everything right. I ate virtually all the time and for thirty-six years of my life, I ate compulsively in the middle of the night. I started using food to cover up my feelings of fear and emotional dependency at the age of four. I began eating in the middle of the night at the age of fourteen, and by the time I was in my twenties I was eating this way every night. (Sometimes I'd go through two or three episodes of binge-eating in one night.)

I learned about Overeaters Anonymous from my sisters when they called me after their first meeting and said, "Jean, this Program is just for you. They talk about God and losing weight at the meetings." I was then straining the seams of size 20 clothing and had stopped getting on a scale at 162 pounds. (I am 5' 2" tall.) But even though I was obese and continued to eat compulsively, I was a successful businesswoman who projected optimism and cheerfulness to others. The truth was that on the inside I was very negative. I was completely dishonest and never even *knew* it. I manipulated and pleased everyone I came in contact with because I had such a desperate need for approval and love. In those days, I could not have a decent conversation with *anyone* who was angry because I would immediately shut down in fear and walk away. I always felt as if I were crawling on the floor, unable to even pick myself up, much less hold my head high.

I reached "bottom" a few days before attending my first OA meeting. On my way to bed that night, I walked past a cake-stand in my kitchen and eyed the cake I had bought for my family earlier in the day. The very next thing I remembered was waking up the next morning with cake crumbs all over my chest. I could barely wobble to the kitchen but once there, I discovered that the entire cake was gone! On this morning-after, I first came to terms with the fact that instead of sleeping through the night for the past three months, I had actually been binge-eating, then blacking out. The panic and desperation I felt was *fierce*.

I attended my first OA meeting on Sunday afternoon, February 16, 1964. The speaker that day was a member of AA who had lived for a time on "skid row." And I identified with this man because my bedroom had really been my "skid row," complete with all the crumbs and grime from my nightly eating binges in bed. The speaker had been in prison for fifteen years for killing someone. I knew that, in a sense, I had been killing myself with food for over forty years, all the while building a prison of my own. Hearing the spiritual aspects of this man's recovery, I thought to myself, I can believe too, and I don't even have to say anything about God to my family members because they will ridicule me if I do. Instead, I can become a quiet *doer* of this Program.

When I arrived home after that first OA meeting, I

did several things I had never done before: I made myself a good, nutritious dinner of reasonable portions; in the evening, after dinner, I drove my car alone and went to the market—without my husband; when I got home, I went to bed early and slept peacefully. In the middle of the night, I awoke with an overwhelming compulsion to run out into the kitchen and eat. I swung my legs over the side of the bed, looked upward and said, "God, help me!" In the split-second that I looked upward, I saw two arms stretched out before me. So I took the heavy emotional burden I had carried for over forty-four years and *threw* it toward the outstretched arms. I felt a wonderful sense of release as the outstretched arms caught my burden. I got out of bed, walked into the kitchen, took a drink of water, walked back to bed, and promptly fell asleep again.

The next morning I was certain that *for the first time in my adult life, I had not gotten up to eat in the middle of the night.* Standing at the foot of my bed, I told God that because of my gratitude at having been released from binge-eating in the middle of the night, I would work the Twelve Steps of Overeaters Anonymous, to the best of my ability, every day of my life. I have been working those steps for over twenty years now, I have maintained a weight loss of over fifty pounds, and I have not eaten during the night. To this day, I do not question how this is possible. *I believe that God can and will help me every time I let go of the problem and am willing to live in the solution.*

In working the OA Program, I learned about the misguided instincts and character defects which had caused all my problems over the years. Through extensive inventory writing, I have made many discoveries: that my fear of confronting angry people actually started in childhood. I was never able to deal with my father's anger; I wanted to be like my mother, who couldn't read, so I failed reading in the second grade and remained a poor reader until I had been in OA for almost eight years. After stealing money from a cafe owner at the age of thirteen in order to buy food, I eventually turned my feelings of guilt inward and they developed into an irrational fear of an agency that represented the authority to punish me —the Internal Revenue Service. My emotional dependency and my manipulative behavior first developed when my younger brother began receiving the attention I had enjoyed and I said to myself, I'll show them; they'll take care of me because I'll *make* them. To my way of thinking, character defects are like trees with many connected branches. My tree trunk was fear, which led to branches of irresponsibility, procrastination, fear of rejection, people-pleasing, pride, perfectionism, manipulation, lying, cheating, stealing, anger, resentment, self-pity, self-loathing, and a total lack of self-worth.

The new awareness I came to have about myself was interesting and wonderful to me, but *awareness is not enough*. I had to be willing to *take action* in order to overcome my old ways of thinking and behaving, and I still do. God has given me the willingness to become a person, and this willingness is necessary to my abstinence. When I feel fearful, I just face that fear, feel it, accept it, and then let it go. I must go through the fear rather than run away from it. God has been very good to me and OA has been my school of learning for over twenty years now. On a daily basis, I know what the truth is in my life and I am learning more and more to be my highest self.

What am I like now? Most of the time, I am a woman instead of a child. I have overcome my fear of confronting angry people. I can express myself *honestly*, without fear of rejection. My priorities and my life are in order and I generally do things minute by minute instead of procrastinating. By learning how to make decisions, I have learned how not to get stuck at the inevitable "forks" in the road. I do what I feel is honest and right and now I can love and accept *myself*. I have learned what it means to accept myself as I am at this moment, and I know that I cannot go forward until I accept what is right there in front of me. I finally understand that no person, place, or thing can ever fix my life; I must depend only on God and myself.

I now know that in order to change, a person must go through the Steps of awareness—knowledge, belief, and trust. I finally came to believe within myself that *I am a worthy person and that God wants the best for me, always*. God brought me to OA to be of service to other people, but I must put God first and myself next, or I will have nothing to give to anyone else. Most of all, I know that without God, I could have done nothing. In the days before OA, my choice was to be fat, lazy, dishonest, and fearful. Now, working with God, I am dealing with my character defects, one by one. And it is all right with me that I am not (and probably never will be) there 100 percent; *I never want to graduate from OA*. I know the Twelve Steps of the OA Program work best when I am willing to give them all that I have to give. On the days that I *do* give my all, I am at peace with myself and at one with God. When I led my first meeting many years ago, I said something that is still true for me and for many others:

> *"As I walk with God, I can stop running.*
> *As I stop running, I can face myself."*

Norrene's Story

...nothing in God's world happens by mistake.

What is it like to know that "something" is wrong, "something" is off-kilter, yet not be able to identify that "something"? The Big Book describes this state of mind as "restless, irritable and discontented." That Big Book description aptly characterizes the first forty-one years of my existence.

I couldn't understand why I was always hungry, particularly right after eating, or why food seemed to be in my every waking thought. I knew that my preoccupation with food was inappropriate, *but I didn't know what to do about it.* I tried to deal with the symptom—weight—in countless ways, but I failed in each of my attempts to lose weight. No matter how hard I tried or how often I screamed and begged God to please help me lose weight, I just could not stay on a diet. Several times a week, I ingested so much food that I felt as if I were suffocating. I was unable to breathe properly after these binges and sometimes I felt as though I might *explode.* It is difficult to describe my self-loathing and my feelings of bewilderment that a religious person like me could do something so destructive to her body. Each time I binged, I vowed that it would be the *last* time, yet deep down in my heart I knew I was completely powerless and that my behavior would continue on as it always had. I entered a state of "dumb resignation"; I had given up all hope. I rationalized that I wasn't the ugliest person on earth and I wasn't the dumbest person on earth, so God must have made me fat in order to give me *some* burden to bear. Believing this released me from all responsibility for my actions. I figured that the responsibility for my obesity really rested with *God* because He knew I didn't want to be fat, yet He had not seen fit to change me.

As my compulsive overeating progressed, so did my medical problems. I spent *months* of my life in the hospital for illnesses directly related to my obesity. Doctors tried various approaches to deal with the symptom of excess weight, but to no avail. It was during one of my hospitalizations ten years ago that I first heard about Overeaters Anonymous. As I sat listening to the hospital dietician explain her interpretation of the Program, I remember thinking to myself that Overeaters Anonymous was certainly a stupid name for a diet group. The name was just so common—it didn't even sound *intelligent*. Even though my obesity was then threatening my life, I promptly dismissed the idea of "membership" in such a group.

Exactly one year later, I saw a notice in the local newspaper about an OA group. Out of curiosity, I decided to attend a meeting. I remember purposely arriving at the meeting late so as not to be noticed. As I parked my car, I wondered how many neighbors were peering out of their windows watching the fat people walk into this "fat" meeting. I felt a real sense of shame to *be* one of them. I was confused by the meeting

302

because there was not much talk about food; there were no scales; and there was very little literature available. To top it off, the leader was very petite and thin—*and I had known her most of my adult life!* At that moment I deeply resented this woman and was disgusted that someone in the group actually *knew* me. Hadn't I prayed to God that no one at this meeting would know me, especially no one from other weight-reduction groups I had attended in the past? I certainly didn't want to be associated with a bunch of unintelligent "losers."

But the "magic" happened that first night at OA and I never stopped returning to meetings. A "miracle" began. Almost immediately the symptom was relieved; my weight started to drop. I was finally able to get out of my size 24½ clothing; then I progressed to a point when I no longer needed half-sizes; then I progressed to size 20 and then to size 18...16...14...12...10. And all the while I was losing weight, I remained very active in the group. I gave service, sponsored "the world" (or so it seemed to me), and imparted my vast knowledge of the Program (or so I thought) to anyone who would listen. Taking Step Four and Step Five showed me how my life had been ruled by resentments, fears, and a multitude of other character defects. For example, my husband works for one of the major airlines, but I had never been *inside* an airplane because of fear, and that was *only one* of the fears that dominated my life. (Actually, I feared everything and everybody.) But just one week after completing the Fifth Step, I took my first flight from Cleveland to Dallas in one day and I have been flying in airplanes ever since that time. God took away that fear just as He has taken away each fear I have asked Him to remove, along with my resentments, my intolerance, my lack of patience, and my powerful need to control and manipulate.

But, slowly and surely, the "miracle" started to fade. Even though I had achieved a predetermined weight-loss goal for the first time in my life, and even though I appeared to be of normal weight, I still felt that uncontrollable hunger all the time. And my defense for fighting that hunger was growing thin. My defense? It consisted of the following: peer group pressure; the knowledge that I had achieved a significant weight-loss goal and had kept the excess weight off for four and a half years; involvement in the politics of a Twelve Step organization; and putting myself on a pedestal. None of these worthwhile gimmicks was working for me anymore. Gradually the weight started coming back, and I was terrified. About this same time, our Intergroup in Ohio invited a speaker to come and share his program of recovery and how he was living the Twelve Steps. I listened to him, smiled, and nodded my head in agreement. But inwardly I doubted *everything* this man said. I felt sure that *he* didn't know what it was like to be hungry all the time and *he* didn't know what it was like to look at television and salivate at the sight of a food commercial. As far as I was concerned, he lost his credibility when he said that by living the Twelve Steps on a daily basis, he had no compulsive desire for sweets. I knew that this man was either lying or he was *not* a compulsive overeater.

The retreat left me feeling challenged and disturbed. But for the first time there was a *glimmer of hope* that this obsession of mine could be relieved—that maybe I *didn't* have to spend the rest of my life feeling hungry and using my time and energy to decide whether or not to eat at any given moment. The speaker at the retreat shared from *Twelve Steps and Twelve Traditions* and the Big Book, and somehow he made those books come alive for me. For the first time I really *studied* those resources. I also read any other AA literature I could get my hands on; I sent for tapes and listened to them; I started putting my thoughts on paper; and I started attending AA meetings. And then it happened. One afternoon, I was sitting at the breakfast bar in my kitchen watching my favorite commercial (the glories of cheesecake with cherry topping). I sat there waiting for the usual salivation and uncontrollable hunger, but I suddenly realized I had absolutely *no desire* for that food. My persistent hunger was gone—it was lifted—and that was a very strange feeling because it was so new to me. I will never forget that afternoon!

There is no way I can adequately put into words what it is to walk through life without having an addiction, without having to seek comfort in appeasing a persistent appetite, and *with* the ability to deal with life on life's terms. I feel that I progress each year I live in the solution brought about through these Twelve Steps. Life is not perfect. There are times when I have to live with circumstances I *never* would have willingly planned for, such as a job transfer that meant leaving family, friends, a beautiful home, an administrative position, and a conservative Midwestern town, and moving to a city that is unlike anything I have ever experienced. There are times when I have to live with situations that are not of my choosing, like when I found out that I had an incurable illness at a time in my life when I thought that everything was "perfect." Through it all, I realized that there are more spiritual journeys ahead for me and that I am being taken care of by God. He knows best what areas of my life I still need to grow in, for nothing in God's world happens by mistake.

I am so very grateful for the Twelve Steps of Alcoholics Anonymous, and to Dr. Bob, Bill W., and the people in all Twelve Step organizations who have shared with me and helped me. I am also grateful for people who are willing to give of themselves by sharing at retreats, for the people God has brought into my life on a sponsorship basis, for an incredible new feeling of happiness and self-worth, for a treasured relationship with my husband (who has been in the Program for eight years), and for a church community that far surpasses any I have known in the past. Above all, I am grateful for the application of a faith that works—really works—under and above all circumstances. With the Twelve Steps, my religion has become a dynamic daily spiritual experience. Having experienced the powerlessness that comes from being totally dominated by an addiction, what a relief it is to have that addiction lifted on a daily basis by living a Twelve Step recovery program. I am grateful for the "delicious" feeling of being able to *think through situations*, rather than allowing my emotions to be in control, then reacting and always being the victim. Even though I have been totally abstinent from alcohol all of my life, *I can now see what a beautiful kinship I have with the sober alcoholic.* In the past I always felt superior to alcoholics, but now I realize that they are indeed my brothers and sisters in the Program. The exact nature of our addictions may be different, but the obsession and the feelings that accompany that obsession are the same. God has indeed done for me what I could not do for myself, *and all I had to do was be willing to change.*

Judy's Story

I have come to believe that my life is a gift.

I believe in miracles. I believe because I *am* a miracle. But life wasn't always like it is today.

I grew up in a loving family and was led to believe that after college I would marry, have children, then live happily ever after. But things didn't work out that way. I *did* marry, but the man I married was diagnosed as having cancer and had to undergo a series of cobalt treatments shortly before our wedding. Being an egotistical and grandiose martyr at the time, I began my married life believing that I could single-handedly deal with any problem that might come our way. After a year of marriage, we adopted a child. I began to block out all feelings, but steadfastly held on to the belief that I could survive *anything* through my own self-will. I was then nineteen years old, filled with plans for the future, and learning to cover up problems and feelings with food. (After all, I reasoned, food is a socially acceptable substance.) When my husband and I divorced, I was 60 pounds heavier than I had been at the time of our marriage three and a half years before.

For the next sixteen years, I alternately gained weight and dieted. During those torturous years, I believed that I was *destined* to be a 300-pound woman without the ability to do things that normal, happy people do. My life was measured by the numbers on the scale, and I continued to eat my way through both happy and sad times. I first came to OA as a favor to someone else: my cousin wanted to attend an OA meeting and didn't want to go alone, so she asked me to accompany her. That meeting was in 1975, and OA is still very much a part of my life.

Not long ago I received the following message from an anonymous source: "We are all molded and re-molded by those who have loved us, and though that love may pass, we remain nonetheless their work...No love, no friendship can ever cross the path of our des-tiny without leaving some mark upon it forever." These words certainly describe what has happened to me in the last ten years. I have met people in OA who love me unconditionally, no matter how I look, what I say, or how I behave. People in the OA fellowship also have taught me how to love myself, not from the out-side, *but from the inside out*. With the example of their own lives, they showed me a path consisting of Twelve Steps. These Twelve Steps adapted from Alcoholics Anonymous helped me to *admit* my powerlessness and helped me to *accept* my inability to solve every problem by myself. I learned to be honest with myself by preparing a written examination of my life, and I acknowledged my personal defects through daily prac-tice of the Twelve Steps. I worked on my relationship with God by allowing my will to become one with His. I carefully surveyed my negative relationships and made amends to those I had harmed. I made a deci-sion to devote myself to helping others in need. Through meditation I sought God's help to practice these principles at all times and to set a direction for my life. Was it easy? Yes, it was—particularly considering the pain and torture I had always felt inside myself. Now I can look at the real me without hiding. Now I know that with God's power, I will always be OK.

Good things happened almost automatically when I changed my attitude and motives through the Twelve Step Program: I lost 170 pounds without even dieting and began having more good days than ever before. In fact, each day is a good day now, because I'm aware of all the things I receive through God's power. Even when my life is difficult, I don't panic. I feel peaceful and still, and I have learned to reach inside myself for God's power and strength, and for the courage to do what is necessary to do.

I have come to believe that my life is a gift. I have a new husband and two children, and we communicate with each other honestly and lovingly. Each day I pray and meditate, and then I exercise for two hours. (I still marvel at the fact that I'm exercising so much; there was a time when I could barely *walk.*) Now I find love in God's many works of art—in my environment and also in the eyes of the people I meet. I have also learned that nothing in life is permanent. What counts is *whether* I live each day and *how* I live each day. I have a choice—life or death. Today I choose to live because I know I'm not alone. I have my family, my friends, OA, and a relationship with God.

Patty's Story

What we are trying to learn is love: the first three Steps teach us to love God, the next six Steps teach us to love ourselves, and the last three Steps teach us to love other people.

From my earliest memories, I was shy and preferred to be alone. By the age of ten, I was an overweight child who was *devastated* by the teasing of other children. I withdrew more and more to being alone, reading, and playing the violin. I suppose that even then, I was showing signs of being overly sensitive, willful, and generally at odds with the world.

By the time I reached my early teens, I was associating with an older crowd and drinking. I drank the first bottle of liquor I ever had with the intention of getting drunk, which of course I did. From that time on, I drank whenever I went out with my friends. And every time I drank, I caused problems. I usually knew that I was making a fool of myself, but I figured I had a good excuse: *I was drunk and therefore I wasn't responsible!* I drank not to be sociable, but to get drunk so that I could avoid the pain of reality. At the age of fifteen, I was raped by an older man who then used intimidation to establish a relationship with me. I was afraid of him, but even more afraid of having my parents find out about the rape and our relationship. The result of all this was an unwanted pregnancy. My parents were so shocked and worried about what the family would think they finally decided that, during my pregnancy, I should stay with an aunt and uncle who lived in another town and were a little more accepting of my situation. But just a short time after I went to live with my aunt and uncle, they were transferred to a location near my parents' home. Consequently there were times I actually had to *hide* so that my relatives wouldn't *see* me while I was pregnant. I gave birth to twins, but they were quickly put up for adoption and I was never even allowed to *see* them. I returned home, but was then too far behind in my studies to graduate from high school with my classmates. I no longer had any friends to drink with, so I spent my time eating (a much more acceptable behavior than drinking, I reasoned). As time went on, though, I became less able to deal with reality and more confused, depressed, and unhappy.

During this period of depression, I began dating a man who drank heavily. A pattern soon developed in our relationship: we got drunk every time we went out and we didn't even go out unless we had enough money to get drunk. With this pattern established, I should have been able to see the serious problems that were ahead for us. Instead, I ignored the signs of trouble and we were married. I deluded myself into thinking that this marriage would make me happy. After we got married, my husband still enjoyed going out to drink, but I was too busy playing at being married to want to go along with him any longer. He would disappear for no apparent reason, and sometimes he'd end up in jail for drunkenness. He spent all of our money on liquor. At that point, I thought I would be happy if only *he* would straighten out or if only I had a baby to care for. I was so miserable and I really didn't want to drink with him anymore, so I returned to my compulsive overeating behavior again. I had a baby girl and enjoyed my role as mother for awhile. But I was still having difficulty coping with my husband's drinking and our financial problems. I began seeing a doctor for my nerves and finally came to the conclusion that I would be happy if I lost some weight. And so the pill routine began: diet pills—more each day—sleeping pills, and nerve pills. And then I let alcohol come back into my life. Each time I started drinking, I continued on until I was drunk; my life was unbearable. No matter how hard I tried and no matter what I did, happiness seemed to elude me. Despite my growing confusion, I managed to get a job. I assumed that if my husband and I had more money, we wouldn't have so many problems and I would finally get to feel good. But I found that the more money we had, the more my husband drank. My second pregnancy really upset me because I knew our marriage was in serious trouble and probably would not last. In my seventh month of pregnancy, I became ill and had to have an operation. My baby boy was born early and died two days later. Of course I was depressed and completely overwhelmed by everything that had happened.

At this point I decided to file for divorce. I had already lost weight, so I thought that a divorce would finally make me happy. But instead of getting happy,

I got drunk. And my drinking continued until my mental condition became so bad that I cut my wrists and was admitted to the psychiatric ward of a hospital. There I was—*twenty-five years old and wishing I could die*. When I was released from the hospital, I went back to work. Then I began to drink and hit the pills heavily again. At the same time, though, I had an active social life and soon met a man who was really good to me. He had two small children of his own, and I figured that with my daughter we could happily settle down to enjoy our newly-formed family. But we didn't get married for some time—we were too busy chasing around, taking pills, and drinking up our unemployment checks. Eventually we married, and for about three years, we got along really well. We actually tried to quit the crazy party scene on several different occasions, but we never succeeded for very long. Our marriage gradually began to deteriorate in the midst of all our partying. I was unfaithful to my husband and the guilt was affecting me. But the guilt didn't get to me as much as the anger I felt when I found out that my husband was being unfaithful to *me*. That was a blow to what little self-esteem I had. So I got another divorce and shortly after that I had another mental breakdown—or so they called it.

I regained all the weight I had lost, got a job in a supper club, and began gorging and drinking myself into oblivion on a nightly basis. After work each morning, at 2:00 A.M., I would go to the grocery store half-smashed and buy enough food to feed a whole family. After I consumed all that food, I'd start drinking again. Using beer for a chaser, I'd drink until I passed out.

Then I'd have a sandwich or a snack of some kind whenever I woke up during the night. This pattern of night eating and drinking went on for a few years and during that period, I tried to commit suicide several times. While in a skid-row bar one night, I met an older man who seemed to be rather dignified. I married him soon after we met and almost right away he began dominating me. My life was a mess again. I soon found out that my new husband was a chronic alcoholic and had some serious mental and behavioral problems that affected both me *and* my teenage daughter. When I became aware of the nature of my husband's problems, I really went off the deep end. It all culminated in an ugly scene with the police, and I was again sent off to the hospital psychiatric ward—this time, for allegedly abusing my husband. After several more months of serious problems, I finally got another divorce. Eventually I went back to work at the supper club and, almost right away, my old pattern of self-destructive behavior returned. *By now I was so depressed I truly did not want to live.*

I began seeing a psychologist. He encouraged me to continue my education, so I quit my job at the supper club and enrolled in a business school. I studied hard and was doing very well—for a while. One of the teachers there became a good friend; she encouraged me and helped me so much by just *believing* in me. Gradually my life began to look better to me and, in retrospect, I think of this period as the "turning point" in my life. I would stop drinking for awhile and then begin once again for no apparent reason. My new friend took me to an AA meeting, but I didn't think I

317

needed *that* kind of help. A member of AA spoke at the school I attended and I was intrigued by his story. After that, people began teasing me and saying I was an alcoholic, but I thought it was a joke. *There was nothing wrong with me, I thought. I was just unhappy.*

I finally received my high school diploma and graduated from a secretarial course with a high grade-point average. My father was so proud of me. I got a job as a bookkeeper and was soon involved with another man. Then the behavior pattern I had started as a teenager returned: I never drank to be sociable, only to get drunk. I began drinking continuously again and lost my job. Life was once more unbearable: I weighed over 300 pounds; the only friends I had were on skid row; I was on welfare; and my mother had to take over the care of my daughter. If there was a God, I thought, He surely didn't like me. I had never believed in God or religion as I knew it. For years my mother had encouraged me to pray, but I thought it was a stupid waste of time because it seemed too much like talking to myself. At that point I did the only thing I felt I *could* do, and that was to go back to skid row for a job as a bartender. That was the perfect place for me, I thought. It would bolster my shattered ego because I would feel like a "big shot" there—better than anyone else. I was as low as I could get and I managed to stay drunk most of the time. One day an attractive man dressed like a hippie walked into the bar and attempted to impress me. This man lived on skid row and was carrying a gun in his boot. His story was interesting and not altogether unlike my own: he had left a family and financial security in an effort to escape reality. In time, he moved in with me and together we began our constant drinking. It seems now that all we did was fight. We were so mean to each other that I sometimes wonder how we stayed together.

One day when this man and I had been together for about a year, he met a man he had once known on skid row who subsequently became a member of AA. This former acquaintance of his was doing *so* well in AA that my friend decided to follow his lead and check it out. He went to an AA meeting, came home, and told me there would be no more drinking. How I quit, I'll never know. I was still bartending on skid row at that time and it was hard for me not to drink in a situation like that. I had been drinking for more than twenty years and had not yet been successful in my attempts to quit. But my friend went to a few AA meetings and then he took me to one. I quit my job, and together we traded drinking for new friends, new interests, and new surroundings.

After a few months of mutual sobriety, we were married. I still wouldn't admit I was an alcoholic because I didn't want people to know there was anything "wrong" with me. I went to Al-anon and tried to pretend I belonged *there* instead. (I was still embarrassed to admit publicly that I was an alcoholic and a year passed before I could openly and freely admit my problem.) I also attended AA meetings whenever I could. I heard Chapter Five of the Big Book read at every meeting, and its message finally penetrated my thick skull. By now, I was free of the obsession to drink and although the physical craving was not completely gone, I was finding it somewhat easier not to drink.

When I finally decided to use the AA Program to lose weight, I lost over 150 pounds. I worked hard to transform my life: I read every self-help book I could get my hands on and even had three major plastic surgery operations to "perfect" my new body. I had convinced myself that I was doing all this to be happier and to make my husband proud of me. Now I know that I was really trying to find my own spirituality and self-esteem. But even *without* the drinking and excess weight, I still felt that everything about me was bad. The growing unhappiness within me was very real and *very painful.*

After a few more years of dieting and trying to make myself better, I was more desperate than ever. I had heard about OA, so some of my AA friends and I started an OA group of our own. Of course we thought we were doing the right things—we *did* lose some weight, but we weren't getting much of a spiritual program. And we were all going nuts trying to stay with our food plans. I knew something was terribly wrong with me, but I wondered how changing my weight could possibly make me *more* than I already was. *I found that in order to change my life, I had to change my way of thinking and that went much deeper.* At AA meetings there was a special look of serenity in some people's eyes and I knew that *I didn't have that.* But instead of asking these people how they got to where they were, I was *jealous* of them. I knew I was missing something, but I didn't know what. When I first came to AA, I had done a Fourth Step and Fifth Step, but they hadn't worked for me. I had done these Steps with a woman I knew and respected, so I left out a lot of information about myself. (I feared that this woman would be shocked if I told her everything about me and my past.) No wonder I didn't get results!

Then one of my friends asked me to go to an OA retreat in Wyoming with her. The retreat leader was a man whose personal story was as bad as mine, yet he seemed to be doing very well. He talked about a Higher Power and how he had at one time been an atheist. I made the decision to believe this man and for once in my life, *I really listened.* I knew that I was near the end of my rope. I *had* to stop lying to myself and do the Steps *as if my life depended on it* because, literally, it did! I went home from the retreat that weekend a different person and immediately started working the Steps. This was the beginning of my life as a recovered compulsive overeater and this was the beginning of my life as a sober, happy alcoholic. I carried the Big Book and *Twelve Steps and Twelve Traditions* around with me and memorized much of the information. I kept repeating the Third Step Prayer to let God know I really needed help! I begged God to help me be happy, but nothing much happened. I was so busy trying to *make* God change me that *He didn't even have a chance.* I began to understand that *a person can get so busy trying to work the Program and so impatient for results that nothing happens.* Results come when we just relax, work the Steps, and enjoy what we are now.

I finally came to that understanding six years ago. I can now see that the positive changes in me were there all along, but I was so busy looking for them I couldn't even see them. Now I have a fulfilling and demanding job, a good family life, and close friendships. Now I really *know* a Higher Power that I had never even *dreamed of* before. I wish I could express how *deeply* I feel this knowledge in my heart and in my mind. No longer do I have to beg God because I know I will get what I need in His time. I feel I am being spiritually *led* through life; I don't feel I am aimlessly drifting. I have a purpose—to be the best me I can be.

The change in me has been dramatic. Recently I attended another OA retreat in Wyoming with some of the same people who were at that first retreat I attended six years ago. This time I felt so *free*—like a totally different person. I felt so much love in me that I had never felt before. I know that I have learned about this love by working the Steps. Another important thing I have learned is that my drinking and my weight ceased to be problems for me when I became willing to seek God and to believe in a power greater than myself. Today I have completely lost the desire to eat and drink compulsively and I no longer weigh 300 pounds. I'm not thin by any means, but that really doesn't bother me. I was thin once and I was crazy even then. Now I'm learning and growing and loving and living every day. I know the meaning of serenity, and I have an inner peace that I was unable to find when I was so busy dieting and following rules.

I truly believe OA is a spiritual Program that can completely change lives. What we are trying to learn is love: the first three Steps teach us to love God, the next six Steps teach us to love ourselves, and the last three Steps teach us to love other people. The thing I am most grateful for is that someone in the Program cared for me enough to accept me unconditionally, be my friend, and make me listen. My husband and I have a relationship that gets deeper as time goes by and far exceeds everything I had ever hoped for. We have had thirteen years of sobriety together. God must have known how *much* each of us needed someone; our marriage is truly one of His gifts. Each of us is first an individual and next a member of a partnership that works in spite of the problems.

Not long ago my husband almost died after having four heart attacks. I thought it was practically the end of the world, but the experience turned into one of growth for us instead. Both of us have learned to calm down, and our inner peace and serenity have given us a greater respect for life and how to live it *today*. Recently I began having seizures. Of course, both of us were frightened by this at first, but now I know it's going to be another lesson for us. The Program has given me a whole new perspective and I finally realize that He is in charge. I know that with His power, I will have the courage to accept whatever might happen in my life. The most wonderful part of my life today? My granddaughters. The total, unconditional love I feel for them is a bonus in my life that I never really expected. It truly amazes me when I think about what I surely would have missed had I not found the Program. And the greatest miracle of all is that I have finally found *happiness*.

Jerry's Story

*I have come to believe that this Program
really begins at home.*

Late in the summer of 1977, my wife told me about a
man who had joined OA and lost a significant amount
of weight; she thought it might be a good idea if I had
a talk with him. I finally met this man a few weeks later
at a cocktail party and, as we chatted, I proceeded to
eat all of the snacks on the table. He told me about
OA that night and suggested that I come to the next
meeting of his OA group a few days later.

Since that September evening in 1977 when I attended my first OA meeting, I have stopped eating
compulsively and *major* changes in my life have taken
place. One of the most significant changes in my life
was reflected by the following incident: when I had
been in the Program for about two weeks, I called my
sponsor one day and told him that I was going to a
party that evening and already knew that the hosts
would be serving lasagna. I told him that since lasagna
was not allowed on my food plan, I was going to eat
dinner *before* I went to the party so that I wouldn't be
tempted to eat it. My OA sponsor said, "What I think
you should do is go to the party and eat small portions
of the food that is served. No one there has to know
that you're on a diet. All you have to do is act like a
normal person." So that is *exactly* what I did at the

party that evening. And it was then I first realized that like many of my friends I, too, can be a normal person when it comes to eating and food.

When I joined OA, I weighed approximately 255 pounds and my goal weight was 225 pounds. After I reached *that* goal, I said to myself, Why not lose a little more? I began to realize that I didn't really know what my optimum weight *was*. After six months in the Program, I had lost 90 pounds—I weighed 165 pounds then and I have maintained that weight for the last six years.

As a child, I was one of the tallest, heaviest boys in my age group. I had learned at home that I should always clean my plate and never, ever waste food because of all the starving people in the world. (I sometimes think I was eating on behalf of *all* those starving people.) Even when I was in elementary school, I had to wear clothing designed for "husky" children. Because of fears I had, I wasn't very good at team sports and I was *never* what one would call "athletic." In fact, when it came to sports, I had very low self-esteem. So, instead of participating in sports activities after school, I would go home and eat instead. I didn't have much success with my first diet, so my mother sent me to a doctor who examined me and prescribed medication. I took the medicine, lost some weight, and became a rather hyperactive person. But when I stopped taking the pills the doctor had prescribed for me, I gained all the weight I had lost, and more! Whenever I tried to lose weight, it was *for* someone or something. There was *pizza* at the end of my rainbow. I started thinking of food as my best friend. It seemed to be the perfect relationship because food couldn't talk back to me. After all, eating was a socially acceptable thing to do, no matter *where* I was. I began to think that I could solve *all* of my problems by eating; food seemed to be the perfect antidote for every feeling I had—happiness, fear, sadness, failure, rejection, and acceptance.

Because I was tall, I could carry much more weight than my friends and yet never really *look* obese. By the time I reached high school, I was a very poor student. Eating seemed to be the *only thing* I was interested in doing. I did not date very much as a teenager. In fact, the only steady date I had then was with the local pizza parlor. In high school I was still one of the tallest, heaviest boys in my age group, but I did not participate in sports. When my friends pressured me to participate, I would react by eating compulsively. I remember always being the first one to arrive at the pizza parlor after school football games. In fact, many times I had already ordered and *finished* eating a whole pizza long before the team *even arrived* at the pizza parlor. I *did* date once or twice each year in high school, but that was about it.

My body size became a way to make sure that other people wouldn't get close to me. Mine was a classic case of being jolly on the outside, scared and crying for help on the inside. After high school, I went to a university in the Midwest. When I got to college, I began to drink beer and became a very serious eater. My body began to show it. I felt then that I was *destined* to be heavy for the rest of my life. I was not very outgoing during my freshman year in college and didn't date much at all. I flunked out of college

327

after only one year.

I tried various diets throughout my school years but failed with each attempt. For some reason, I could never stay on a diet. After I left college, I entered the army, hoping I would come out as a *man*. Following the rigorous exercise of boot camp, I was down to a relatively "svelte" 201 pounds. That was the least I had weighed since my first year in high school. Then I was sent overseas on a military assignment and, for the next two and a half years, I *ate* my way through Europe and consequently gained back all of the weight I had lost during boot camp. After completing military service, my only real goal was to go back to school, so I enrolled in another college on probationary status. At that time, college students were experimenting with drugs. But I didn't have the time to experiment with drugs, *I was too busy eating!*

During my sophomore year in college, I met a wonderful woman and we got married in my senior year. I continued to eat compulsively and got bigger and bigger. I finally *did* graduate from college and we moved to Detroit for a job in a family business. It was then I began to feel family pressure. I was told that working in the family business was my best opportunity, but I was *miserable* with the arrangement. Despite my unhappiness, I was afraid to leave the family business because I wasn't sure I could be successful without the help of the family. During this time of frustration and conflict, my weight was steadily increasing. I would lose pounds, then gain pounds. In desperation, I tried a few of the commerical weight-loss programs but they didn't work for me—I didn't like even *half* the food items these programs recommended.

When I finally came to OA, I was at rock-bottom. I was a "mess" physically, emotionally, and spiritually. I was told at the first OA meeting I attended that I would lose weight if I ate only three meals a day. After six months, I reached my goal weight, but my head said that I was still fat. I simply could not believe that I was now living in a thin body. Some people said I must be sick and suggested that I try to regain some of the weight I had lost. People who had not known me when I was fat thought I was just normal. *Losing weight was not the recovery I really thought I wanted.* I finally learned that the *Steps* of the Program—not a diet— would help me recover. When I finally admitted to myself that I *was* a compulsive overeater, I began to find out what that was really all about. I learned that I had to do more than just mouth the words of the Program, *I had to believe it 100 percent.* I had to learn the meaning of total commitment to recovery and I had to learn how to maintain that recovery once I achieved it.

Step Two and Step Three were probably the most difficult Steps for me. I simply could not accept the idea that God was going to take care of me, nor could I even accept the concept of His existence. I was an "agnostic" which, in my case, meant that I was unfamiliar with the concept of God. It wasn't that I *denied* God, I just didn't know anything about Him. The first thing I had to do was to find a sponsor who was working the Program. It wasn't easy. Actually, I didn't even know the meaning of "working the Program" until I gained some new insights. Then I began to realize that "working the Program" means that a person is living the promises of the Big Book. It took me a while to find such a person, but I *did* and that relationship helped me to really start recovering. Initially, I worked the first few steps because I was desperate. I was told that I must learn the Steps just the way people do in the AA Program. Food was only the *vehicle* of my real problem. I had to find out the reasons why I wanted to destroy my body and shorten my life.

The Third Step was a growing experience for me. The realization did not happen overnight but gradually, over a long period of time. I began to realize that recovery did not mean losing control but recognizing that the power of my spirituality controls my destiny. I had to really understand that *I have to do the action but the power comes from God.* I had to turn my will and my life over to God before I destroyed my God-given life. I found out that I must do His work and keep my mind and body in the best possible physical and mental condition. I learned to believe in a God. I read somewhere that when I had completed the first three Steps to the best of my ability, then the Fourth Step would come easily and I would not be afraid of what I might find out about my past. I had to accept the fact that the fears I continued to hold onto originated in my *past*, not in my *present*. I had to accept the fact that who I was and the decisions I made many years before were based on what I thought was best for me *at that time.*

Step Five was also relatively easy for me because I trusted the people I was talking with in OA. Sharing my inventory with others was not a difficult thing for me to do. Step Six and Step Seven were probably the most difficult Steps for me because I was not aware of having any character defects *at all*; I thought I was *perfect*. After I wrote my inventory, I realized just how many shortcomings I had and continued to have. Then I had to prepare myself to live my life *without* those character defects. I had to learn the appropriate action for me to take in order to live each day as a mature human being.

Step Eight and Step Nine were *very* difficult for me, but I knew that I had to work through them if I really wanted recovery. When I started making amends, I began to see that my perception of the world was quite different from other people's. I was *floored* when I realized that I was allowing my past to destroy me when most of my fears were just a product of my imagination. The Big Book says that after you take the Ninth Step, the promises of the Program will begin to come true and the design for living will come to you. In other words, eating and food will be put in their proper perspective. I have to say that this is exactly what happened for me.

Steps Ten, Eleven, and Twelve supply my guidance for daily living. I try to live by these steps one day at a time and to the best of my ability. I am far from being perfect, yet my goal is to *strive* for perfection. I have a long way to go, but if I pray for the strength, courage, and the power of God within me *and* if I do God's will, then the results of my life will be happy, joyous, and free.

I am slowly learning how to be a man. Having been in the Program for over six years now, I sometimes feel like a six-year-old child. I know I have a long way to go. I guess that is why I keep going back to meetings every week. I don't have to make a conscious effort to attend OA meetings anymore for they have become an ongoing part of my life. I want to keep on doing the work and sharing myself with others. The more I share myself, the more sane I will be. *I have come to believe that this Program really begins at home.* If I cannot live the life of a recovered person with my family and friends and with my colleagues at work, *then I have learned nothing.* I must treat others as family and I must treat family with the care and understanding and patience I have learned to extend to others. The real lessons of recovery are not limited to meetings; they intertwine with every aspect of my life. I have learned that sanity is not selective and, therefore, I cannot just work on eating or work habits, or any other aspect of my life without working on *all* aspects of my life. In order to maintain recovery—living within the Tenth, Eleventh, and Twelfth Steps—I must work the Twelve Steps at all times, in all places, and with all the people who come into my life.

Donna's Story

*The hardest thing to do is to grow up and
face life.*

Sometime around the age of five or six, I decided to
check out of my world. The fantasy world I created
was exciting and safe: people didn't make me cry and
they didn't hurt or reject me. Being alone became a
goal, my idea of happiness. When I walked into my
first OA meeting, I was in tremendous pain because of
my weight, *or so I thought.* I had no job, and I could
not manage school. By the time I was twenty-one, I
was still living at home and had no friends. At that
point in my life, I had only been on about four or five
dates. I'd never had a relationship with a member of
the opposite sex and had never even been kissed by
a man. If someone had asked me then what my interests or hobbies were, I would have been unable to
think of a single *thing.* All of my energies went into my
fantasy world. Reality, the things I *had* done and
achieved, seemed less real than my fantasies. I felt that
there was no validity whatsoever to the things that
were real in my life. I really hated myself and anything
associated with me. I believed that my self-hatred was
the result of my fatness, and that if I could just be thin,
my life would be fine. Fat was not just fat; being fat
meant to me that I was stupid, ugly, and unpopular
with people my own age. I believed that the only

reason I did not do anything productive with my life was because of my obesity. I was convinced that every unhappiness and inadequacy I felt was due to my fatness and that all the unpleasantness in my life would magically disappear forever *if I could just lose weight.*

I *tried* to lose weight; I went on my first diet at the age of six. I subsequently tried dozens of weight-loss plans: grapefruit regimens, diabetic diets, diets developed by famous doctors, my own starvation diet (one frozen dinner and diet sodas each day), and special diets prescribed by my own doctor. My last "diet" attempt prior to getting out of this insanity involved special injections and a 500-calorie-per-day diet. Some of these schemes worked for a time; some did not. But one thing remained consistent in all my efforts: I ultimately gained back every pound I lost, *along with extra pounds.* In effect, I "dieted" my way up to 224 pounds.

I felt then that nothing I did was *ever* good enough. When I was a student, I won several awards for art, poetry, speaking, and school work. Later I taught disadvantaged children, and several times I was asked to lead one committee or another at the church I attended. But I always discounted the awards and opportunities that came to me and, instead, retreated to my fantasy world. I just shut down and decided to live my own kind of life—in my head. In my fantasy kingdom, my father was always home; my mother did not yell at me and verbally insult me; and my brother did not beat me up and call me "fatso" every day. This make-believe world was wonderful, and it still holds a certain appeal for me. In my fantasies, I always had *perfect control.* I could decide exactly what I wanted people to say to me. I could change anything at the very moment I decided to: I could be a different person, or have a different boyfriend, or live in a different place, or have a different job. Everything was so easy—*I just changed my mind and changed my fantasy.*

In fact, as I look back on it, any popularity I had in high school came from my ability to sustain the attention of other people with the fabrications I conjured up. I would spend my lunch hour telling stories, then go home after school, eat, lock myself in my room, and sing along with Elvis Presley. I related best to objects and also to people who had absolutely no involvement in my *real* life. I had little interest in creating relationships with my family or with the kids at school. I was terrified of men to the point that I refused to go anywhere, other than church, for fear of meeting them.

When I reached puberty, I turned my normal sexual feelings into an obsession with a particular religion that told me it was *good* that I was not dating. The dogma consumed me, and I threw myself into learning more about it. I felt if only I could know and understand God perfectly, I would be fine. I began to use my fantasies and my religion to keep me from living in the real world.

As often as I said that I wanted to lose weight and break the hellish cycle of food consumption, guilt, and bad feelings I was into, I was never able to do it. *I was the ultimate victim.* I felt there was nothing wrong with me except for the fact that I ate too much. But I also hated everybody and everything. I went away to the college of my dreams and was actually quite happy there for the first three months. Then I began to hate the place. Towards the end of my stay there, I could only manage five units of school, and it was a good day for me if I managed to even drag myself out of the house. I was consuming thousands of calories each day. I outgrew every outfit I had and my roommate made long, flowing caftans for me to wear because I was unable to find clothing in department stores that fit me. I fought with everyone. I spent most of the day in bed fantasizing, and the rest of my time feeling guilty about my fantasies. Often I stayed in bed until everyone else left the house, then I'd sneak out of my room, turn the stereo on, and eat.

When my parents moved out of state, I decided that moving *with* them would be the answer for me: I would leave my school, start school in a new location, get a job, and meet people who were exciting and understood me. But I hated reality in the new location, too. The reasons were different, but my feelings were the same as always. And almost as soon as I got to the new location, I spent most of my time trying to figure out how to return to the place I had just left—the same place I had blamed for my misery in the first place!

Shortly after moving back to where I formerly had lived, I went to an OA meeting. At first, I dieted. I called it "abstaining," but it was nothing more or less than dieting. I was very rigid and felt my program completely revolved around what I ate, or better yet, *what I did not eat.* I was afraid that if I broke my abstinence, all would be lost because I had this hideous disease that was beyond my control. So I tried very hard to do

everything OA said and I tried to do it perfectly. I learned the language; I knew what to say; I read the books
that were recommended to me. I salute those early
days in OA; they were exciting. For the first time in my
life, I felt loved and understood.

My first sponsor, God love her, kept me in OA all
by herself. She showered me with unconditional love
and never judged me. I felt safe in that I could tell her
anything. She was the first human being I had ever
really trusted. My first year in the Program, I *lived* for
the meetings and sometimes attended two in one day.
It was a way for me to feel as if I were being close to
people without *really* having to be close to them. Eventually I found that I could participate within the struc-
ture of the OA meeting. But I continued to have a
difficult time really letting people into my life. Just
being with someone and having a good time was
foreign to me and also very frightening. Aside from my
sponsor and one friend, I still chose to stay pretty much
to myself outside of meetings. I had people call me in
my sponsorship capacity, yet those relationships were
all rather formal. I felt comfortable sharing as long as I
could talk about program aphorisms and food. This all
worked well for quite awhile.

The sharing I managed to do during that time allowed me to take my first baby steps toward integrating
with the real world. I got a job, went back to school,
and got a car. I started doing things I had always
wanted to do but always thought I was too fat for:
voice lessons, theater classes, even ballet. I was terrified, *but I did it anyway.* I wrote an inventory, started
making amends, and found a faith that was more

comfortable than the religious dogma I had used to protect myself from reality.

Then, my brother died of cancer. It was a painful experience that brought up unresolved family issues. Again, I focused on food. I felt I wasn't abstaining in the "right way," so I started calling in my food again, and began to work out at a gym. I saw a doctor who put me on a carrot juice fast and a health regimen. *I gained more than 30 pounds.* I felt miserable, and was consumed with bitterness, sadness, and fear. I had thought OA was different, unlike all the other diet clubs, and that I would never have to "go out there again." At this same time the sponsor I had depended on so much was gradually leaving OA herself.

As a final, last-ditch effort, I went with my sponsor to an OA marathon in our area. I went there feeling resistant and defeated. I no longer had any hope. I was only half-listening to a speaker at the marathon when he said that recovery had nothing to do with food and weight. I listened more intently when he said: "Why are you trying to control your food when the First Step says that you are *powerless* over your food compulsion? Only God can remove the obsession and that happens when we work the Twelve Step Program." His words were a revelation to me. From that point on, I stopped using food as an *excuse.* I stopped dieting or restricting my food in any way. I refused to allow food to be the reason for feeling either good or bad. Food became just food. This new way of thinking was scary for me at first, because it seemed to conflict with the concepts of OA as I had learned them. But I knew that the old way had not worked in my life for any significant period of time.

With this change in my thinking and attitude, I lost my food obsession and, in turn, food lost its power to dictate what was wrong with me and why I was or wasn't doing something in my life. I made a commitment that with God's help, I would face life and be willing to start *experiencing* life as it really was, not as I fantasized it. Obviously, life cannot always be as exciting as my fantasies, yet in many ways life is *much more rewarding and fulfilling* than any fantasy I could ever dream up. I get a deep, warm feeling when I share and listen to others and I have learned to cherish my friendships.

The hardest thing to do is to grow up and face life. I don't always like the things that happen in my life, but now my life is *real*. What I didn't realize was that in my desire to shield myself from pain, rejection, and disappointment, I had also denied myself feelings of love, caring, and joy. I have learned that *all* feelings are valid. Allowing myself and others to be human has freed me from my own prison. I don't have to eat and live in a "dream world" in order to survive today. By consistently working the Twelve Steps, I have been able to create healthier survival mechanisms for myself. I ask God to help me accept reality and I know that I can have peace of mind no matter what is going on in my life. I don't do this perfectly, but I know what to do in any given situation. I call it "practicing life." I'm not doing this to get an award; I'm doing this so that I can live with peace of mind and so that I will never be tempted to return to destructive behaviors in order to cope with life.

I have found that meditation and daily writing are very helpful and therapeutic for me. I had always denied my feelings so strongly, thinking they were *wrong*. Now, my growing ability to write and tell the truth has dissipated my fear of feelings. Probably the most important change is that I am learning how to be with people and how to have fun. After all those years in self-imposed isolation, being with others does not come naturally to me, so I have to work at it. I have also developed a keen interest in both recreational walking and white water rafting. I like old movies and the beach. I even go dancing now and then to help me get rid of my old fears of rejection. I date now; I am no longer afraid of men. I'm still learning, and when I get upset with myself for not being further along in a certain area of growth, I just stop, remind myself where I was only a short time ago, and then I feel grateful again.

The Twelve Steps have helped me *transform* my old ideas, enabling me to live a sane and happy life. I now know that I am a *miracle*, not in the sense that I'm perfect, but in the sense that I have gained peace of mind. The Twelve Steps have taken away my obsession with food. They have given me the courage and trust to take risks. And all of these gains are by-products of practicing a way of life that is basically simple and requires honesty and faith. *I am Donna and today I like myself.*

I have come so far—light years, in fact—from the girl who walked into OA and thought *food* was her problem, but still I have compassion for the person I was because that was all I *knew* at the time. The gift

shown to me is the same gift I now share with others—
there are alternatives. I believe that with faith in God,
all things are possible. There is an inner power that
knows more perfectly what and how to do things than
I could ever know on my own. This inner power has
helped me through good and bad times in work,
school, and relationships. I believe that there is an infi-
nite "knowingness" that is part of each and every one
of us and it can transcend all our old ideas, fears, and
resentments. It is the perfect spirit of love and understanding that nurtures me and allows me to continue
to be and do and grow and face the realities of life.

Marlys's Story

The old excuses just don't work anymore.

From my earliest memories on, I had feelings of fear and powerlessness. I felt that somehow I just didn't fit into the world the way other people did. I felt insignificant and invisible—as if life were a game but I didn't know the rules. I believe that I was loved, but not in a way I could fully *understand*. In my family, children represented a source of pride and entertainment; expressions of innermost feelings were met with disapproval or denial. I soon learned to protect my inner self from pain by building a wall that blocked out feelings. In time, I even lost sight of the fact that I had built that wall, yet the most vital and essential part of me was behind it. In order to survive within my family unit, I did what my parents expected me to do. But I developed an emptiness inside myself that *longed* to be filled. Food—the main source of entertainment, comfort, and pleasure in my family—neatly served that purpose. By the time I was five years old, I was obese and other children ridiculed me. Being fat, feeling insignificant, and hurting became part of my reality. I went on my first diet when I was seven years old—the first of countless attempts to ease my pain and make everything right.

As a teenager, I grew tall and became thin, but that didn't alter the reality I had created: that I felt bad because I was fat. Regardless of how thin I was, I could always find a fat spot on my body and convince myself that this fat was the reason I felt bad, alone, and invisible. To compensate for my lack of self-worth, I concentrated on being a "good girl" even more than I had in the past. I worked very hard in school. But even the academic achievement that brought me approval wasn't enough to fill the emptiness I felt inside. The idea of leaving the relative security of home and going to college *terrified* me. Again, I attributed my bad feelings to my weight, so I dieted and became extremely thin. But I discovered that thinness didn't make me happy, and I became so depressed I was unable to function at all. Psychiatric help and medication eventually restored me to what I considered "normal," but the relief I felt was only temporary. At this time in my life, I had no excess body fat to justify my bad feelings. My fear of independence was *incredible*; the thought that I was actually responsible for my own feelings and my own life was *terrifying. What if I made a mistake?*

The only safety seemed to be in finding someone who would take responsibility for my life—someone who would make me happy and take responsibility for my mistakes. Marriage seemed to be the answer to my problems and my fears. I assumed that all I'd have to do would be to stay at home and have children. The added benefit was that I'd be safe from responsibility, safe from making mistakes, and insulated from pain. *But my marriage didn't work that way.* The withdrawal from life that I chose out of fear kept me from developing the inner resources I needed to really *live*. In other words, the price I had to pay for safety was too high.

Marlys's Story

I became angry, resentful, more afraid, and more compulsive. Again, I tried to fill my inner emptiness with food and I tried to "stuff" the fear and feelings of powerlessness I had. At first it worked; a cookie could fix *anything*, at least temporarily. But soon there weren't enough cookies in the world to make me feel better. I gained weight and again used fat to justify my bad feelings and my withdrawal from life. (After all, what could be expected of a fat person?) And so the cycle began: The worse I felt, the more I ate. The more weight I gained, the worse I felt. I became a victim of this cycle, *a victim of the circumstances of my life*.

I spent *years* gaining and losing, always confident that if only I were thin, I'd be happy. But when I *did* lose weight, nothing in my life changed, so I always regained the weight I had lost *and more*. During this time, I discovered diet drugs. They worked, but not for permanent weight loss. Instead, diet drugs gave me *temporary* feelings of power and freedom. I thought they would allow me to be happy at last. But the novelty of the drugs soon wore off, guilt for using them set in, and I became addicted. The drugs and food actually began to *control* me and I spent the next fifteen years taking drugs and overeating. All those years, I wondered how *anyone* could live without either one. *I knew that I certainly couldn't.* I lived in a constant state of fear, guilt, self-hatred, and anger. These feelings manifested themselves in all areas of my life and my family suffered right along with me. After all, I was *certain* that my unhappiness was partly the fault of my family situation. I assumed I would be thin and, therefore, happy if only things were different: if I didn't have small children, or if they were different, or if we had more money. *Of course, I could never get my family to change enough to make me happy.*

When I came to OA, I was still clinging to the belief that fat was my problem, food was my enemy, and those around me were in some way responsible for my unhappiness. The anger and resentment I felt at that time were surpassed only by my fear of living. No longer could food, drugs, or emotions conquer my fear or fill the terrible emptiness I felt. *The victim role that had shielded me from life was now destroying me.*

But the fellowship of OA was *wonderful*. At last I found other people who felt the way I did. I got a food plan, reluctantly stopped using drugs, lost weight, and became absolutely convinced that thin was well. But then when I started to gain back some of the weight I'd lost, I bought a Big Book and started reading it regularly. My obsession with food and eating was still there and even though I talked about my abstinence when I shared with others, I lived in fear that I'd wake up one morning without the will power I needed for abstinence. So I covered all the bases: I read, went to meetings, became a sponsor in OA, made phone calls, and then just crossed my fingers and hoped that I'd be able to resist the desire to eat compulsively. I was working the Twelve Steps, so my life was getting better in many areas. Whenever I relapsed—with compulsive eating or old ways of thinking—I berated myself. But I have learned that compliance through fear is not much better than compulsive behavior. I was not at peace in those days, even though I was abstaining from compulsive overeating. *I was still a victim.* I believed that what I needed to be happy was somewhere "out there" and that if I just tried hard enough, I'd find someone or something to save me. How could I possibly recover if I hadn't yet found that special someone or something? I was still blaming other things and other people for my problems, but that was becoming more difficult and uncomfortable to do. *Being a victim wasn't working anymore.*

Through my efforts to be safe and to hide from life, I had refused to acknowledge the power of God within me. For years I had denied the concept of God, at least as it related to *my* life. The God of my childhood religion had brought me no help, so I was very resistant to the idea that there was a God. I felt it would be easier not to believe *at all* than to risk feeling betrayed again. After all, I had prayed as a child and what had it brought me? I was still alone and afraid. I was able to talk about God in OA, but only in abstract terms. The God I could talk about had little to do with my inner power.

I was at an OA retreat when I finally came to understand that God isn't "out there," inaccessible to me. I finally discovered that I have, within me, the power of God that is my birthright. At that point I finally realized that I had *chosen* to be a victim and, in doing so, I had denied God's power within me. Now I know that acknowledging His power gives me the freedom to choose everything: life, love, joy, and even pain. No longer do I have to wander around, looking for "magic" to make me well. I already have the power I need within me. Making choices to live, to love, to be responsible for my decisions, to be in control of my reactions to life—that is my expression of God within me. *Becoming a victim is to deny God.*

I have undergone a complete change in my ideas, attitudes, and emotions. The world hasn't changed, but my perception of the world has changed *dramatically.* By virtue of God's power within me, I can now choose life. Because I have the power to choose, I am now free of compulsions and free of a crippling inability to deal with anger, resentment, fear, ego, and self-pity. I still have negative feelings now and then, but I am no longer a *victim* of those negative feelings. Now, instead of using negative feelings to prove how *terrible* I am, I use them as opportunities to grow and learn.

Life is not perfect, but now I can choose how I respond to pain and to a world that isn't fair. I have power to choose the relatively brief pain of change rather than the lifelong pain of denying myself and God. My self-worth no longer disintegrates if I eat too much or gain weight. If I do either, I just acknowledge the fact, change my behavior, then go on. I am no longer a *victim* of my compulsion. The awareness of my growth and change and the awareness of God's power bring me a joy in living that no drug or food has ever been able to give me. I am alive in a way that I had never even dreamed about. I am free to love, choose, risk, and be myself. That freedom can be painful and unsettling, but it's worth every uncomfortable moment. The relationships I have with my family are becoming *growing* relationships. It is not an overnight process. Family life and relationships will always be a challenge, but these challenges can be opportunities for each one of us to grow. When I gave up the control

I wanted to have over my family, I was able to see each individual as a human being who is worthy of love.

After twenty years I have now returned to college. Doing this involved confronting fears and risks, but I decided I was unwilling to continue living as a victim—no longer would I tell myself that I couldn't return to school because of money, time, challenge, or the needs of my family. *The old excuses just don't work anymore.* Now if I want to do something that I think is good for me, *I do it.* I still try out my old excuses at times, but I eventually discard them. I have no idea what life has in store for me, but I'm no longer afraid. Whatever life brings, I know I am free to choose my response to it, free to be aware of God's power within me, and free to go on in spite of my disappointment or fear or pain. In my awareness of God's power within me, I have everything I need to survive and to be happy, joyous, and free.

Eva's Story

Food is not an issue anymore; living is.

I had a *living* disorder long before I was even *aware* of many of the substances I later abused. I lived in Germany as a child and I somehow felt different, special. I suffered from something that I later learned was called "terminal uniqueness." Attacks of grandiose daydreams compensated for my lack of self-worth and my feelings of not being wanted. One day, I'll show them all, I thought. Then they'll be sorry they didn't appreciate me.

I started drinking and using drugs at the age of twelve, and I think I was hooked on those substances immediately. Ten years later I walked into an Alcoholics Anonymous meeting as a "hopeless" alcoholic and drug addict, emotionally dead and spiritually non-existent. I had given up my university education and was living on the street. I had attempted suicide several times and had even spent some time locked up in mental institutions and prisons.

When I joined AA, I stopped drinking and using drugs immediately. But after a year in the Program, I began using drugs again. I saw a psychiatrist who offered me a softer, easier way and provided me with an "excuse" for my behavior and a label, a fancy and scientific-sounding name for my illness. Again, I became convinced of my uniqueness as a person. I don't blame the psychiatrist for the problems I had after that. *I* was the one who chose to use mind-altering drugs. I went back to hospitals, mental institutions, and feelings of complete despair. It was awful. But through it all, I stayed in AA because I knew it was the only place I would ever make it. *And I did.* After a dreadful withdrawal from drugs and alcohol, I broke the habit and have not taken a drink or a drug since that time. I got more involved in AA, got a sponsor, worked the Steps, had good relationships and good work experiences, and generally lived the most satisfactory years of my life.

This productive, positive lifestyle lasted for five years. During that time I fulfilled a dream and moved to a place I had always wanted to live. I went back and began my college education all over again. I successfully completed college coursework in a foreign country. But then, slowly and gradually, I started to go off the Twelve Step Program. My priorities were confused. My college professor became a Higher Power, and so did men, and so did all the people I wanted to be accepted by. It became important for me to do the "right" things, be with the "right" people, say the "right" thing, read the "right" newspaper, and so on. Once again, I became very dishonest with myself. I even denied myself the opportunity to experience love because I feared dependence. Instead, I put my energies into pretending that I was a completely self-sufficient intellectual. I continued to attend AA meetings once a week. It just so happened that I did not like my new AA group as much as my first AA group and complained that my early years of sobriety had been much more exciting and happy. I told people that I wanted to get back that joy of living I had known in the past. (Be careful what you pray for, because you might get it. The process of getting that joy back into my life took me through a lot of pain.) Now I see this slip into a painful eating disorder as a loving act of God that served to remind me of my *real priorities.* Because I had stopped working the Twelve Steps, my old personality came back in the form of a different symptom of the same disease. It happened in the summer of 1979. I woke up one day feeling that I was overweight and promptly decided to go on a diet. Despite my former dependencies, I had never been obsessed with food. Up to that time, I had always been naturally slim. I remember feeling anger towards women who seemed to have nothing to talk about other than calories and losing weight.

My new problem with food and eating lasted three years. During that time I went through alternating cycles of compulsive eating and compulsive dieting. I lost and then regained a considerable amount of weight *five times.* Then I completely lost my appetite. I'd go straight from a diet into compulsive starvation. I was obsessed with both my work and the man in my life, so it seemed there was no room left for food. It was sheer madness, and by then I knew it. I knew I was suicidal, so I even contemplated getting myself locked up for self-protection. *Nobody has to tell me that "thin is not necessarily well."* That phase of being unable to eat passed, and I went back to bingeing and fasting. Then I became bulimic; I alternately binged and threw up. I recognized that something was terribly wrong with me and my attitude toward food. Knowing that, I felt I *had* to do something. I cannot tell you what it felt like when after ten years of abstinence from alcohol, the toilet bowl again became my "higher power." I was literally kneeling in front of it and praying for it to help me, to relieve me from the pain that my last binge had caused. I *knew* I was insane, and that eating was only *one* aspect of my insanity. My entire life began to revolve around food, calories, and my weight.

Though I could not see the connection at the time, my problems with food were very much a part of my emotional illness, the anger and frustration I felt, and my need to control relationships. I'd reject someone simply to avoid being rejected by that person. I became compulsive in all areas of my life and stopped living in the here and now. I was always looking to the next hour, the next day, the next week, the next year. I was depressed, hopeless, and had completely lost the joy of living. Worst of all, I actually became *accustomed* to living in this state of anxiety and misery. Once again, I was dying from the inside out. For the first time in ten years, I fantasized about drugs and alcohol. I knew I had to do something.

I joined OA and hated it. All these thin women without *half* as glamorous a career as I'd had with alcohol and drugs dared to tell me that they were not particularly interested in the fact that I'd been abstinent from alcohol for ten years. I was determined to "show them all," so I restricted myself to three meals a day because I mistakenly thought that was what OA recovery was all about. I binged once in a fortnight. When I look back on it now, it really didn't make any difference whether I binged or not; I was miserable either way. I was obsessed with food all the time anyway, so I figured I might as well eat, because at least then I would have a *reason* to feel bad about myself. This is what the illness of compulsive overeating did for me: it kept me from living, from facing myself and the world. It enabled me to live my life in my head, to project that life would really begin when I was thin again in four or six or eight weeks time. It helped me to feel like a failure *all the time*.

Six months after I joined OA, I moved to London England. The move ultimately turned out to be a lifesaving one, but I walked into my first meeting there terrified of bingeing to death in this foreign country. I went to the OA meeting in London very humble and willing to listen. When I saw the people in this group, memories came flooding back of what life *could* be like and what the fellowship *could* be like for me. There was an atmosphere of acceptance and love in the room. Several overweight people shared their gratitude for the fact that, since they found the Program, they no longer had to eat compulsively. Thin people shared how they applied the Twelve Steps to their problems and they laughed about the hang-ups they still had. The hope expressed by all of these people was *contagious*. I kept going back to the meetings because I needed to have the people there tell me that if I kept working the Program, the Program would work for me. I got involved in OA-London and became compulsive about attending meetings. I got a sponsor and considered myself a complete newcomer to the Twelve Step Program. I stopped eating and was even *afraid* of food for a time. Then I committed myself to a food plan that involved two months of phoning in and writing. I gave up that plan after only three days. Then I binged again. I believe I did it because I was dishonest and because I was hurt but too proud to admit it. There was nothing else to turn to after bingeing, so I blacked out emotionally and put myself to sleep at two in the morning. It was a dreadful experience, but I think it was a necessary one for me at the time. I needed to come to an understanding that no food plan and no food sponsor could have prevented that binge. Since that time, I have never again tried to "get control" over my food.

But the novelties of not overeating, living in London, and attending OA and AA meetings wore off after a few months. I felt disappointed and wondered if this was all there was to life. On my way to an OA meeting one evening, I sat in the Underground and thought to myself, "Why am I going to this meeting? Why do I choose to be with these people? Why do I put all this effort into the fellowship?" Suddenly, it occurred to me that I might as well *Do It*—I might as well do the Twelve Steps without any reservations. *I JUST DID IT.* I was so sick and tired of my own rationalizations, procrastinations, and avoidance. At that point, I had nothing to lose. I started doing what the people who had what I wanted had done—I *acted as if.* I took the first three Steps. I wrote an inventory without having any expectations and set myself a deadline to share it with my sponsor. When the deadline came, the inventory was finished and I did a Fifth Step with my sponsor. I took Step Six and Step Seven formally. Then I made a list of all the people I had harmed, and I made my amends. This whole process took a few months, but I just kept right on working the Program.

Since then, I have experienced dramatic changes in myself and in my life. In fact, I feel as though I have nothing to do with the person I was when I first came to OA. I do not have to *act as if* anymore. God has become a reality in my life. God is there when I choose to turn to Him. Unlike human beings, God is perfect. To me, He is infallible. And, whether or not I understand it, God loves me. Looking back, I can see that everything that has happened in my life now makes sense. I feel the need to keep my life simple, and to work Steps Ten, Eleven, and Twelve on a daily basis. The fact that in order to live, I have to eat two, three, or four times a day now has nothing whatsoever to do with the fact that I used to abuse food. I do not avoid any foods. I stopped weighing myself. I am neither overweight nor underweight. I try to eat balanced and nutritious meals, but I am not obsessive about it. *Food is not an issue anymore; living is.*

I do not know *how* it all happened, but I can tell you what *has* happened since I have really been working this Program. There is a lot less fear in my life; my relationships are a lot better; I feel I am useful and worthy by just *being*, not only by doing; and I am completely free of compulsive thoughts and behavior much of the time. Occasionally I slip and become compulsive about food, working, or sleeping, but my compulsion is a lot less severe and long-lasting than it was. I feel I have a message to carry to other people and I have hope for myself. To enjoy life is not to experience or expect a bed of roses all the time, but to appreciate the good parts and *face* the problems instead of avoiding them. My character defects still get in the way, and then I become willing to have them removed and I pray to God to have them removed. It works, in God's own way. It takes courage and trust, but I have those things now. Through experience, I have found that disaster results when I seize control through sheer will. After all those years of struggle, I eventually got to where I am today. I have learned to live without turning to excess food for sedation and support. All it took was *total surrender*—without reservations—to a power greater than myself. It feels good to know that I am OK, that I am another compulsive eater in the OA fellowship, and that I am another human being in this beautiful world. Now I feel I am worthy enough to share my story with others.

Morris's Story

Life, for me, is the wonder of gratitude and the affirmation of service. Today I choose life.

I was born just after World War II. My father grew up during the Great Depression of the 1930s, so he was determined to give his family a better, more secure life than *he* had known as a child. The year I was born, my father started a wholesale toy business that soon became successful. In fact, when I was a young boy—about six years old—we were able to move into our own home and I even had a room of my own. My father operated his business from our home, and it began to dominate our lives. For example, my mother considered business phone calls top priority. She once turned on me for making noise during a business call: she shoved me against a door and beat my head against the door so hard that the door cracked. I remember a home environment filled with tension and anxiety. When my father's business began to fail, things went from bad to worse: my father had a heart attack, my mother had a nervous breakdown, my older sister left home, and we lost our house. By the time I was fourteen years old, my parents had separated and reconciled several times. It seemed as if we were *constantly* moving from one apartment to another.

It was during one of my parents' many separations

that my own crisis occurred: because of the anxiety I was experiencing, I found it impossible to stay in school for a whole day. I felt guilty going to the school nurse, but I was too anxious to sit in the classroom. Finally, the nurse would send me home. One night, for no apparent reason, I became violent and tore my room apart. Afterwards I cried uncontrollably. Following that episode, I found it difficult to function at all. I was subsequently placed in therapy. Although the therapist who worked with me was a good one, the therapy was not particularly effective. I became an isolated fantasizer. The one friend I had at that time was a boy whose intellectual ability I admired. I became his shadow.

When I graduated from high school, I was determined to live out my fantasies as soon as possible. I suppose I was bright enough to convince people I knew what I was doing. I really believed I could do *anything*, and no one tried to stop me. So I got a job, made money, and traveled to Europe just after my eighteenth birthday. In Europe I endured nine months of miserable deprivation, and encountered dangers there I was hardly aware of. In those days, I thought of myself as a literary vagabond. Traveling helped to reinforce my belief that I was special. I was looking for a life of "special meaning" and I felt I could realize my dream if only I could be successful as a writer.

I returned to the United States with feelings of relief that I was home. But I soon realized I was alone at "home" in America too. There was no one I could call. I worked six days a week. On my day off, I'd dress in my best clothes and spend my time wandering around outdoors like a traveler with no place to go. Later on, when I had some new friends, I felt eclipsed by them. In order to find myself, I figured I'd have to "escape" and be completely alone again. I moved to a small desert town in California and spent three years there working as a nurse's aide in a hospital. I told myself I was doing this for the "life experience," to help me be a more sensitive writer. Truthfully, the hospital environment represented a surrogate home to me. I felt good there—safe, useful, and connected to other people. I enjoyed my work and decided to become a registered nurse. But almost as soon as I started school, I felt the same anxiety I'd felt in the classroom as a teenager. So, every week while I was in nursing school, I commuted by bus to see the same therapist who'd treated me when I was a child. I never would have finished school had it not been for my therapist.

My eating habits became an obvious problem for me while I was in nursing school. After one particularly bad binge, I felt that I could no longer control my sugar intake, so I decided to stop eating all sweets. When I had successfully abstained from sugar for several months, I decided that I would celebrate my achievement by eating a cake. After all those months of abstinence, I was sure that I could take sugar or leave it. But at the stroke of midnight on the day I was to celebrate, I was off on a binge that lasted for months.

After I graduated from nursing school and got my first professional job, I had the longest and most successful relationship I'd ever had with a woman. This woman was attractive, intelligent, and dedicated to me, but I knew that my plans for the future didn't include her. At that time, I was again obsessed with thoughts of becoming an actor/writer/artist. *Nothing was going to stop me.* I was unwilling to acknowledge my relationship with this woman. After almost a year with her, I left for New York alone.

I ate compulsively and gained weight while I was in New York. I withdrew, isolated, quit the job I had there, and left on what would become a haphazard trip through Europe. And so it was that one year after I'd left California and a loving relationship, I had to wire my parents for money so that I could return home. I was broke and exhausted and there was nowhere else I could go. When I got back to the United States, I pursued an acting career. But the things I hoped for just didn't happen. *I couldn't get my life to work.* I had a job as a professional nurse and participated in acting workshops. But I knew no one and I had no real desire to work as an actor. I felt a tremendous sense of expectancy, but I was actually stagnating. I had a series of roommates; I was fired from my job; I gained weight, lost it, then gained it back again. I traveled to Thailand to help rescue refugees. When I returned after three months overseas, I told people I was going back to school. But I dropped my classes after only one week. I went back into therapy and there I began to realize— slowly and painfully—that *I was putting my life on hold.* Week after week, I cried that my life was over. Then, for the second time in my life, I crashed. I stopped going to work and I stopped taking care of myself. For two months, I did almost nothing but lie on the living room floor.

Then my father died unexpectedly. We had reconciled our differences some time before, and the grief I felt was distant and somewhat ambiguous. I took on a religious obligation in his behalf, saying a series of daily prayers for him that are part of the teachings of my religion. I was looking for a spiritual experience. The religious community offered me a sense of belonging. But when the year was over and I was no longer obligated to remain in it for my father, I just drifted out. It was as if the year had never even happened: no bridges were crossed; no faith had been created or strengthened; I had made no friends with whom I could share my feelings. In fact, I hardly understood my *own* feelings. All this time, I continued to gain weight. I was close to my previous top weight of 220 pounds, and fearful that I would surpass *that*. Even though I was undergoing treatment for acute stomach pains, I continued to eat compulsively. It was in this condition that I walked into my first OA meeting. I realized I needed the OA Program for more than just my eating problem.

The Program has helped me develop an ability to tolerate painful experiences. I now have friends, and I'm attending to my development as a human being. I am becoming a person others care about and *I* care about. There are many rewards: serenity, a wider range of emotional experiences, and life experiences I never even *anticipated* before. I have been recovered and aware of my growth for eighteen months now. Each day I pray that my recovery and growth will continue. *Life, for me, is the wonder of gratitude and the affirmation of service. Today I choose life.*

Grace's Story

In order to keep recovery, I must share it with others.

Here we are with the eternal pattern of paradoxes: at the very same time I state that recovery isn't a light matter, I experience wonder, joy, freedom, and peace flowing through me and a mysterious smile appears on my face. One moment I'm saying this recovery business isn't a light matter and the next moment I'm describing how light and free I am as a recovered compulsive overeater. It is this kind of paradox that I misunderstood for so many years and that became such a monumental barrier to my recovery. I was sure that things could be only one way at a time. If a situation appeared to be a certain way, *that was it* and there was no room for anything else. If I was sad about *anything* in my life, then I thought I had to be sad about *everything*. If I was jubilant about *something* in my life, then I thought I had to be jubilant about *everything*. That all or nothing mind-set was deeply ingrained in me. Then there was a long period of time in my life when I didn't feel anything, or so I thought. *I mastered that!* I was determined that nothing would bother *ME*. Perfect self-control is the image of me other people saw and the image I dedicated my life to perpetuating. No matter *what* happened, I acted calm and in control for others while inside me a tornado was raging.

Sometimes the conflict between the inner and outer me was unbearable!

I discovered there were certain foods that could, for a time, quiet the violent storm inside me. With ice cream or doughnuts or peanut butter or raw spaghetti noodles, I'd be just fine *for a while*. This system of quieting myself with certain foods and compulsive overeating worked in my life for quite a long time. My weight was manageable. Whenever I felt the need, I would go on a weight-loss diet. The binge fat would "magically" disappear, and everything would be fine. For a few days, anyway. Then I would start binge-eating again to cover up the fact that being thin *didn't* make me feel terrific about myself. The conflict would begin again. Get thin and feel terrific. But instead of feeling terrific, I felt *lonely*. I was scared, too, because I knew the cycle that awaited me: I would go back to compulsive overeating and then back to another diet. I was sick of it.

This cycle continued on for a few years with lots of blame going in many different directions: If only my husband would...if only my mother would...if only the world would...if only...*if only*. Then one hot summer day, I was mowing the lawn dressed in an old pair of shorts and feeling very fat. Suddenly, I quietly said just one word—"help." My plea that day was not directed anywhere in particular, but I was finally led to OA. I gained and lost 50 pounds three times during my first few years in OA. I was dutifully following the recommended methods for losing weight, but that old conflict between the inner me and the outer me *was stronger than ever*. At first I became resentful that "it" (the

Program) didn't work for me. Then I decided that somehow I had not measured up to the Program. I became extremely hard on myself. But for some reason, I stayed in OA. I got to the point where I knew I would never call in *one more ounce* of food to a sponsor. (This is what some of us used to do in the Program. It was supposed to give us discipline or something, but I never really figured out how it worked.) For the first time in my life, I truly could state that I felt resentful, guilty, angry, bitter, embarrassed, and antagonistic. Imagine that! *I had feelings after all.* In order to cover up all of those intense feelings I was experiencing for the first time, I ate compulsively. Who could stand it?

I started reaching out *because I had to.* I started going to AA meetings because it seemed to me that the people at those meetings took the problem of alcoholism very seriously. The people in that AA group I found were really something else. They were there for anyone who really wanted to stop drinking. And they gave of *themselves*—not just a lot of talk. They were *there* for the newcomer who wanted to stop drinking. They were *there* sharing, sharing, sharing— not telling people how to live their lives, but sharing just how they recovered. I listened because there was something to listen *to.* After a while, I even started to share some of what I learned at AA with people at my OA meetings. I must admit that this was risky. Little did I know *then* that my recovery was already in process. I was speaking up, *no matter what other people thought.* I needed to do this for myself. The word "recovery" started popping up here and there. About this time, some friends of mine told me about a man who led retreats and talked about recovery. I wanted to know more. The same friends later went to a convention and brought one of this man's tapes titled "There Is a Solution" home for me. What wonderful "*music*"! After hearing the tape, I realized there were other people out there who wanted what I wanted and were going for it. I made a decision then and there: *I WANT TO RECOVER!* So the path turned, and my journey of recovery continued on to another level.

I started reaching out to others in a way I never had before in my entire life. *I knew that my life depended on it.* I listened. I questioned. I shared. I stumbled. I cried. I smiled. I felt a conflict of emotions I had never felt before. I was really scared...but *trusting.* I now trusted that no matter what was going on with me, I was okay and *God* was there for me, even when it didn't seem that way. I learned from beautiful people sharing their hearts and souls that recovery is outlined in the Big Book. I decided to follow what the Big Book said. I realized that I may not agree or like what is said in the Big Book, but *I would not argue with what these recovered people had to say. I wanted to recover and I didn't even know what that meant anymore.* But about this time, I think I began to understand that recovery meant much more than losing weight again. After all, I had already done that. Just losing weight was not the answer for me, that's for sure. There was more: the joy of living; being alive and truly enjoying that for no other reason than just to be alive. It's that simple and it means as long as I'm alive, I have joy. It doesn't mean experiencing the joy of living only when everything is going well. This joy of living does not deny the fact that there are difficulties in *all* our lives. Problems and difficulties are *everywhere*. The difference for me now is that I can acknowledge that I have conflicts and problems and I accept the fact that this is not a perfect world. So what? There are also wondrous things in my life and in this world. I have learned not to allow the joy in my life to be dependent upon the absence of problems or the presence of wonderful things. *Today I am joyful simply because I am alive.* When I forget this—and believe me, I have my moments—I ask the people who love me to hold my hand or give me a swift kick while I go through whatever I have to go through in order to "lighten up."

I haven't talked much about food in my story...and there's a reason for that. Food is as important as air and water. It helps me sustain my life and my health. The fact *is* that some foods happen to taste better than others. That's nice, but it's certainly no big deal. I *need* food. I also enjoy eating special meals that are prepared with love in celebration of special occasions and I enjoy eating at a nice restaurant with good friends and family. That's it!

Whenever food takes on more importance in my life than just sustenance and simple pleasure, I take that as a sign that I am avoiding *me*. And at that point, I actually can choose what I'm going to do about it. Fortunately I have this beautiful Program known as the Twelve Steps that gives me wonderful guidance. When I choose to live and stay on that path of guidance, I am living in harmony with the universe. When I choose to ignore the guidance of the Steps, I again become caught up in myself and then the old conflict returns. When I get off track today—and I do—all I need to do is choose to get back on the track. It's as simple as that. I began my journey to recovery with a simple request for help. Since that summer day more than eight years ago, I have been given the opportunity to share the answer to that spontaneous prayer with other people. There is one hitch to all of this: *in order to keep recovery, I must share it with others.* This sharing is not a burden, but an opportunity to discover the magnificence that is in each one of us. Today I am in partnership with my God and together we are doing what I never could have done on my own.

Epilogue

*Our journey ends with the beginning of a
new journey.*

As I have tried to illustrate in this book, our journey to
recovery is filled with tempting obstacles—delusions,
fantasies, lies, fears, guilt, and resentment. I used to
cling to the hope that one day I would no longer have
to be vigilant in order to resist the obstacles and keep
myself from slipping back into the hellish existence I'd
known for so many years. *But that was not to be.*
There is no respite, no station of safety we ultimately
arrive at that symbolizes the end of our work. I know
for a fact that I cannot "rest on my laurels." Instead, I
found that I had to reach a new level of awareness in
my life. Now, even though I know there will always be
work ahead, the past seems less burdensome; the
future seems less frightening; and I find so much joy
and satisfaction in the present. All this has happened,
yet nothing in my world has changed. (Nothing in my
world, that is, except *me*.)

Recovery signals the beginning of a lifelong journey
that will certainly be interrupted from time to time by
"easier, softer ways." But most of us will quickly discover that these "easier, softer ways" divert us from
our chosen path. Sometimes we'll find that we're
unable to sustain even the simple trust and faith that
the Program requires of us and that we're filled with
fear and self-doubt instead. And these negative feelings
may be unknowingly reinforced by well-meaning

371

people in the Program—people who may *themselves* be filled with fear and self-doubt.

I have made the decision that I will no longer allow my self-worth to be determined by my ability to conform to specific behavioral criteria such as perfect adherence to a food plan or regular reporting on food intake. I know that I am a human being made in the image of God, and I will not denigrate that gift. I am no longer willing to exist in a "living death" whereby I am a victim of my history and dependent on the expectations and approval of others. I want to live my life and celebrate it each day as a testament to God's power within me.

The Program set forth by two alcoholics more than fifty years ago continues to amaze me for its relevance to contemporary problems and contemporary lives. *The Program continues to succeed where nothing else does. Recovery is our goal, weight loss the result.* Through our work in the Program, we learn that in order to *maintain* recovery, we must first *attain* recovery and that we attain recovery through a daily practice of the Twelve Steps. As your journey continues onward, relieved of the bondage of obsessions and compulsions and relieved of the bondage of the past, I pray that you will fully engage in the great adventure of living and that you will be *free* at last.

Bill B.
Los Angeles, California
June, 1986